the last
single woman
in america

cindy guidry

A PLUME BOOK

PLUME
Published by the Penguin Group
Penguin Group (USA) Inc., 375 Hudson Street, New York, New York 10014, U.S.A. •
Penguin Group (Canada), 90 Eglinton Avenue East, Suite 700, Toronto, Ontario, Canada
M4P 2Y3 (a division of Pearson Penguin Canada Inc.) • Penguin Books Ltd., 80 Strand,
London WC2R 0RL, England • Penguin Ireland, 25 St. Stephen's Green, Dublin 2, Ireland
(a division of Penguin Books Ltd.) • Penguin Group (Australia), 250 Camberwell Road,
Camberwell, Victoria 3124, Australia (a division of Pearson Australia Group Pty. Ltd.) •
Penguin Books India Pvt. Ltd., 11 Community Centre, Panchsheel Park,
New Delhi – 110 017, India • Penguin Group (NZ), 67 Apollo Drive, Rosedale, North
Shore 0632, New Zealand (a division of Pearson New Zealand Ltd.) • Penguin Books
(South Africa) (Pty.) Ltd., 24 Sturdee Avenue, Rosebank, Johannesburg 2196, South Africa

Penguin Books Ltd., Registered Offices: 80 Strand, London WC2R 0RL, England

Published by Plume, a member of Penguin Group (USA) Inc. Previously published in a
Dutton edition.

First Plume Printing, February 2009
10 9 8 7 6 5 4 3 2 1

Ⓟ REGISTERED TRADEMARK — MARCA REGISTRADA

The Library of Congress has catalogued the Dutton edition as follows:

Guidry, Cindy.
   The last single woman in America / by Cindy Guidry.
      p. cm.
ISBN 978-0-525-95052-3 (hc.)
ISBN 978-0-452-29001-3 (pbk.)
1. Guidry, Cindy. 2. Single women—United States—Biography. 3. Guidry, Cindy—
Relations with men. 4. Man-woman relationships—United States. I. Title.
HQ800.2.G85 2008
306.81'53092—dc22   2007034491
[B]

Printed in the United States of America
Set in Fairfield

author's note

This is not a courtroom transcript!
The essays contained within were written over a period of many years. They were written for me. Writing is my way of making sense of myself, and the world around me.

There is far more fact than fiction on these pages, but under oath, my account of these events would be somewhat different. This is creative writing, and I have used creative license in telling these stories. In some cases I've exaggerated the truth to make a point, other times I've done it just for fun. Some names and identifying details have been changed, some characters are composites, and in some instances time has been compressed or otherwise altered for dramatic effect. What's important to me is that these stories are all emotionally true. I am more interested in conveying feelings than I am in presenting cold, hard facts.

That said, truth is a funny thing. Ask two people about the same event, and they'll give you two different stories. When emotions are involved, those individual "truths" will diverge even further. The passage of time poses additional challenges; memory is not an airtight storage container. Even if I were trying to tell the whole truth and nothing but the truth, I could only hope to give an accurate account of *my* truth. These stories are simply my retelling of certain events, creatively altered through my own internal kaleidoscope. And they weren't all written in real time, some were based on memories.

You do the math.

For my parents,
in heartfelt appreciation for their unconditional love,
which I will now continue to test with
the following 300 pages

contents

Define Yourself 1

Yin and Yang 11

Overqualified 23

Never Never Land 35

Welcome to Earth 49

For Sale by Owner 58

Thanks for Sharing 71

The Greek 82

The Most Beautiful Girl in the World 90

Men Are the New Women 103

This Is Pilates 114

Klimax 121

Something Shiny 138

Buddhist 147

What's Your Hook? 156

The Cat Whisperer 167

Rob Marciano Is Hot! 175

Under My Roof 188

It's Only Natural 207

Future Ex-Husband 211

Hell 219

The Last Single Woman in America 236

Love 250

Simon Says 268

Acknowledgments 291

define yourself

Everyone told me to quit saying I'd been fired. They insisted that I should tell people I'd been "let go" or "downsized." In addition to this, I was supposed to act like I was still on great terms with my former employer. I couldn't understand it for the life of me. "They're assholes," I'd respond. "I was wrongly fired and given a shitty severance package to boot. Why should I justify someone else's unjust actions?"

The truth is, in the film business, injustices are the norm and terminations occur willy-nilly. It was probably just my turn, but that didn't make it any easier to stomach. Indignation was my prerogative. I'd earned it and no one was taking it away from me. I was Fired, after all.

When I persisted in bandying the *F* word about, my friends started throwing Mom-isms at me. "You're cutting off your nose to spite your face," they'd warn. But really, I wasn't. Trust me, nose-cutting is something I know a thing or two about: I've elevated it to an art form. And until I come up with something else I do just as well, I'll probably keep doing it.

Their warning didn't apply. Bad behavior is de rigueur in this town, and usually rewarded, so even if I ran around Los Angeles bad-mouthing my former employer to everyone in sight, it wouldn't have been nose-cutting. And it wasn't like I was telling anyone anything they didn't already know, anyway. *Variety,* the entertainment industry trade paper that *everyone* reads *every* morning, had already openly announced that I would no longer be working for the film studio that had employed me for the better part of ten years. It was no secret that I was on the streets with a hobo stick. There are no secrets in Hollywood.

So why pretend? Sure, I was told that they were letting me go due to downsizing, but they didn't downsize everyone. When I told them I didn't have to go, they still made me go. And just for the record, I don't think my fellow "downsizers" were all that concerned about me at the time, anyway. They simply didn't want the *F* word rubbing off on them. But hey, everybody, guess what? We were all Fired!

Finding myself job-free, I delighted in a smorgasbord of arts & crafts by day and flitted off to parties every night. My friend Dylan dubbed me "the poster child for unemployment." He was amazed at the way I'd blossomed in the wake of a pink slip. "I don't know, maybe they did me a favor," I'd confess. "But I still think they suck."

My happiness was both a mystery and an affront to Dylan. He too had been "downsized," but, unlike me, the event absolutely devastated him. While I was merrily making stickers of my own happy face on my new color printer, he was experiencing such a heightened and unrelenting degree of panic that, frankly, just being in the same room with him made *my* palms sweat. He would spend all day typing up wildly inflated résumés and calling everyone in town begging them to shoot off an e-mail to this person or that in the hope of landing an interview. Then he'd spend all night dreaming up more lies that he could add to his résumé and wondering if there was anyone he'd forgotten to call. I told him that while I couldn't give a definitive answer as to why I'd been visited by the spirit of joy, I could make a pretty good guess as to why he hadn't. "You're letting some stupid job define you," I said. "Chill out. Something will happen."

In truth, I think the reason getting fired didn't crush me was because I'd already been reduced to rubble a year earlier. I was seeing a man who was technically married but legally separated, when, lo and behold, his wife got pregnant. So that was the end of that. Then, just as I'd begun licking my wounds, an old boyfriend appeared on my doorstep and proposed marriage. His timing couldn't have been worse. I declined, but three days later, it struck me that I may have spoken too soon. I mean I still loved him, even if I wasn't *in love* with him. Hoping to buy some time, I called him to change my *no* to a *maybe* and learned that he'd accidentally impregnated some woman I'd never even heard of, and she would soon be moving in with him. The marriage proposal was off the table. Then, while I was trying to decide between a noose and a bottle of sleeping pills, my best friend swept in and alerted me to the fact that he'd *always* been in love with me. Unfortunately, shortly after consummating our relationship, he hooked up with some chick at a bar. And now she, too, was pregnant. In little more than a month I'd lost ten years' worth of beloved men to faceless women with growing bellies.

Getting fired is a cakewalk compared to that.

"It's fine not to be crushed," said Dylan. "But you seem downright happy about it, and that's just weird."

Unable to provide Dylan with an acceptable explanation, and beginning to wonder myself if it wasn't just a little fishy, I paid a visit to Michael, the psychiatrist who'd talked me off the ledge after the previous year's indisputably crushing romantic turmoil. I think it's OK to say Michael's name, because it's only his first name, plus I'm pretty sure that doctor-patient confidentiality thing only works in one direction anyway. Still, I told Michael he's free to use my *whole name* whenever he likes because I just don't give a shit what anyone thinks anymore.

Being that Michael had already stuck a gold star on my head and declared me fixed after six ugly months of his own tough love, he didn't think it was weird that I was happy, but he was interested in hearing about my plans for the future. I told him I didn't think it was any coincidence that the Dave Matthews tour schedule came out the same day I was fired.

Oddly enough, Michael didn't seem to think that following Dave across America was a viable alternative to work. Oh, he didn't actually say it—therapy is like yoga and Buddhism: It's judgment-free. But I saw it in his eyes. I heard it in his cackle. I know how he operates. He just went on and on about how it might be better if I fixated on a *real* person.

I told him that I was offended on Dave's behalf, and that I considered Dave a lot more *real* than a lot of the guys I've actually gone out with. And let me tell you, after hearing about my entire clown-speckled past the last time around, Michael wasn't about to argue that point. When I proceeded to explain that I didn't have any *real* interest in hooking up with Dave—that I just like his concerts because of the high concentration of good vibes and strapping young men—he backed off.

But, in truth, I was offended on *my* behalf, too. It really bugs me when people act like I have some delusional romantic interest in Dave Matthews, because I don't. I just like his music. In fact, I like his music way too much to ever have anything to do with the man. I know because I was at a dinner party once and he was there.

I'm not easily intimidated, and working in the film industry you meet famous people all the time, but when Dave Matthews walked in, everything changed. To think people have actually had the gall to say *I'm* intimidating. Those fools obviously didn't know what real intimidation felt like. Oh, but I did. Standing there before Dave, I knew exactly what it felt like. Suddenly, I was twelve years old. I was the ugly girl with acne and braces, the straight-F student, the clumsy kid nobody wants on their kickball team, and the goofball in the dunce cap all rolled into one. And I'm 5 foot 10. It's hard to conceal that much angst and insecurity. So when Dave introduced himself, I grunted. Then I did an about-face, walked directly into the kitchen, grabbed the wooden spoon from my host's hand, and demanded that he let me finish up the risotto.

When the only liquid left that I hadn't tossed into the pot was Liquid-Plumr, and the grains of Arborio rice had blown up to the size of lipstick tubes, I knew I had only two options remaining: I could emerge from hiding and dine with a man whose fan club I belonged to, or I could jump out the window.

The window was my first choice. I peered out. The house was on the side of a cliff; the cliff was steep. I reluctantly accepted my fate.

With downcast eyes and my body aquiver, I entered the dining room and seated myself—a feat that I considered nothing short of a miracle, given the situation. It may have been Michael who helped me sort through the wreckage after losing three men in forty days, but it was Dave who sang to me every night as I cried myself to sleep. And it was Dave who, when I had to wake up and face a world that I no longer recognized, lifted my spirits and assured me that there was still hope. I'd listened to his life-affirming lyrics on a continuous loop through what was arguably the darkest period of my life. His music became my religion.

So it's no surprise that, finding myself sitting at a table with the man, I felt like, well, like I was breaking bread with Jesus. Except that, while I can't be sure, I would suspect that Jesus doesn't revel in scatological humor and, more to the point, with Jesus I would have feared no judgment. I mean, Dave was, without a doubt, the most unassuming celebrity I've ever met, and he seemed a lot more interested in drinking than judging, but let's face it, the guy's still human, and with humans there's always the risk of judgment.

There I was, overwhelmed with gratitude for a gift Dave didn't even know he'd given me, wanting nothing more than to return it, to tie it all up with a bow and give it right back to him. I wanted him not just to *know*, but to actually *feel* the enormous spiritual effect his music had had on me, but there was simply no way for me to express that much emotion without falling to my knees, kissing his feet and bursting into tears—which frankly, would have been totally inappropriate at a dinner party. Even though it was just a party of five, I was the only girl, and girls can usually get away with that kind of thing.

So I did what I had to do. I channeled Helen Keller. We ate dinner. We had drinks. And throughout I spoke not a word. It was weird, too, because I'd never spent that much time with myself without hearing me talk. At one point, I wondered if I hadn't disappeared entirely. But apparently not, because suddenly I heard Dave and his friend asking me if I could give them a ride back to their hotel. I haven't the foggiest clue how I replied, or if I even opened my mouth, but I must have given them some positive indicator, because they sent their driver home, and an hour later, they were getting into *my* car with *me*.

Being in a house with Dave wigged me out, but being in a car the size of a refrigerator box with him wigged me out a whole lot more. What really did me in, however, was the realization that all six CDs in my six-CD changer were Dave Matthews Band

CDs. *Good God, is there no rest for the weary?* I mean, really, try-ing to contain that much emotion is like trying to contain a pterodactyl in a Tupperware container. I was pooped out. And now my very own car was threatening to undermine my efforts and expose me for the obsessive freak I am? Do the injustices never end? Mustering every ounce of indignation I could, I rammed my fist through the dashboard, making sure the CD player was turned OFF.

I tuned the radio to KCRW, and we listened in silence as I sped down La Cienega, making a beeline for the Hotel Nikko at 100 mph. All the while, I kept an eagle eye on that evil CD player in the event of a freak electrical accident or maybe just a random act of defiance, while at the same time, fighting an almost uncontrol-lable urge to turn the CD player ON because what I wanted *more than anything* was to listen to #41, the quintessential Dave Mat-thews song and the only thing in the world guaranteed to calm me down and put things back into perspective. I knew if I could only listen to #41, *everything would be OK.*

But I couldn't listen to #41, because the man who'd written the song was in my car and the song was in a CD player with every other song he'd ever recorded. I felt like a stalker. My fists looked like two prizewinning beets. I had them wrapped so tightly around the steering wheel that I feared my skin might burst at any moment. I looked in the rearview mirror; my pupils were dilated from the pressure. It wasn't good. Something had to give. Maybe if I opened my mouth, let out just one, quick casual remark, I could release enough tension to prevent a blowout. But I knew that was just wishful thinking. It was all or nothing with me, and besides, that was no longer an option. I'd already doomed myself to silence. Anything I said at that point was going to sound freak-ish simply because I was *saying* something.

I couldn't have been more disappointed in myself. I couldn't even be happy that the Hotel Nikko was coming into view. I couldn't believe I was going to let Dave Matthews out of my car without even telling him *thank you*. But that's exactly what I did. I pulled into the hotel, slammed on the brakes, kicked Dave and friend to the curb, peeled out, rounded the corner, threw my car into park and cranked the volume. #41 came on, Dave's voice filled my car, for the first time in over six hours my heart rate dropped below 170, and there I sat, feeling like a complete loser and wondering if maybe now wouldn't be a good time to start addressing my vulnerability issues. It was without a doubt *the worst night of my life*. The whole thing from beginning to end felt like that moment of sheer terror during a nightmare when you're trying to scream but nothing will come out.

So it really offends me when people act like I want Dave to be my man because truly, what kind of masochistic nincompoop would want to go through life like that?

Michael, of all people, should know better. And anyway, as I pointed out to him, I was already planning to marry Mark, the guy from the Holiday Inn commercials.

Of course, Michael then felt obligated to point out to me that we'd never met.

"Technicality," I replied. "Minor technicality."

I assured Michael that I had it all figured out. First I was going to lure Mark to my apartment with promises of brand-name merchandise. Then I'd send him down the hall to fill the ice bucket while I slipped into something provocative. When he came back, I'd offer him full access to my dataport. If that didn't seal the deal, I'd make him a skillet breakfast the next morning.

Michael eyed me and said, "You know his name's not Mark, right?"

"Who?" I asked. "The actor?"

Michael nodded.

"Yeah, I know. His name's Ross. I'm not crazy. But I'm not going to marry Ross, I'm going to marry Mark."

With only two minutes left to my session, Michael just decided to go with it. "OK," he said, tapping a pencil on his desk. "This takes us back to the original question. Assuming this plan of yours does work, and you do marry a fictional character from a television commercial, what are you going to do about money? I mean, isn't the whole premise of the commercials that Mark's parents are desperately trying motivate him because, like you, he's thirty-seven years old and has no job?"

"Oh," I said, "you mustn't have seen all of them. He's working on this Internet thing that's going to be giant. His parents don't have a lot of faith in it, but you're a shrink—you know how parents like to quash dreams. Plus, I'm only thirty-six."

Just then, Michael's buzzer went off, marking the end of my session. Before I could get up to leave, he asked if he could have his gold star back.

I arrived home to a message from Dylan begging me to make a work call on his behalf. When I phoned him back, he asked how it had gone with the shrink. I told him I was pretty sure Michael thought I was in denial of something, but I wouldn't know exactly what until the following week.

Dylan instantly assumed credit. "Yeah, I figured you were in denial, too," he said.

"Oh really," I replied. "Then maybe you should add that to your résumé right after the bit where you talk about how you swam up Niagara Falls after single-handedly carving Mt. Rushmore with a razor blade."

A week later I returned to Michael. I told him that I'd thought about our last session and what a giant waste of money it had been. "Look," I said, "I know there's no future for me and the Holiday Inn guy; it's just a lot safer to love someone who can never hurt you. And I know that following a band across America isn't a reasonable substitute for an actual job; it's just that no one can take it away from me. I don't really think it's denial if you know what you're doing."

I told Michael I'd been called in for a job interview a few days earlier, but when I got there the woman wanted nothing more than to goad me into confirming some dirt she'd heard about my former employer.

"Did you?"

"No," I replied. "It was none of her business. So we just did the interview thing for a while, and in the end she asked me how I would define myself."

"*And?*"

"I told her I would define myself as someone who could have pretty much everything taken away from her and be OK, as long as I still had me and a handful of Dave Matthews CDs."

Michael smiled. "You can keep your gold star."

"Thanks," I said. "But it wasn't the right answer. My friend Dylan got the job."

"Does that bother you?"

"Nope. Still happy. It's a real brainteaser."

He nodded his head. "I think you'll figure it out."

"I don't know about that," I said, "but I'll bet you a hundred bucks Dylan told that woman everything she wanted to hear and then some."

yin and yang

I have this friend Ben who lives in New York. When we first met, I got the feeling that Ben thought he'd made contact with an alien. We are opposites, bound by a mutual fascination. He's a Rhodes scholar; I'm a college dropout. His life has been a series of plans, goals and accomplishments. My life has been more like a series of 911 calls—totally random and unplanned; I whip into action when called upon, when moments announce their importance, when some*thing* suddenly eclipses all else.

My life is like a collage. It might not look like anything yet, but like I told Ben, I've followed my heart, I've done what I needed to do, and I have to believe that at some point the collage is going to form a pretty picture. I mean, really, I *have* to.

Tomas doesn't make it easy.

Tomas lives in the "twin" building next door. Surely at some point the twins had the same parents, but apparently they divorced, and from what I can tell it was a pretty ugly divorce, because it caused enough friction to create a crack in the earth just wide enough to allow the river Styx to come a-flowin' through. The only thing the twins share at this point is a floor plan.

On my side, you have a soothing peach and terra-cotta color scheme, lush tropical foliage, a meticulous landlord who spends every weekend going to flea markets in search of vintage lighting

and fixtures, and a team of overworked Mexicans under his command who can't possibly be getting paid enough to put up with
the unrelenting demands of a madman who takes on home
improvement with a fervor better suited to eradicating world hunger and demands military precision in its execution.

On the other side, you have a sort of brownish-gray block set
upon a barren wasteland, a family of inmates running the asylum,
some juicy drama unfolding every other day, and cheap rent.

And it's not just me who sees it that way. My cat, Frankie, walks
outside, sniffs the flowers, dances with the hummingbirds, lounges
in paradise, and then, when he's ready to do his business, he wades
across the river, scans his vast personal postapocalyptic litter box,
chooses his detonation location, slinks over—always on full alert
as he snakes through the passing tumbleweeds—digs a quick hole,
drops his bomb, then hauls ass back to the land of the living just
as fast as he can. Even with nine lives, Frankie's not dicking around
on the other side.

But Tomas, he *lives* on the other side.

Tomas is a weird combination of friend, enemy, neighbor and
peeping Tom. And talk about annoying.

Like the other day, I spotted him messing around in my driveway, snipping jasmine or something. Then he was gone, only to
reappear in my living room. I was working at the dining room table.
He walked straight past me and over to my desk. I saw him eyeing
the bulletin board, and braced myself for his theatrics.

Sure enough, he cleared his throat, tossed back his imaginary
hair, and launched into a dramatic reading. " 'Hers was a singular
life. It had no achievements other than itself. It declared, in its
own way, that there are things that matter and these are the things
one must do. Life is energy, it proclaimed; life is desire. You are

not meant to understand everything but to live and do certain things.'" Then he paused, adding, "Interesting quote. Where's it from?"

I moved not a muscle, as I called upon my inner lizard, hoping to blend in with my surroundings, thus sparing me the inevitable debate. Sometimes they're educational and entertaining, sometimes not. The last one wasn't; we already had another one on the books, and the forecast was grim. Tomas had been especially dark as of late.

A black cloud moved over the dining room table; Tomas waved his hand before my unblinking eyes. My lizard act was getting to him. It pleased me mightily.

"You've got this Medusa thing all wrong," he said. "She's supposed to turn *other people* into stone."

"Oh, if only it were that easy," I replied, letting out a laugh. Then I turned to him and said, "You know, the Chinese consider Yin the principle of femininity and darkness, while Yang is supposed to be the principle of masculinity and *light*. You'd really throw 'em for a loop in Beijing. You should go there."

"Where's the quote from?" he asked again.

I kept it simple. You have to with Tomas. Anything you give him just comes back to bite you in the ass at some later date. "It's from a book," I replied.

"I saw you leaving to go out last night. You looked really hot. Much better than you do right now."

"That's because there are no interesting men around right now," I countered, as I turned back to my computer, wondering all the while what it is that compels him to dole out compliments with his right hand, then take them away with his left. But *that* is his signature move.

"What book is the quote from?"

"James Salter's memoirs."

"*James Salter?* I'm impressed. I'd have thought you were more the Bridget Jones type."

"Right, well, I think I may have mentioned this before, but uh, *you don't know jackshit about me.*"

And really, he doesn't. He thinks he does, but he doesn't. Why? Because, unlike Ben, Tomas refuses to accept our differences, much less find anything even remotely fascinating about them. The other night I told him I was happy; he told me I wasn't, his proof being that I, like him, am single. I told him I enjoyed spending time alone; he told me I was lonely. I told him I thought happiness was a choice; he insisted that I was wrong and debated me until the sun came up. It never ends. I tell him I'm not sure I want to stay in the film business; he tells me I have to because that's where *our* passion lies. I tell him I don't feel passionate about film; he tells me it's just because I'm depressed. Then he tries to claim it's a location issue, christening our street the place "where dreams go to die."

But really, it isn't. It's just like that on his side.

So I tell him again that I'm happy, and the whole thing repeats itself with some weird new twist. It literally *never ends.*

"You keep that quote up to make you feel better about not accomplishing anything?" asked Tomas.

"How'd you get in here?"

"The front door was wide open."

"Yeah, well, that's because I like to keep it airy *and light* in here."

Then he said something about how he just came in to scratch Frankie, who was clearly visible through the window, *outside* my apartment, in the driveway.

"You stepped over him on your way in," I replied.

"Oh, *that's* what that was."

Then he chuckled past me and plopped down on the couch.

"So who's the quote about?" he asked.

"Some woman he based a character on."

"From which book?"

"Light Years."

"I read that book."

"Of course you did."

That's another thing about Tomas. He's smarter and more literate than you. And it's even worse when he's drinking.

"Was it Nancy? No, Nedra! Was that the character?"

"Yep."

Then he walked into the kitchen and started snooping around in my refrigerator.

"Nedra was married, right?" he called out, as I heard him pop open a Tupperware container and mumble something about its contents. "And she had kids?"

Oh, and not only is he smarter and more literate than you; he remembers everything he reads and stores it in his mental arsenal. I read things and only ever remember how they made me feel; Tomas can recall every annoying detail.

"Uh-huh," I replied, as I waited for what I knew was coming.

"Then she accomplished at least two things you haven't!" concluded Tomas.

"I guess she didn't see it that way."

"I guess *James Salter* didn't see it that way."

"Getting pregnant was God's accomplishment, not Nedra's."

"That only works if you believe in God."

"Actually, to a believer, God exists regardless of who believes in Him. But if it'll get us closer to the finish line, we can just call it Nature."

"Ah, but what if Nedra had to *really work at it*?"

"It was either Nature or a fertility specialist. Nedra was only a vessel."

"I thought you liked Nedra," challenged Tomas.

"I do like Nedra, but, like me, she didn't think getting pregnant was an accomplishment. If a cat goes out and gets knocked up, you call that an accomplishment?"

He returned with a banana and sat right next to me.

"Depends on the kittens," he replied. "If you're talking about Frankie's *biological* mother, then yes."

"Doing a good job *raising* children is an accomplishment, but who knows? Maybe the woman Nedra was based on didn't even have children. You're a writer—have you never heard of creative license?"

"What about getting married?" asked Tomas. "That was Nedra's doing."

"It's not really an accomplishment," I replied. "Unless your whole goal is simply to *get married*."

"What about *staying married*—would you call that an accomplishment?"

"I don't know, would you?"

"Definitely."

"Great, then I would, too."

"You're no fun," pooh-poohed Tomas, as he got up and headed toward my DVD collection.

"I guess that's why I've never been married," I replied, brightly. "Oh no, wait, that doesn't work because you're no fun and you have been married. You just couldn't *stay married*. So I guess that's one thing Nedra accomplished that you haven't."

"My ex-wife *begged me* to come back to her."

Finally, the wound revealed itself. I had him. And it would have been *so easy* to go in for the kill. But I didn't, because I actually like Tomas. Long before we ever became whatever the hell we are, I would see him tooling around on his motorcycle and think that he had a very kind face. And he is kind and he is smart and he is literate and I do often use him as my personal thesaurus and encyclopedia, but man, can he go to some dark places. And when he does, you better not even think about offering a torch because he'll snatch it right out of your hand and piss all over it.

But then the tide always turns. I'll hear circus music coming from the evil twin, I'll peer through the hibiscus, and I'll see Tomas—tucked safely in his apartment, watching some movie, his face filled with nothing but wonder, his black cloak and scythe nowhere to be found. Just a little boy lost in a magical world.

Tomas is a screenwriter. Movies are his passion; they are his escape and inspiration. And I envy him for that, for knowing exactly what he wants to do, while I sit here living off my severance pay, trying to figure it all out.

I'm not sure movies are the answer. I didn't come here with stars in my eyes or dreams of working in the film industry. I left New Orleans to expand my horizons. I left San Diego to escape a bad relationship. I just ended up in Hollywood. Eleven years ago.

Until recently, most of my life here had been spent working at the same movie studio—from receptionist on up to development executive. But all things come to an end, and frankly, the thought of getting another job in the film industry just isn't doing it for me right now. It wouldn't be the same. We were a family. We were a totally dysfunctional family, and "Dad" ultimately saw fit to kick me out of the house, but we were a family.

I take that back. We still are a family. Still dysfunctional, now scattered, but since when did that stop people from being connected?

It's not just nostalgia that's holding me back, though. Hollywood is one big game. Some people are good at playing that game, and some people aren't. I'm not. So I've decided that they can keep their game; I'm playing my own game. What it is, I have no idea.

I feel like a giant Etch a Sketch that's been shaken clean, but there is a strange beauty in this emptiness, and in the unexpected reveal that I don't actually need a man or a job to define me. I can't remember ever feeling this way before.

Then again, I can't remember much.

My mother's always calling me from New Orleans with some breaking news about one person or another—someone I went to seventh grade with, someone from summer camp. I never have any idea who she's talking about. And every time I tell her this, her response is always the same. "That's a good trick," she says. "I'd like to forget half the stuff that's happened in my life, too. Can you teach me how to do that?"

"Well, Mom," I reply. "First you have to be born to you and Dad. Once you've pulled that off, come back and I'll give you step 2."

But while I don't remember details, I do remember feelings. And try as I might, I can't remember ever feeling like I wasn't running from something, or trying to get somewhere. Now suddenly, everything is still. Maybe even still enough for me to finally hear my own voice.

Although, like I said, Tomas doesn't make it easy.

"Can I borrow this?" he called out, while snatching a DVD.

I looked over. He had *Amélie* in his clutches. "Sure, if you promise not to hurt her," I replied.

"What are you working on over there, anyway?"

"Nothing."

"That's not an answer," he snapped.

"Oh, I'm sorry, I didn't think you needed an answer. I thought you already had them all."

"No. I've got a lot of 'em, but *you've* got all of 'em."

"Oh, right," I replied. "I just don't have the slightest clue which questions they match up with."

"So what are you writing?" he asked again.

"Nothing. I just like writing. It's sort of like therapy, but cheaper."

"*Like therapy,* but without the objective outside party to offer any valuable insight."

"Exactly. That's the beauty of it. There's no one contradicting me. I get enough of that from you."

"So what is it, like a journal?"

"I guess, in a way, but it's more like a story."

"Is it about a mean girl who lives alone with her cat?" he asked, excitedly.

"No," I said. "It's about an obnoxious boy who gets drunk and cracks his skull open. The mean girl who lives alone with her cat is just an ancillary character who washes his bloodied shirt fifteen times to get the stain out."

"Well maybe we can count that as your first accomplishment!" exclaimed Tomas.

"Washing your shirt wasn't an accomplishment, Tomas. It was a mistake."

"You know," he said, "you're not very nice to your guests. Where I come from . . ."

"*Not again!*" I cried out, desperate for it to finally just end. Because that right there is the mother of them all.

Tomas is Canadian, and he reminds you of it about twelve times a day. *This would never happen in Canada; that would never happen in Canada.* Honestly, the guy morphs into Garrison Keillor every time he talks about Canada. Oh, Canada, where all the women are strong, all the men are good-looking and all the children are above average. And not only that, everyone is polite, the streets are all spotless, the sun always shines, and magic elves leap from red polka-dotted mushroom caps to sprinkle golden fairy dust into the air whenever anything less-than-perfect threatens to go down in the utopia that is Canada. Because that's just how Canadians are—community-minded, through and through, be they human or elfin.

And yet the fool lives here.

I told him if America sucked so hard, he should take his ass back to his beloved Canada. But no, he can't do that, because this is where his chosen career path has taken him (read: They don't pay as well in Canada). I told him if he was going to stay in this hellhole, he should become a citizen and try to make a difference with his vote. But no, he can't do that, because his heart belongs to Canada (read: I just like to bitch and complain). I told him if he was going to cling to his green card until it disintegrated, he could still "be the change he wants to see in the world" by getting off his socialist rump and volunteering to actually *do something*. But no, he can't do that, because he's too busy (read: After gazing into my navel for six hours a day, bothering you for four, and writing maybe two, I have to walk over to The Dime, get tanked, and pontificate until they sweep me out the door).

Tomas is also a trained actor, and if his impersonation of his father is as spot-on as he claims it is, Tomas baked his bloody brains in Cape Cod during the summer of '72. So maybe that's how he got this way. I don't know. All I know is that he walked out of my front door with *three* DVDs in his hand.

Then, as I was sighing with relief, he peeped through the window.

"What time's dinner?" he asked.

Yep, that's right, there's a sucker born every minute, and I actually serve my Canadian neighbor piping hot meals on occasion. Even though the last time I had him over for dinner, all he did was talk about how wretched it was that we were *forced*—by virtue of the fact that we are both so pathetically single—to dine together, with an accent, of course, on the heartbreaking level of pity he feels for me. And that was while being *forced* to chow down on steak au poivre and potato gratin, which, for him, was gratis.

If I had any sense at all I'd just leave him alone in his den of darkness to gnaw the night away on peameal bacon and ketchup chips. But I don't.

Although, in all fairness, attributing these dinner invitations solely to masochistic charity, or even charitable masochism, would not only be inaccurate, it would be wrong, because when Tomas is good, he is very, very good. In fact, he's a delight. He makes the joke, he gets the joke, and, most admirably, he is not above *being* the joke.

He demonstrated this enviable quality at a recent party.

Tomas and I were swordfighting with swizzle sticks when a drunken buffoon stumbled over and asked Tomas if he was gay. Now I'm the first to admit that I have no *gaydar* whatsoever. My brain waves are far too congested with thoughts of my own sex life to pick up any outside signals. But to me, there's nothing overtly gay about Tomas, who cheerfully informed the buffoon that he was not, in fact, gay, he was merely a "nonpracticing heterosexual."

"Oh, so you're celibate," slurred the buffoon.

"Wrong again," said Tomas, smiling like a jack-o'-lantern, "just unlucky."

Then they clinked glasses.

That's my Canadian neighbor—happy to toast his own misfortune, and even happier to have another injustice heaped atop that heavy wooden cross he's been lugging around on his back for God knows how long.

And then there's me, giggling gleefully beside him, until, inevitably, he goes too far and *forces* me to bitch, complain, and wonder if there's any way I could possibly trick Ben into doing an apartment swap with him.

Clinging to the belief that good would ultimately prevail in the battle for Tomas's soul, I called back through the window that dinner would be ready at 8:00.

"Should I bring anything?"

"*From over there?*" I gasped.

"Tonight's meal doesn't call for a tablespoon of hemlock?" he chimed. "Or perhaps a pinch of deadly nightshade?"

I smiled back sweetly. "I'd be more than happy to add it to yours."

"No, no. I don't want to put you out. I'll just bring myself."

"If you insist," I replied.

Then I got up and ran to the front door.

"Tomas, do you prefer green beans or asparagus?"

"Blue lake or French?"

"French."

"Let's go with the green beans."

"You got it," I replied, "but Yin's not invited tonight, only Yang."

I thought for sure that would provoke a barb, but no. Tomas simply blew me a kiss and crossed over to the other side.

Why the parting kiss, I have no idea. Maybe he's in the Canadian mafia. I didn't dare ask. Like I said, it's best to keep it simple when dealing with the Prince of Darkness.

Instead, I retreated to my computer and turned the whole silly mess into a story. I don't know why—it's just what I do.

overqualified

I am a Dragon. I know this because my Persian waxing lady is constantly yapping at me about Chinese astrology. Her name is Gisou, which means hair or ringlets or something. I find it strange that a Gisou would be in the business of *removing* hair; it reeks of self-loathing, if you ask me. But that's how it is, and I saw her today.

I'd barely assumed the position when Gisou started going off on her favorite subject.

Frankly, I've had my fill of Chinese astrology. I'm not interested in hearing that male Dragon babies were celebrated in ancient China, or that female Dragon babies were killed. Not when I'm naked from the waist down. And not when the person telling me this is brandishing hot wax and behaving as if she has both a direct connection to the ancient Chinese *and* the authority to reinstitute the practice of Dragon slaying. What do I care? This is America. And I'm not even Chinese. If I were, I wouldn't need a bikini wax before hitting the beach.

Mostly I think she's just mad because I'm a Dragon and she's not.

Desperate to change the subject, I told Gisou that I was considering going back to therapy for real, *regularly*. But she didn't like that idea. She told me that only crazy people go to therapy, and advised me to spend my money on a very nice pair of shoes instead. According to Gisou, I don't need therapy to figure out why I haven't been in a relationship in almost two years, the answer is obvious: I'm overqualified.

I am a Dragon, after all.

Content with this diagnosis, I began flipping through an ancient copy of *Vogue* magazine. That is until Gisou alerted me to the fact that she'd just spoken to Freddie Mercury.
"The guy from Queen?" I asked.
Gisou smiled, pleased that I knew him.
"I hate to be the one to break this to you, but he's dead."
"Yes," she replied, "but he is also Persian."

And then she just went silent, leaving me to assume *what?* That Persians are exempt from the laws of nature? "Yeah," I snorted, " a *dead* Persian." Then I scratched and sniffed a Beautiful perfume sample, surprised to find that it actually did smell like an exact combination of Elizabeth Hurley and a golden retriever puppy. I know because I was once in an enclosed space with Elizabeth Hurley.

I checked out of Hollywood in 1994, leaving my post as assistant to the president of production to pursue a romantic endeavor in San Francisco. Things went awry; my attempted escape was thwarted. So I drove back down in 1997, listening to "Hotel California," wondering if it were true that I could never leave, and trying to make peace with my potential fate.

Shortly thereafter, I found myself interviewing for a job. I was totally out of the loop on all things Hollywood, and it was the first time I had ever interviewed for a real job. The last interview I'd been on was in 1990, and that was just for a receptionist position, which doesn't count, because really, who doesn't know how to answer a phone?

But this was for a real job—development executive—and it

required that I actually know something. Granted, there's not that much to know—most movies are proof of that—but they do expect you to be up-to-date on all the hot new writers, which I wasn't. On top of that, I was meeting with America's favorite couple— Hugh and Elizabeth. The whole thing made me a little nervous.

Let me just say that I've been doing yoga for three years and I still go to beginner classes. Why? Because I *hate* being unprepared. In Yoga 101, I never have to worry about that because I'm totally overqualified for the class, thus negating the possibility of me ever fucking up, and worse, looking stupid. That said, even being prepared is no guarantee that I won't *feel* unprepared. Back in grammar school, where I was consistently prepared, whenever the teacher would ask a question, I'd whisper the answer to some kid next to me then urge him to raise his hand. The answer was always right—I wouldn't have dared whisper it otherwise—and the ignoramus next to me would go on to receive *my* praise, as I sat back feeling both vindicated and robbed.

So anyway, I was pacing around my apartment, trying to psych myself up for the interview by reminding myself that everyone in Hollywood is full of shit, when Melanie called. And Melanie and I weren't really even friends. She's just one of those people who has to "help" her way into everybody's business.

"You're meeting with them today, right?" confirmed Melanie.

"Yeah, I've got to leave in about five minutes," I replied.

"Perfect. Hugh's a big history buff and he hates the South."

"*What?*"

"That's all I was able to dig up."

"Are you fucking kidding? How could you do this to me? I don't know jack about history, and *I'm from the South!*"

"Not really. You're from New Orleans."

"Well, then, you obviously don't know jack about geography because New Orleans is in the Deep *South*."

"I know, but it's not the same. Anyway, you sound like you're from New York, so just don't bring it up. And everybody knows *something* about history."

"Yeah, I know something. I know that the South is supposed to rise again. Maybe I'll use that as my opening line. 'So Hugh, when do you think the South is . . .'"

Melanie cut me off. "Stop worrying," she said. "I majored in history. I'm happy to help."

"Oh God no, I couldn't possibly trouble you. You've already helped more than enough."

I hung up the phone, went to my car and spent ten minutes trying to still my shaking hands long enough to get the key into the ignition. On my way to Simian Films—Hugh and Elizabeth's production company—I drove past a forty-foot Elizabeth Hurley. She was looking down on me from her Estée Lauder billboard. I laughed the hysterical laughter of someone who knows that disaster is just around the corner.

Then I turned the corner and pulled into the parking lot.

Hugh and Elizabeth couldn't have been lovelier, but that didn't stop the interview from going down exactly as anticipated. I don't really remember much about it, except that I'd never heard of a single writer they mentioned, and I may have voluntarily confessed to being a historical ignoramus at one point, in the hope of avoiding a pop quiz and causing Hugh any further disappointment. I may have brought up the Southern thing too, because I seem to remember Hugh saying "fiddlesticks" or some such word not often uttered in America, and I can't imagine what else it would have been in response to, if not the accusation that he *hated* an entire quadrant of the United States.

We did have a few laughs along the way, but I could never tell if they were laughing with me or at me, and I left not knowing whether they thought I was a complete imbecile, or if perhaps they had seen me for the quick-witted but ill-prepared Southern belle that I was. But I'm going to assume the latter; they seemed pretty smart.

Needless to say, I didn't get the job. But I did get a condolence letter from Elizabeth, because apparently, even in Hollywood where etiquette is considered an outdated convention, the Brits sometimes adhere to it in a nod to history. And in a nod to the Brits, I now sign all my letters with a red Sharpie, just like Elizabeth did. I think it looks pretty cool.

So while I can't claim that she and Hugh actually had a golden retriever puppy present during the interview, puppies, like babies, all smell basically the same, and it's easy enough to imagine what one would smell like if combined with Elizabeth's scent. Or I don't know, maybe Elizabeth was wearing Beautiful that day. Maybe Hugh was, too. Maybe they bathed in the stuff. All I really know is that scratching that perfume sample in Gisou's waxing room transported me back to another time and place, forcing me to relive an interview that I never needed to relive, an interview that left me feeling decidedly *under*qualified, despite the fact that I then checked back in with my old boss, who quickly rehired me *as a development executive*, no interview required.

As I was reliving all this, Gisou yanked me back to the present with the removal of a linen strip, and informed me that it was their mutual Persianness—hers and Freddie's—that allowed them to converse beyond the grave. Who knew? I didn't, and I still don't know if this is specific to Persians or if anyone can do it with any dead person from their own country. But I'd sure like to find out.

What I did learn was that Freddie Mercury bears a striking

resemblance to Gisou's father, who is also dead. I wanted to tell her that *all skeletons* bear a striking resemblance to each other, but I feared that a comment like that would most likely leave me with third-degree burns. So I asked if her father ever wore leather chaps around the house instead.

As usual, Gisou had zero interest in expanding the conversation to include anything that actually interested me, and instead reverted back to her own line of chatter, proudly announcing that she had all of Freddie's tapes. *Tapes?* "What, like eight-tracks?" I asked. And to that she responded, "Don't be ridiculous."

As Gisou slathered me with boiling wax, I eked out that "Under Pressure" (Freddie's duet with David Bowie) was one of my all-time favorite songs. Gisou stared back at me, bewildered. She'd never heard of David Bowie, but I guess that makes sense, given that he is neither dead nor Persian.

I tried to ring a bell by humming a few bars for her, but she quickly shut me up with another yank at yet another linen strip. Once she had my attention, she confided in me that Freddie Mercury and her father come to her in her dreams and advise her on love and life. "Well, no wonder you don't need therapy!" I blurted out. "If I was getting free advice from a pair of ghosts, I wouldn't need it either."

Then I asked her what they ate when they came over and if they looked like the people in the Haunted Mansion at Disneyland.

Gisou slapped my ass, scolding me for mocking the dead, and insisting that Freddie Mercury was a very nice man. I defended myself, replying that there was little doubt in my mind that this was true, as I had read as much in a November 1978 (!) issue of *Rolling Stone*. "It's your father I'm not so sure about. Why the hell does he need Freddie Mercury to talk to his daughter? Isn't his own advice good enough? And not for nothing, but birds of a feather do flock together."

Gisou stuck her tongue out at me in response. But really, what more can you expect from a Snake?

Waxing complete, I suggested that Gisou clear her schedule for the rest of the day and run to the nearest therapist. And what did she do? She threw me a curveball. She does it every time. Just when I'm convinced that she is 100 percent crazy, she lets loose with something oddly wise, completely out of the blue, and frankly, a little disorienting.

As I was lifting myself off the waxing table, she pushed me back down, got in my face, and said, "You have good genes. You are a beautiful, intelligent young woman, thanks to your parents, and yet you complain that they are not supportive enough."

"So?" I replied, attempting to disguise my complete lack of preparation as a complete lack of interest.

"Let me ask you something," she added, somewhat venomously. "If your parents were more supportive but you were an ugly, stupid pig, do you think you'd be better off?"

Forget disoriented, now I was irritated, because really, getting waxed, much like answering a telephone, shouldn't require any skill or preparation whatsoever. But Gisou is only a Snake; it wouldn't have been fair for me to engage in battle with her. So I simply slipped into my skirt and told her I didn't know, adding, however, that I did know that "Fat-bottomed girls make this rockin' world go round."

She stared back vacantly as I forked over a check. It was crazy. Here I was quoting Freddie Mercury, and his #1 fan had absolutely no idea what I was talking about.

I drove home thinking about how it always baffles me when people claim to be Persian because if you look on a map, there is no Persia. It no longer exists. It's ancient history, just like Freddie Mercury.

I was left to wonder, how could someone have all of Queen's tapes and not be familiar with some of their most famous lyrics? And why would anyone lie about something like that? What was there to gain? Did Gisou really exist? And if not, did it make me any less overqualified? Had I just been waxed? Was I dead, too? Why was it that my mother never returned my calls? Could it be that she considered me a stupid, ugly pig, despite the fact that I'd taken a dip in her very own gene pool? Was there a slice in time somewhere near the intersection of Doheny and Santa Monica that allowed entrance to empires of days gone by? Why was Gisou so obsessed with the ancient Chinese? Did she have ancient Chinese clients? And if so, what the hell did they need from a waxing lady? I wanted to stop for a smoothie, but what was the point if I would be drinking a smoothie that didn't really exist, paid for with money that didn't really exist?

That nonexistent money thing was the first thought that made any sense at all. I remembered that I had no job. But maybe I never did. I started to get a headache.

I arrived home and collapsed on the couch, completely spent. It was all I could do to grab the Magic 8 Ball and ask it if I was real. After a quick twirl, the words appeared: REPLY HAZY. TRY AGAIN LATER. I thought about asking it again but I knew that wasn't what *later* meant and everybody knows it's only the first answer that counts anyway. So I chucked it.

Then I fell into a deep sleep and dreamt that I was a Persian princess.

I lived in an elaborate beachfront castle on the Caspian Sea. The gate surrounding it was made of pure gold. Camels frolicked in the crystal blue water, while sheep and goats made merry on the shore.

The beach was speckled with billboards—forty-foot images of me, sprouting up from the sand like giant wildflowers. I'm not usually a fan of billboards—and I'm pretty sure they were invented post-Persia—but as I gazed upon them through the velvet-draped windows of my boudoir, I thought to myself, those billboards look pretty damn good.

I was eating a bowlful of rubies while lusting after a hot young servant whose sole purpose in life was weaving me a magic carpet. His muscles shimmered with sweat as he wove the golden threads in and out on his massive loom. I longed for him, but he dare not look at me. I tried to tell him that just because I was overqualified didn't mean I wasn't willing to stoop for sex, assuring him that I'd done so once, maybe twice. But it was if he felt his ears were not even worthy of hearing me speak. He simply cast his eyes to the ground.

To hell with that, I thought. I was not about to be ignored just because I was beautiful *and* intelligent. So I brushed my freshly waxed leg across his handsome face as I placed my flower-painted toes on the magic carpet and asked if he thought my bottom was fat enough to make this rockin' world go round. The poor guy looked super confused, which is when it dawned on me that they probably didn't speak English in Persia. And I'm assuming they didn't have razors either, because he was absolutely awed by my silky-smooth skin.

So drawing on what little high school Farsi I could remember, I begged him to kiss me, just once, promising him in return a ride on my magic carpet to a place called Los Angeles, where there are thousands of women who are just as well waxed but infinitely less qualified. Then I pulled his mouth to mine and awoke to a ringing telephone and Frankie trying to lick the cherry Life Saver that was lodged between my slightly parted lips.

Talk about a buzz kill.

———

Thoroughly disgusted and completely discombobulated from my recent time travel, I could not have been less prepared for what awaited me on the other end of the line: my mother.

"How was the job interview?" she asked.

What? Why was she bringing that up? "It was awful," I replied. "Hugh and Elizabeth thought I was an idiot."

"*Hugh and Elizabeth?*"

Emerging from my post-nap confusion, I updated my response. "Oh, you mean the one *today*. I had to cancel it. It was the only time Gisou could take me."

"Oh, for Christ's sake!"

"Mom, *it's summertime!* And where have you been, anyway? I've left like seventeen messages. I could have actually needed you."

"I've been busy. Look, I'm trying to clean up this house and I need to know what you want to keep."

"Do I have to decide right now?"

"Yes."

"Well, then, I don't know. You decide. Or throw it all away. I don't care."

"I have two words for you: Fry Baby."

"Please. Don't remind me. And that was yours, anyway. If you want to talk about your stuff, I know exactly what I want."

"I'm not dead yet," she announced. (It's one of her favorite lines.)

"I know," I replied. "If you were, I wouldn't need a therapist."

"I don't know what the hell that's supposed to mean, but I've got a box here that appears to contain some old records. You want it?"

"What's the point? You probably already gave my turntable away."

"That turntable is only one-third yours."

"Wrong. It's all mine, but even so I'd settle for one-third."

"You got it, Solomon. Let me just find my saw and I'll send your third right out."

"*No, don't!*" I cried. "Pitch it. I have too much junk already."

"All right, we're moving on to records. Here's one: 'Fat Bottomed Girls.' Want it?"

I couldn't believe my ears. Was the big guy trying to tell me something? "Oh my God, Mom, you have no idea how spooky that is."

"Trust me," she replied. "It's not nearly as spooky as some of the stuff I've found."

Fearing what she may have unearthed, I thought it best to end the conversation.

"Alrighty. I think this is my cue to say good-bye."

"Good idea. Call me when you have some money in the bank."

"OK, if that's how you want to be. But first I'm going to have to call you to *get* the money."

"I don't think so. Your allowance days are over, baby. And don't call your father, either."

"Oh, fiddlesticks," I replied. "Why can't you people be more supportive?"

"I am being supportive. I'm being supportive of the idea that you're capable of earning an income."

"If you insist. But I may need some interview-aversion therapy first. Wanna pitch in for that?"

"No!" she replied. "I'm going dancing. I've *earned* my leisure time."

"But Mom, interviews freak me out. I'm not good at selling myself."

"Get over it."

Then the line went dead.

———

I hung up the phone, rolled over, and picked up the Dragon literature Gisou had shoved in my purse as I was limping out the door. One glance confirmed my suspicions: My mother was also a Dragon. It made perfect sense, given the battle of wills that's been raging between us since the '70s, but didn't lead me to believe that we were any closer to a resolution.

Overtaxed by the day's events, Frankie and I headed into the kitchen in search of comfort food. A lone fortune cookie and half a bottle of red wine awaited us. Frankie plopped down and started licking his cat hole just to remind me where his tongue has been, while I returned to the couch with a glass of vino and proceeded to seek my fortune.

A PENNY SAVED IS A PENNY EARNED

Hmm, I thought, very interesting. Still, I didn't know quite how it applied to me since I had no pennies saved and wasn't earning any, either. Nor could I see what bearing it had on my romantic life.

I momentarily considered going to Tibet, thinking it might be easier to figure it all out there, but I knew even if I could afford it, Frankie would never allow it. If only Elvis Presley and old Uncle Ronald would come to me in my dreams to advise me on love and life. But they never did. They just left me to my own devices, much like my live mother. According to her, I was more than qualified to solve my own problems. That's what adults do.

never never land

My younger brother Blair came out to visit me once, for oh, I don't know, thirty-six hours. Not long, just long enough to meet my friend Alice and dub us the "spinster sisters." But he's wrong about Alice; she's a divorcée.

Alice lives seven blocks east in the homeowner section of our neighborhood. Our neighborhood is technically called The Fairfax District, but I once heard a woman call it The Scale + 10 District, as most of the residents are unknown, out-of-work actors who, on the rare occasion that they do work, are paid scale + 10 percent. Everyone else is either Alice, Tomas, me, or a Hasid.

When I first moved to this neighborhood, I was excited about the prospect of befriending a Hasid. *Why not?* Having been raised in New Orleans, a predominantly Catholic/Bacchanalian blend, I figured this was the perfect opportunity to add a little cultural texture to my social circle, and maybe even learn something in the process. But after almost two years, all I've really learned is that Hasids have very little interest in befriending me. Maybe it's the shorts and tank tops—I have no idea. I try to make eye contact when I pass them on the street, but it never works. A couple of months ago one of them scraped the paint off the side of my car with his minivan while pulling out of Canter's Deli, but even he didn't look at me. He just drove away. Places to go, things to do, I imagine. He was a lot like Alice in that way.

Alice is one of those people who have to be in constant motion, like a shark. She can't sit still for two seconds; she's always sniffing out action.

Case in point: An airplane recently crashed into an apartment building two blocks from my place. And yet, in a neighborhood where nearly everyone is out of work, Alice, who lives more than five blocks from the crash site, was the first person on the scene. She claimed that she just happened to be looking up at the sky when the plane started going down, but no one just looks up at the sky in The Fairfax District.

This is due to the overabundance of ravens that give life here a spooky Hitchcockian slant. They're giant, they're menacing, and, apparently, their wings don't work. I have never seen a single one of them take flight. They just strut along on the pavement like the badasses they are, and your eyes damn well better be down there with them if you know what's good for you. Occasionally, you may catch one hopping up onto the hood of a car and ripping the antenna out of its socket for sport, but that's as high as I've seen them go. Alice wasn't looking up at the sky; she's just got a nose for drama.

Lately, though, things have changed in our neighborhood. The Grove, a fabulous new Disney-esque mall, now towers over the old Farmer's Market, announcing the arrival of higher rents that will force the next shipment of out-of-work actors to find housing elsewhere. A nasty breakup has prompted Alice to renounce drama. And I, who have always skipped from one man to another, have not had one for the last 736, *count 'em*, 736 (!) days.

Not wanting to dwell on that particular change, I called Alice and we walked over to The Grove to see *Adaptation*. What a great movie. The twists, the turns, the fabulously flawed characters, I couldn't have loved it more. I didn't understand half of it, but I couldn't have loved it more. I was still trying to put the pieces together when Alice and I left the theater and made our way to Wetzel's Pretzels. And it was there, at Wetzel's, while squirting mustard on my pretzel, that everything came into focus.

"Fuck me!" I screamed out, *"I'm Charlie Kaufman!"*

The mustard container fell from my hand and bounced off the pavement; I staggered over to a park bench and began to weep. It was all so obvious. Why did I need a movie to see it? Just like Charlie, I'd been sitting on the sidelines of life, trying to psych myself up, but really just psyching myself out.

Alice, of course, was infinitely more troubled by the flying mustard that had now landed on her jeans. She hates condiments.

"What's your problem?" she barked, while trying to remove the vile yellow goop without actually touching it.

"I'm Charlie Kaufman!" I cried. "How much further explanation does a tragedy like that require? I've been doing myself in! I've been sitting around for the last two and a half years wondering what had changed, why I wasn't getting any action, and now I find out that I've actually been hiding in plain sight while my life slips away!"

"It's not just you," assured Alice. "We live in Never Never Land."

"Is that supposed to make me feel better?"

"I don't know, but for what it's worth, I thought you were more like the Chris Cooper character. He was more like Blair, but he was a little like you, too."

I couldn't believe my ears. The character played by Chris Cooper was heartbreakingly human and thoroughly fascinating, but talk about a piece of work! The guy made Tomas seem carefree and uncomplicated by comparison. And here was *my friend*, Alice, remarking, *nonchalantly*, that Chris and I were cut from the same cloth. I was devastated.

"What?" continued Alice. "I thought he was a fun character."

"Please, just go away."

Everything was all wrong, but was it all me? I may have been sitting on the sidelines, but wouldn't I at least have noticed an interesting passerby? Wouldn't that have driven me to action? Was the kooky post-credit reveal that *I'm Charlie Kaufman* a legitimate turning point in my own story? Or was it some sort of red herring tossed in by my subconscious?

Alice was wrong about me, but she was right about us living in Never Never Land. Hollywood is the high school quarterback that you later discover maxed out at eighteen, a Peter Pan cloning experiment gone amok. The common belief seems to be that Hollywood messes people up. The thing is, many—if not most—of the men in Hollywood came from somewhere else. So while I realize that the concept of personal responsibility isn't all that popular these days, I think it may be more accurate to say that what really messes people up is their own willing surrender to a messed-up environment. And I often wonder, is America's fascination with Hollywood a foreshadowing of where the whole damn county is headed? Or are things already messed up across the board and men with a fondness for green tights merely migrating to Hollywood?

I worked on a television show for about five minutes. My partner and I were going over one of the episodes, when he turned to me and said, "I just realized what your problem is. You're like Jason Schwartzman in *Rushmore*. You want this to be art, but it's not. It's the opposite of art—it's TV."

Call it surrender, call it adaptation, call it whatever you like, I couldn't do it. But he was right. If the show hadn't been canceled, I'd have been hanged for mutiny. And while I know I don't respond well to authority, that doesn't negate the fact that integrity—artistic or otherwise—just doesn't get you anywhere in this environment. In fact, it's usually a detriment. Oh people may notice it and comment on its quaintness—it's possible they may even admire it—but they're not likely to adopt it as part of their own repertoire, since it doesn't have much practical value. Even just run-of-the-mill decency is an oddity. It's really quite something the way people will get downright celebratory when they stumble across anyone who isn't a complete and utter asshole. *Oh my God, your boss didn't fire you for buying him peanut M&M's instead of plain? What a great guy!*

Forget passion. This town is powered by an alternate fuel, equal parts ambition and desperation. And I think Silly Putty is used as a thickening agent. Otherwise, I have no way of accounting for the incredible shape-shifting some of these characters seem to be capable of at the drop of a hat.

Hollywood is a magnet for men with a hunger for money, power and fame—those are the prizes on offer—which makes it about as cozy as a snake pit. No one really trusts anyone, so insecurity permeates the already toxic air. Those on the rise are largely interested in grabbing onto the coattails of those who can further their careers, creating "friendships" that are both self-serving and sycophantic in nature.

There are exceptions, of course, but that's the rule. I'm sure a lot of people come out here with grander aspirations, but for the most part they just adapt to the environment. The women are just as bad, and they've got the added option of sleeping their way up the ladder—a market I think they've still got cornered, but since I'm not looking to hook up with a woman, I'm not going to concern myself with them for now.

People get lucky here every day, but making it in Hollywood requires more than luck. It's a tough job in that it requires thick skin and an iron stomach. In addition to that, the line separating one's personal and professional lives is virtually nonexistent, making it a round-the-clock job.

So how much time does a man really have left to give after that? Probably not enough if you're looking for an actual life partner in a loving and lasting relationship.

You hear women talk about men and their fear of commitment, and while I'm sure that's valid in some cases, from where I'm sitting, the problem seems a little more complicated than that. Because in any supercompetitive environment, in any environment where one's "value" is in a constant state of flux and always in danger of plummeting, it's easy to get beaten down, it's easy to feel *not quite good enough.* And from what I can tell, living in an industry town where one's perceived value at any point in time is common knowledge only makes matters worse. It's also an idea that is supported by the constant cry of men who aren't rich, powerful or famous—or perhaps just not rich, powerful or famous *enough*— that women in this town only want to go out with men who are. So a lot of them don't even make the effort, or maybe they're just too weary to try, instead waiting for the day that they are *enough.*

But what is *enough*?

It has been said that the best things in life are free. They don't require money, power or fame. Things like *love, happiness, inner peace,* things that I have a hard time believing anyone *doesn't* want. So when I see people giving up all else to make their mark in the film industry, when I see people committing their lives to achieving greatness simply for the sake of greatness and its tangible by-products, that mark strikes me as decidedly *un*remarkable, that achievement in all probability hollow, and I can't help but wonder if those people aren't operating under the misguided belief that their "greatness" will bring them the very love, happiness and inner peace that they never needed money, power or fame to attain in the first place, and that have likely become more distant and elusive in the process.

This is something I like to refer to as the Hollow Chocolate Bunny Syndrome. Always a disappointment, and yet, no matter how many hollow chocolate bunnies are cracked open, their bogus nature revealed—in the form of miserable millionaires, hideous highly publicized breakups, and overdosing celebrities—people fall for it over and over again because, I don't know, *that bunny really looked solid?*

Passion, I get. Slithering through a snake pit in order to land a hollow chocolate bunny, I don't. The whole thing reeks of Greek mythology, if you ask me. It's like one of those stories where a young man seeking some profound truth is sent on a series of life-threatening missions by a three-headed monster only to return years later a beaten man and find out that he missed the whole fucking point.

Money. Money. Money. It's all right, but I'm beginning to wonder if materialism hasn't put us in a weird holding pattern. Hollywood often feels like one big waiting game. Only once X, Y and Z have occurred can *life* actually begin. To make matters worse, the wait itself seems to produce yet another problem:

It used to be that there was Ragú and maybe Prego. Now, there's an entire aisle of spaghetti sauces. It's a bit overwhelming and a recent study revealed that, when faced with many options, people were *less likely to make a choice* than when faced with only a few. *I thought I wanted spaghetti sauce, but fuck it, this is just too confusing.* Likewise, it used to be that when a person found someone they thought would make a good spouse, they just cut bait and got on with it. Now, it seems like a lot of people are holding out for a *better* mate. But I wonder if it's not so much a conscious decision as an inability to even make a decision, for fear that it might not be the *right* decision, meaning the *very best* decision. A fear that I would imagine only intensifies with the passage of time and exposure to ever more possibilities.

Maybe we always sucked at making decisions and there was just a lot of coin-flipping going on in the past, but it would appear that our seemingly unlimited number of choices has caused something along the lines of paralysis. It calls to mind the old expression *shit or get off the pot*. There's a lot of protracted pot-sitting going on around here, and given the vast amount of available reading material, I wonder if half these guys are ever going to just get on with it. People may have made decisions too hastily in the past, but is spending one's entire life in the bathroom really the right response?

And I know it's not just men. I've had girlfriends who held out for Mr. Right, then, once they were ready to have a baby, hooked up with the first joker who came along, someone who would have never made the cut previously, a *worse* mate than she could have had were she not holding out for the *very best* mate. Now, there could be some out there, but I personally don't know any men who have been struck by the sudden urgent need to reproduce. So if not that, what does it take to get a man off the pot?

I've got a friend in New Orleans whose divorced mother hooked up with an old high school boyfriend, a widower. Then, after a few months of newfound relationship bliss, her boyfriend, Carl, told her that he couldn't commit to anything because he wanted to date other people. *Carl was seventy-two years old!*

Edna Mae told him to take a hike, and I guess once left empty-handed Carl realized that he might *die* before he found anyone else *to date* because he eventually came around, but I mean, it really does beg the question: *Does this shit never end?*

It's a sorry situation, but at least Edna Mae had the Grim Reaper on her side. I too have had some experience with pot-sitters, but not having death looming quite so large, they took a tad longer to come around, giving me just enough time to lose all interest.

Unfortunately, I don't see things changing anytime soon, and they'll probably only get worse before they do. But maybe I'm wrong. Maybe history will in fact prove my generation to be *the absolute worst* at entering into and maintaining relationships. Maybe hundreds of years from now people will look back and scratch their heads, unable to fathom how we could have possibly screwed things up so royally.

I was born in 1964 and was raised to believe that I could do anything a man could do. It was a new curriculum for us girls, but I'm pretty sure the boys of my generation were still being taught the same old stuff—don't cry, be strong, prepare to provide. I guess that works if the whole point was to pull a quick sucker punch on the male population, but in terms of me actually finding a partner, I think that may have been slightly less than helpful. Because if I were a man today, I might be somewhat unsure of my value to a generation of women raised to believe that they could do it all— women who, in many cases, are doing it all *without men* —providing for themselves, having babies by themselves, yada, yada, yada— and frankly, I might be just a wee bit intimidated by the whole situation.

Now, from what I've been able to gather, since somewhere around, oh, the beginning of time, men have been in awe of (a.k.a. intimidated by) women, this usually attributed to the fact that woman are able to give birth, and sometimes attributed to the fact that women can have sex with just about anyone they want, anytime they want. So it would appear that feminism isn't the foot that tripped men—men were doing that on their own long before then. No, feminism is more like the laughter that ensues after the fall, laughter that typically results in making the person on the ground (A) feel like an even bigger loser, and (B) not like the laugher very much.

But who knows? Maybe the reason I haven't seen any action in the last two years has nothing to do with any of that. Maybe it *is* just me.

A few months ago a friend of mine was going through a divorce and having a really hard time with it. We were talking, when suddenly she asked, "Has anyone ever wanted to have anal sex with you?"

Needless to say, I was a little taken aback, but she wanted an answer, so I gave her one. "Only my first boyfriend and every boyfriend since," I replied.

She, in turn, burst into tears. *"No one's ever asked me to have anal sex!"* she blubbered.

Why this was a problem for her is beyond me, but she was really undone by it.

"Don't cry. Maybe no one else gets asked either. Did a guy ever want you to pee on him?" I asked.

She shook her head.

"Well, you see, I've gotten that one a lot, too. Everybody wants me to pee on them. So maybe it's just me. I've often wondered if perhaps men see me as a symbol of authority, and are torn between wanting to dominate me and be dominated by me, because I just can't shake the feeling that those two requests are oddly related."

I mean, come on, there's obviously something going on there. Or at least there was, so what the hell happened? My friend Pierre recently felt compelled to warn me that it's going to be difficult for me to find a man because most men are intimidated by independent women. And I guess I'm stuck with that Catch-22; one doesn't really have any option other than independence when there's no man around to depend on.

Then there's my friend Dan, who claims that I'm just plain

intimidating. Why? I don't know. When I suggested that just because he was intimidated *by me* didn't necessarily mean that I was intimidating, he laughed it off. According to Dan, it's going to be hard for me to find a man because most men need to be lured into a relationship, and I'm the kind of woman whose mere presence demands a choice—whatever the hell that means; he didn't elaborate. But according to Dan, no man in his right mind is going to fuck around with me. In my defense, I'd just like to point out that I have, in fact, been significantly fucked around with by numerous men over the years. Still, it's quite possible that none of those guys were in their right minds, and well, I probably wasn't either.

My mother called yesterday to inform me that she'd heard on the radio that men *really are* intimidated by strong women, beautiful women and intelligent women. And she delivered this news as if it were just that. Of course, in the past, whenever I've hinted at any of these things, she's acted like I'm trying to pull a fast one on her, maintaining that I'm simply not trying hard enough or, her favorite, that I'm too aloof.

I'm not aloof; I'm blind. Beyond three feet everything's a blur, and contacts are out of the question because I have "dry eye syndrome," which is basically a load of crap because every time I step one foot outside of Los Angeles, my eyes are downright dewy. I'm afraid to have laser surgery because they say it can dry your eyes out, and if these chalkballs I've got lodged in my eye sockets get any drier, they'll turn to dust and blow right out of my head.

So I get called names. Last week for example, a friend of Alice's reported to her that he'd seen me at the YMCA. Apparently, I'd looked straight at him then rudely turned away without so much as a nod of the head. I asked Alice if he said I was aloof. "No," replied Alice. "He called you a bitch."

And sure, I could wear glasses, but frankly, making eye contact with men isn't always a wise idea. Just the other day, I was walking through Chaya, a popular restaurant adjacent to Cedars-Sinai, when I passed a table of grown men in scrubs. One of them said hello, I returned his hello, and then he followed it up with. "Nice tits," which his fellow frat boys, I mean doctors, met with uproarious laughter and, I swear to God, a high five.

Meanwhile, my friend Jay told me that he's heard some pretty raunchy locker-room talk about me as of late. Of course, when I begged him to *please* spill the beans, hoping for a vicarious thrill in the absence of any real sex, all he would say was, "Well, it usually starts with 'I'd like to . . .' and ends with fluids."

Yet none of these virile men approach me. Why?

Why should any of this stuff matter now if it never prevented me from having a boyfriend in the past? Is it a product of age or time? Is this what the pool's been reduced to? Men who are capable of harassing women and using them as locker-room fodder, but can't actually engage with women? Is the thrill of impressing the boys really better than sex? Have women become so scary that men can only find strength in numbers? Or are they all closet homosexuals like my gay friends keep insisting? I have no idea. I only know that once I started to think about everything, it really started to bug me that I didn't have a man, and well, here I am in my sexual prime, and this honey pot's going untapped. At the risk of sounding self-centered, I've got to tell you, I consider that one of the greatest American tragedies of all time.

Since he was closest, I called Tomas over to shed some light on the intimidation issue.

After confirming that men are intimidated by any woman with a uterus or a vagina, their own mothers, some of their friends' mothers, the occasional sister, independent women, each other, strong women, beautiful women, intelligent women, women with nice tits, women with not-so-nice tits, and authority figures, and after Tomas agreed with me that any woman who was able to get through all those hoops would be completely repellent to men anyway, I asked. "How about this? Can you think of anything that men *aren't* intimidated by?"

Tomas thought about that for a minute then said, "Little people. You know, midgets and stuff. But that could just be me. I can't speak for all men."

"Good to know."

"That's the thing, you're not particularly intimidating in and of yourself, but you are tall, and that's *really* intimidating."

"Oh, well," I replied. "It's probably for the best. At least that way men won't come near me, which is better than having them run for the hills only once they've confirmed the presence of girly parts."

It seemed pretty bleak, I'll admit, but I refused to believe that last call had occurred without my knowledge. I just had to get off the sidelines and enter the field. I mean, if *Adaptation* could get made in Hollywood, I had to be able to find a man here.

So I put on my glasses and went for a walk.

The Hasids were all in for the night; it was mostly out-of-work actors on the streets. So why was no one meeting my eyes?

Were we an entire neighborhood of Charlie Kaufmans, too timid to engage? Were we a neighborhood of Chris Coopers, hiding our fragile hearts behind gruff veneers? What was Hollywood really producing more of—entertainment or alienation?

And what was up with all those dogs? Were they just dogs, or were they substitutes for the human connection that seems to be slipping further and further away with each passing day? Nothing against dogs, but is that really what it's come to? I guess it could be worse; I know people who love dogs but won't allow themselves a dog solely because losing it would be *unbearable*. And what does that tell you about their likelihood of entering into a meaningful *human* relationship?

I couldn't help but wonder—was everyone just biding their time until their ships come in, carrying another load of hollow chocolate bunnies? And what the hell was I doing here if I knew the bunnies weren't solid?

welcome to earth

Making fire was child's play, thanks to my gas stove. Even gathering food was a cinch. Still, there was *something* missing. And my inner cavewoman was doing her damnedest to bring it to my attention.

Let's face it, whacking tennis balls around can only relieve so much tension; I don't care what setting you've got the ball machine on. And then there's the vanity issue. When the muscles in my right arm doubled in size to those in my left, I decided I needed a new outlet.

At first I thought about buying a vibrator. It saddened me deeply, as I could remember once laughing uproariously at the very suggestion, given that the real thing was readily available. But only an idiot never changes his mind. Someone said that. I think it was Karl Marx, but I'm not sure. Whoever it was, he wasn't here now.

So I got in my car and drove over to the Hustler store. And there I sat, on Sunset Boulevard, casing the joint. People came, people went, and they all acted as if loading up on sex toys was perfectly normal. *Fascinating.* I wondered if perhaps I could get away with that, too.

I knew there was a smoothie bar in there, or so I'd heard. A girlfriend told me. And she was a writer on *Sex and the City*, so I saw no reason to doubt her.

I imagined myself sidling up to the smoothie bar, just as innocent as a lamb. I'd order something red, engage in a little innocuous small talk with the soda jerk, discreetly eye the aisles, and locate the object of my desire. I'd casually suck on my straw, careful to avoid any attention-grabbing slurping sounds, as I sauntered down the chosen aisle, snatched that baby up, cruised past the front register, sliding my vibrator across the bar code reader, lobbing my American Express card to the checkout guy and hauling ass out the front door. The next day I'd send Alice back to retrieve my credit card. If she wouldn't do it, big whoop, I'd just cancel it and get a new one. My plan was flawless, and I was the little engine that could.

Unfortunately, just as I was thinking I could, a meter maid appeared out of nowhere, leaping in front of my car, ordering me to either feed the meter or get moving, and stripping me of my nerve in the process. My inner cavewoman wanted to club her; my outer wimp started the car up and wormed her way into the ever-present "flow" of traffic on Sunset. I gave the Hustler store a final parting glance, as I kissed my vibrator good-bye.

Back at home, I considered my options: I could order one on the Internet. I knew they always wrapped that kind of stuff up in plain brown paper, so that was no problem. But then I thought about the actual vibrator packaging. They couldn't just throw something like that in a box with a bunch of Styrofoam peanuts, could they? It seemed highly unlikely, and I imagined that the actual packaging could be pretty risqué. It was then that I realized my previous plan had not, in fact, been flawless; this packaging problem would have haunted me either way.

Sure, I have a shredder. I got it a few months back when I spotted some shady character rooting around in my garbage. And it's a nice shredder, but it can't handle cardboard.

Cardboard packaging was a real problem for me. I thought

about my fellow apartment dwellers trotting out to our shared garbage cans, spotting the vibrator box and instantly linking it to me—the single chick. I thought about Tomas skulking around in my driveway and catching a glimpse of it. *That,* I definitely didn't need. No, the only way out that I could see was to sit in my living room with a pair of gardening shears hacking the package into Chiclet-sized pieces, but that was no good either. By the time I'd turned the stupid cardboard box into confetti *by hand,* I would have had to stare at the package for far too long. Realizing that this is what it had come to would have caused me to sink into a deep depression, killing my libido, and rendering the item *inside* the package 100 percent useless to me, much like the sea urchin cracker I bought while on vacation in Ibiza that hasn't cracked a single sea urchin since; it's only peeked out from a drawer on occasion to remind me what a fool I am.

Only one option remained: the real thing. And that was all right, it was just that attached to the real thing would be a man. And while I've heard it said that tragedy + time = comedy, for me, those things had added up to something more along the lines of terror. Of course, I was also terrified by the prospect of never having sex again.

It was a big circular mess.

What the hell, I thought, flying terrifies me too and that never stopped me from boarding a plane. It didn't really apply, but it was all I had. So I went with it.

I wasn't looking for anything too flashy; that had never been my thing. In fact, I'd decided to go even further in the other direction. I reckoned that the more I simplified my needs, the easier it would be to make the relationship work, thus ensuring myself a steady piece of ass.

Modern man is still like 90 percent caveman, content with a hot meal and primitive sex (preferably unprotected) after a long day of taking down bison. I learned that much the last time out, and I figured it gave me a leg up on all the women who think it's the duty of men to pretend to enjoy things like shopping and decorating and endless blathering. Guys don't want to talk about the relationship. And that was fine with me because what I wanted predated language.

I was looking for someone cavemanish—someone with a passion for life's primal pleasures, but who wouldn't leave a pelt's worth of black hairs all over my sheets. No, I was looking for something in the blonde-to-sandy range, and I'd come to believe that a Viking was the answer.

Alice was off God knows where, probably either helping someone or getting some help for herself. It's always one or the other. So I rang up Stephanie, who's just as selfish and OK with it as I am.

"A *what?*" asked Stephanie, incredulously.

"A Viking," I replied.

"Do you know how stupid that sounds?"

"Too bad, I already carved it in stone. I like Vikings."

"You can like 'em all you want. I like dinosaurs. It doesn't mean I get to have one as a pet."

"I'm sorry to hear that, but I'm not looking for a pet."

"Then let's hit the fjords, baby. Shall we take your drakkar or mine?"

"I'm not talking about an *actual* Viking with a horned cap and all that stuff. I'm just talking about a type. Come pick me up."

The deal was that we had to go somewhere neither one of us had been in at least three years, in the hope of seeing at least *one new face*. Obviously, a Scandinavian bar would have been the optimal choice, but my Internet research had resulted in a big fat zilch.

Stephanie wanted to go to an English pub in Hollywood, but English guys don't generally do it for me, and beer never does, so I wasn't too keen on that idea. I tossed out a few other suggestions, Stephanie vetoed them all, and we ended up at the English pub.

The first sign of trouble greeted us at the entrance. As the doorman was checking our licenses, he smiled at Stephanie, commenting on how incredibly young she looked for her age. Then to me he said absolutely nothing whatsoever on the subject. And it really got my goat because, hey, guess what, I'm the single chick. Not Stephanie. Stephanie's got a boyfriend. She doesn't need compliments from the outside world. She's wearing her validation. It's that rock the size of Nebraska she's got weighing her hand down like a lead glove.

Be that as it may, the doorman then handed her back her license and said, "Here you go, Steph."

And I thought to myself, that's peculiar, a complete stranger shortening her name like that. Except that it wasn't. Because she, in turn, winked right back at him, like they had a little secret that the new girl wasn't in on. Which they would have, had the new girl not been so darn observant.

"You selfish witch," I blurted out. "You come here all the time, don't you?"

"I haven't been here in three years," replied Stephanie, avoiding eye contact throughout.

"Whatever you say, *Steph*. Wink. Wink."

"Who cares?" she replied. "*You* haven't been here in three years."

"Yeah, because it's an *English pub*. I only agreed to this because you acted like you were dying to revisit your old college stomping ground. If I wanted to go to an English pub, I'd go to England. I don't need some half-assed L.A. version of the real thing."

"Just pretend."

"*Just pretend?* I'm sick of pretense. I'm trying to cut through the bullshit and get to the meat. That was the whole point of the excursion."

"I thought we were looking for Vikings."

"We are! It's all the same thing."

"If you can convince yourself that you're going to find a Viking . . ."

I cut her off, shaking my head. "I can't make this England. I don't know how. *I don't even want to.*"

"Do what you can," she replied.

"Fine. Here we are at *Walt Disney's Epcot*," I chimed, fanning my arms out. "Now if you could be so kind as to point me in the direction of the Norway Pavilion, I'd be more than happy to piss off and leave you to suck down Boddingtons with your mates."

"We're here now. Get over it."

"Oh, I was *over it* five minutes ago when One-Eyed Jack failed to notice how young *I* looked for my age."

"*Who?*"

"Your buddy, back at the front door. He's only got one eye. I guess you're so used to seeing him that you no longer notice . . ."

"He's got two eyes."

"*Technically*," I replied, "but I assure you one of them was, much like this English pub, not real. It wasn't even a good fake. It looked like a pool ball."

"What do you want to drink?" asked Stephanie.

What did I want to drink? What did it even matter? The guys at the bar were so busy talking about some stupid game they couldn't be bothered to move aside and allow us to even order a drink. Unbelievable, except that this is a problem of epic proportions in Los Angeles and I'm so used to opening doors for myself and having some *male* agent with a goddamned headset shove in past me that I would have to actually *act* surprised by rude behavior at this point, and I can't act worth a damn so instead I just shook my head and dreamt of days gone by, days when there was at least some surface acknowledgment that men and women are, in fact, two different sexes. Days when men not only opened doors for women, they actually stood up when a woman approached!

But to be fair, they weren't all talking about the big game. Some of them were "cracking up," thumbing away on their CrackBerries, perhaps trying to hook something up, perhaps just trying to look important. Only the good Lord knows for sure. They could have been playing *Space Invaders* for all I know.

And I'm not ragging on the English, because, in truth, probably only 2 percent of the bar crowd had ever stepped foot on the Queen's soil. Everyone else was just pretending.

Thank God for Stephanie's rock is all I can say. It was only once she knocked a few goofballs unconscious with that thing that we were able to get close enough to the bartender to snag two glasses of wine. Two glasses of wine that Stephanie was not asked to pay for, I might add. No, they were "on the house," another clear indication that Stephanie was, in fact, a regular. "Feel free to pay for the drinks if it'll make you feel better," said Stephanie, breezing past me.

We moved on to the patio and scoped out the scene. It was a large gathering of incredibly average-looking guys, peppered with a smattering of super sketchy foreign-accented men. I felt as if I'd accidentally stumbled into an open casting call for the next Bond villain. Knowing that Stephanie was an aficionada of all things Bond-related, I wondered if she was picking up on the parallel and figured this was a perfect opportunity to test her powers of perception. "What do you think?" I asked. Stephanie scanned the patio and said, "Sheer magnetism, darling."

And that's when it hit me that, once again, my plan resembled nothing as much as a slice of Swiss cheese.

How can you test someone when you have no knowledge base of your own? I'd only ever seen one James Bond movie in my life. I imagine I probably would have seen more if my older brother Stephen hadn't been *completely obsessed with James Bond*. In truth, my most vivid 007 memory is that of me, laughing my head off, as my mother took pictures of Stephen—at an age when he was barely sporting peach fuzz—dressed in a suit and brandishing one of my father's guns, while leaping around the living room adopting various Bond poses. I didn't have to go to the movies; I had all the entertainment I needed at home.

Stephanie, on the other hand, was an only child.

Sheer magnetism, darling? That didn't sound like Stephanie, but I couldn't be sure if she was quoting Bond or not. So I figured I'd just press on; the truth would be revealed eventually.

"Pretty villainous bunch, wouldn't you say?" I continued, baiting her.

"Shocking. Positively shocking."

Damn her. I had no idea whether she was speaking in Bond-isms or not; I just knew she was acting weird.

Suddenly, her eyes lit up. "Wait, I think I see him. Yep, I've found your Viking."

I followed her gaze and landed on a two-eyed Cyclops wearing a fuzzy, leopard-print, poncho-type thing that could have once been the upholstery of a low rider. The words *Mortal Kombat* pounded through my brain. I spat up my wine.

Stephanie slapped my ass. "Run along now, dear. Men talk."

Her new lexicon was lost on me, *but a slap on the ass?* That was a Bond move if ever there was one. "Are you quoting someone, by any chance?" I asked.

"I'm very impressed," she replied. "There's a lot more to you than I imagined." Then after a quick pause, she added, "I'm getting a martini. Be right back."

"*But James, I need you!*" I called out.

"So does England," replied Stephanie.

As I awaited my spy friend, it dawned on me that I'd been terrified for all the wrong reasons. If this place was any indication, it could be *ages* before I even found another man to shatter me. There wasn't a Viking in the lot, and with all the Bond villains skulking around, where the hell was 007? I mean, he's English, but there are exceptions to every rule.

To make matters worse, there were a couple of chicks who probably could have given some of the lesser Bond girls a run for their money. They weren't me, of course, but taste is subjective, guys are weird, and it was pretty clear that even if Bond were to make an appearance, the odds were not in my favor. I pointed this out to Stephanie when she returned.

"Oh, you innocent little lamb," she replied. "Welcome to Earth."

Welcome to Earth? America maybe, but . . .

"Not so fast," I cried, quickly adopting one of Stephen's more famous poses. "There's still Scandinavia."

"If you say so," replied Stephanie. "But if I were you, I'd just buy a vibrator."

for sale by owner

My mother called to inform me that they were selling my childhood home. She and my father had been saying they wanted to sell it for a long time, but I never expected anything to actually *happen*. This was due to the fact that I'd never actually heard both of them say it at the same time, and frankly, I couldn't remember a single instance when they'd ever agreed on anything. One year she wanted to sell it, the next year he wanted to sell it, and I just figured they'd go to their graves passing off the baton.

My parents have been separated for twenty years. When it first happened, my dad moved into an apartment. He was allowed to return home once a week, on Sundays between noon and 5 P.M., to do his laundry; and was called on occasionally to fix things around the house. Kind of like one of those Rent-a-Husbands except that we actually owned ours. Regardless of the reason for his visit, however, my father, a chain-smoker, was no longer allowed to smoke in his own home. Instead, he would do what work needed to be done and then retreat to the garage, where he'd suck down half a pack of Winstons before returning to his apartment.

I found it fascinating that my father had agreed to this, given that the house was half his, so I asked my mom how she managed to get him to go along with it. "I just told him he couldn't smoke in my house," she replied. *Your house?* "Look," she said. "If he can

58

figure out a way to make the smoke only stay in his half of the house, I'm open to it. Otherwise, he can do it in the garage. I don't care if that thing burns to the ground."

Before long, my mom decided that it wasn't fair that she had to clean a whole house and my dad only had to clean an apartment. So she moved into an apartment and he moved back into the house. But the no-smoking law stayed in effect, and he continued to abide by it. My mother returned to the house whenever she damn well pleased to do whatever she damn well pleased, and she often left her dogs there, too. They needed a yard to run around in, after all.

Every few years they'd switch again for one reason or another, and I guess twenty years of that would be enough to get any two people to agree to anything. The house had been sold. But I had already been living in California for a good fifteen years. It wasn't like they were selling my home out from underneath me. I didn't care. They could do whatever they wanted. Despite my indifference, I decided to go home, not so much out of duty, but because it seemed like it *should* be important. Plus, there was going to be a garage sale. *This*, I thought, was going to be something to see. My parents were sixty years old, they'd been married for twenty years, separated for another twenty years, and only *now* were they going to divide the stuff. Knowing what a nightmare it was when two people who'd lived together for only two years broke up and tried to figure out who owned which CD, I thought this might be the thing that finally drove them to divorce.

I arrived to my sold home on a Friday to find a FOR SALE sign still poking out of the front lawn. I wondered if I'd been tricked, but soon learned that my mom was planning to keep it there until the day she moved out to see if she could get a better offer. The fact that it was too late to actually *accept* a better offer was, to her,

beside the point. The garage sale was set for Sunday and prepara-
tions got under way soon after I'd satisfied my deep, painful
longing for a *real* shrimp po-boy, the kind you can only get in New
Orleans.

We dug through the attic, pulling out box after box and piling
them up in the garage, which, after twenty years of chain-smoking
and humidity, no longer smelled simply like smoke but like a wet
ashtray. As we went through the boxes, each new discovery was
more shocking than the last, but two stood out in particular—one
because it so clearly indicated that my mother was a heartless beast,
and another because it was the kind of thing one might expect to
hear about in a trailer park, but not in one's own sold home.

The first was the discovery that my mother was intending to sell
my old Playskool people *and* the yacht *and* the school bus *and* the
dog who barbecues. I was outraged. I insisted that her intention
to sell was little more than confirmation of what I'd long suspected. "You never cared about me!" My mother held her ground,
insisting that anything Playskool was only one-third mine, but if
it meant that much to me I could just take it, adding charitably,
"You don't have to give me a dime."

The second horror came in the form of a bag of old used
underwear—mine. I never got a straight answer as to why they
had been saved in the first place, I only remember my mother
telling me, "Some people, *a certain kind of people,* buy them."
What she didn't seem to understand was that only some people,
a certain kind of people, sell them—a kind of person I didn't believe
myself to be, a kind of people I was trying hard not to think the
rest of my family were either. My mother, on the other hand,
thought the whole thing was hilarious and could barely get through
her laughter long enough to let loose with the fact that there used
to be *two bags* until Blair threw a bunch of them off a Mardi Gras
float a few years earlier.

Blair showed up a few hours later, not to actually *help*, but apparently just to tell me that if I wanted to make up for the loss of revenue from the bag of underwear, I could always sell lap dances during the garage sale. Then he pulled my dad's list—stuff he needed for an upcoming fishing trip—off the deep freezer, scribbled *box of condoms* at the bottom of the list, replaced it, and went home.

I asked my mom if she wanted to start pricing stuff, which is when I learned that we were going with a different system. We were just going to let everyone show up and ask how much things cost, then we'd give them the once-over, determining a price right there on the spot based on appearance and imagined income of customer, compatibility with item, need, desire, medical history, projected life span, age, rank, serial number, general likeability and whether or not their name added up to an even or odd number.

"There's too many fucking variables," I muttered.

"Stop overcomplicating it," ordered my mother. "Just look at them, decide what you think and make up a price. And stop cursing." How could she think that was OK? "What ever happened to not judging a book by its cover?" I screeched. "Oh, you can," she replied.

Maybe, but I couldn't live with her system. It was so imprecise. "But Mom," I said, "it's all so subjective and . . . *gray*. I hate it. I like black and white. What if I accidentally charge someone twenty-five cents for something and later find out you wanted fifty?" She just pulled my Lite-Brite out of a box and said, "I trust you."

Saturday, we picked up where we'd left off. Only my dad was there. When I arrived at 7:00 A.M., he was in the backyard, smoking a cigarette, drinking something orange (and suspiciously *on the rocks*), and lining up all his tools against the fence. He was in the process of figuring out how to display his sander, turning it this way and that, trying to determine its best side. Everything was perfectly spaced out and he had signs clearly marking the non-negotiable price of every item. It brought a tear to my eye. "Dad, that's the most beautiful thing I've ever seen."

My dad turned, saw me, stood up and stated unequivocally, "Presentation is everything, Tidbit." Two inches of ash tumbled down his chest and onto his stomach, which was bursting through the bottom of a shirt whose buttons had abandoned ship long ago. He was wearing high-water polyester pants and slippers that he had bought on a trip to Gatlinburg, Tennessee, when I was six. Presentation is indeed everything.

Two barking dogs—one, the love child of a poodle and a brick, the other a jackal/gremlin mix—announced the arrival of my mother. "What's that bamboo screen doing in the living room?" she wanted to know. My dad piped up, telling her that he'd put it there to remind himself to take it back to his place when he left. My mom claimed that is was *her* screen, but she offered to sell it to him for $20. My dad told her to go to hell. A fight ensued with her calling him a cheapskate, thanking God that she wasn't married to him anymore (even though, technically, she was) and telling him to take the damn thing. He called her a bitch and said he didn't want it. She said he had to take it. He told her that if she could get $20 for the fucking thing she should sell it. She insisted that it was no longer hers to sell and he said something back to her, but I don't know where it was left because I was already on my way to get coffee and beignets.

The day was long and ugly. Blair returned for another three-minute visit, during which he again did nothing. When I pointed this out, he simply responded, "Stephen's not doing anything either." And while it was true that Stephen wasn't doing anything either, I never really expected him to do anything. In fact, I think the last time I saw him he was driving away in a car with the words JUST MARRIED painted on the back windshield.

At the end of the day, I was informed that the garage sale would begin at 9:00 A.M. the following morning. I told my mother she was crazy, that a garage sale had to start way earlier than that. She told me that we had to wake up at 5:45 A.M. to get things ready and I quickly decided that arguing for an earlier start time wasn't really in my best interest. I comforted myself with the thought that it would all be over soon and slipped under my favorite strawberry sheets for a few hours of sleep.

At 6:00 A.M., I found my mother dragging a seventy-five-pound cement planter across the lawn and my father sitting in a lawn chair flipping through cruise brochures. It seemed strange to me, but what didn't? When I asked my dad why he wasn't helping, my mother answered, "Because he's got a pain in the ass," an ailment more commonly referred to as sciatica in the civilized world. My mother and I did all the work.

Nine A.M. rolled around to find my entire childhood up for sale, my father still glued to his chair, my mother applying lipstick in front of my old Barbie vanity, and me, with a banana in one hand and a pair of clackers in the other, clacking away, as I looked up and down the street for any sign of life.

My mother joined me on the sidewalk looking perplexed. "I wonder why no one's here." Did it really warrant wonder? "I don't know, Mom, maybe because all the people who shop at garage sales have already gone back to bed?" Then she told me to go put on a bikini and stand at the nearest intersection with a sign, but really, now that my teenage underwear had already been distributed to half the population of New Orleans, why even bother with a bikini?

Our first customer, an obvious garage sale junkie, arrived at 10:15 A.M., and with him came the realization that not only was our pricing system whacked, my mother's value system was, too. He made a beeline to my old turntable and my mother promptly screamed out, "One dollar." I couldn't believe my ears, not only was it *my* old turntable—not one-third mine, but all mine, a birthday present—it was also one of the few items of real value. The thing looked like it had been purchased yesterday. My mother still had all the original packaging, an extra pack of needles *and* the yellowed receipt. I had no idea what something like that was actually worth, but that didn't stop me from calling the guy a thief and my mother a fool, insisting that she could have gotten at least $50 for it on eBay. My mother just smiled at me and said, "Well, we're not on eBay, we're on the front lawn." Then the junkie hightailed it to his car with *my* turntable.

The other side of this coin was my old pilgrim costume. My mother made it for me one Halloween. At the time I was about eleven, and while I don't remember exactly what I wanted to be instead, I do remember that I definitely did *not* want to be a pilgrim. My mother, knowing that I remember virtually nothing about my childhood, maintains that I very much *wanted* to be a pilgrim and asked her to make the costume, but I know it's a lie. You don't always remember details, but you remember feelings, and I remember feeling like a complete loser. There's nothing spooky about pilgrims unless you're a turkey or an Indian, and, more importantly, there's nothing cool about pilgrims. Everybody knows that, even eleven-year-olds, especially eleven-year-olds. There's no way I wanted to be a pilgrim and yet, I was. I seem to recall the words "I made the damn thing and you're wearing it." Oh how I hated that pilgrim costume, and oh how it floored me that someone in the world actually wanted to buy it now.

"Don't do it," I warned the misguided fool. "Your daughter will only hate you for it." She asked me how much it was. I laughed. "A nickel, but it's nonreturnable." My mother heard me laughing, spotted the pilgrim costume and was at my side in a flash, telling the woman about how many yards of fabric went into the thing, what kind of thread she'd used, how many hours it had taken her to make it, how cute I looked in it. The woman laughed. "All that for a nickel? Fine, I'll take it." My mother glared at me as she snatched the pilgrim costume out of the woman's hand. "A *nickel*? Are you crazy? It's $95." The woman turned to leave. "And you're calling *me* crazy?"

Other people came and went. I watched my Snoopy Sno-Cone machine leave in the bicycle basket of a cute little black boy, my Easy-Bake Oven take off in a truck with a Mexican family and my mother disappear into the house with a strange redheaded woman who appeared to be of Irish descent. I figured she was going to try to sell her the staircase, so I just plopped down in a lawn chair next to my dad. He still hadn't moved, and he was still reading cruise brochures. "Where ya going?" I asked. He had it narrowed down to two: a thirteen-day Alaskan cruise or a seventeen-day cruise through the Panama Canal. "Alaska's too cold," I said. "I'd go to the Panama Canal." He put the Alaskan brochure down and started showing me pictures of different cabin configurations on the Panama ship. "I was favoring the Panama Canal, too," he said. "It starts in Miami and ends in Los Angeles." *What!?!* "I figured Mom and I would just stay out there with you for a week or so after that." I was dumbfounded. "You're going with *my* mom?" He gave me a curious look and said, "You know any other moms?" I just shook my head. "*Great!*"

Blair swung by shortly after that to give our setup a quick once-over and tell us we were doing everything wrong. I leapt up from my lawn chair. "Is that all you came to do?" I demanded. He then gave me a quick once-over and said, "No. I came to see if there were any cute girls here, but there aren't." "Bite me!" I screamed back at him, as I stomped into the house to see what the hell my mother was doing. What she was doing was having tea with the strange redheaded woman. "This is Mary Jane," my mother blurted out. "We haven't seen each other since third grade!" How these two recognized each other is a mystery to me. My mom looks exceptionally young for her age, but not that young, and Mary Jane looked like exactly what she was—a sixty-year-old woman with flames coming out the top of her head. I stared at my mother and said, "I don't know if you're aware of this, but there's a garage sale taking place on your front lawn *right now*."

"It's not my front lawn anymore," she replied.

"Mom!" I screamed, "Why are you doing this? I don't know how to price this shit." She gave me the evil eye and said very calmly, "I told you I trust you."

"But why?" I screamed back. "Why now? You never trusted me when I wanted you to!"

She gave me an eviler eye and said, "You can go now." As I stomped out, I heard her say to Mary Jane, "She talks like a sailor and I can assure you she doesn't get that from me."

Then I slammed the damn door shut.

My mom finally emerged as I was selling off Stephen's old Nintendo set to a young couple. I'd instantly recognized the guy for the nerd he was and told him it was going for $60, pointing out that it was still in its original packaging and insisting that it had barely been used. "It was purchased in the hopes of improving my brother's hand-eye coordination, but he showed no improvement after a week so really, what was the point?"

The nerd had negotiated me down to $30 just about the time

my mom appeared. She saw what was happening, grabbed another box and dashed over to the nerd. "Did you see these?" she asked. It was a box containing every single Nintendo game ever made. The nerd's eyes lit up as if someone had told him he'd just won an all-expense-paid trip to the Star Trek convention, and I guess my mother liked that because she followed up her question with a quick, "You can have them. Lagniappe. The set's no good without the games." The nerd looked like he was going to wet himself. He opened his wallet and handed over a $10 and a $20. My mom looked at the bills and said, "Oh, that's too much," as she handed him back the $20.

The nerd and his wife left looking like two Lotto winners, and my mother turned to me. "Why'd you do that?" she snapped. "What?" I asked. "Try to make money at a garage sale? I have absolutely no idea what came over me."

My mom settled down in a lawn chair next to my dad, and started looking through his brochures. "What time is it?" she asked. It was 3:00 P.M. Closing time. All my dad's stuff was gone, but most of what my mom had for sale was still on the front lawn. "What are we going to do with all this stuff?" I asked. My mom got up and said, "We'll just pack it back up. I'll go call Salvation Army."

Pack it back up? Hadn't we just unpacked it? Why was this happening? What was the point? Was she trying to do me in once and for all?

As I was throwing things back into boxes, I heard my mom say, "Be careful with that stuff." *The crap you're giving away?* I didn't even bother to respond. A few minutes later I looked up to find my mother wrapping something in tissue. She looked like she was handling Tutankhamen's treasures. "Can't you move any faster than that?" I asked, completely annoyed.

Her voice came back whisper soft, as she said, "No. I can't."

———————

That's when it dawned on me that maybe this *was* something important.

We continued packing boxes in silence until the Salvation Army truck arrived. The driver lifted the back door. My mother slowly walked over and very carefully placed a box in the truck. The driver picked up another one and pitched it in on top of an old washing machine. There was a distinct crashing sound. I looked up. And that's when my mother lost it. Tears came streaming down her face as she grabbed the driver and started beating on his chest. *"Do you have any idea what's in those boxes!?!"* she screamed. And then she just crumbled to the ground. The driver didn't know what hit him, or maybe he did. Maybe he'd seen it all before, but I hadn't. And in that moment, I silently retracted every mean thing I'd ever said to or about my mother. I no longer cared what she did to me, what she hadn't done for me, what she was or what she wasn't. She was my mother, and our family, the family I'd complained about my whole life, meant *everything* to her. My dad was off his lawn chair and at her side before I regained command of my motor skills.

My mom and dad went inside the house. The driver offered to come back first thing in the morning with an empty truck. He said we could take as long as we needed to pack it up. I began carrying boxes back to the garage, and as I did, my mother's value system started to make sense. My mother didn't want to price anything because my mother didn't want to sell anything. She had to get rid of it because there was nowhere to keep it anymore, but the garage sale was just a cover. She wasn't interested in making money. She just wanted to see where everything was going. The stuff I was carrying may have looked like junk to anyone else, but to my mother it was priceless. If she thought you were going to give her son's Nintendo game a good life, you could have it. But if you weren't going to give her daughter's pilgrim costume a good home then she'd have cut off her own arm before letting you buy it for any price. It wasn't the nickel that offended my mother. It was the fact that her memories were being laughed at. Mary Jane was just a cover, too. The minute she was gone my mom said the woman talked too much. My mom wasn't interested in catching up with Flame Top. I guess in the end it was just easier than watching her life disappear before her very eyes.

When all the boxes were safely in the garage for the night, I started walking toward the sliding glass doors that led into the kitchen. My mom and dad were sitting at the table, fighting. I slid the door open and quickly learned that my father had managed to sell the bamboo screen for $30! My mother insisted that it was *her* screen and she wanted the money. My dad insisted that she gave it to him, which made it his money. Things went on like that for some time, with my dad ultimately offering to put the $30 toward dinner. My mother wanted Italian food; my dad wanted Chinese. "What do you want, Tidbit?" he asked. I told him all I really wanted was something that tasted like home. "Fine," said my mother, as she grabbed her purse, "Let's go to Acme." And that's exactly what we did. We ate fried oysters and gumbo.

I left two days later, and as my mom was dropping me off at the airport, she handed me a paper bag. "Here," she said. "I saved you something." I looked inside the bag and saw the Playskool dog, his barbecue, a table with an umbrella, two lounge chairs and two little Playskool people—a blonde and a redhead. "Hey," I said, "It looks like you and Mary Jane." I kissed my mother good-bye and boarded my plane.

———

It used to be that every time I went home, I went home hoping and praying to find that my family had somehow magically morphed into the kind of family I wanted and thought you were supposed to have, like the Waltons. My prayers were never answered. I was disappointed again and again, and my return flight was invariably spent crying under a cheap blanket.

My family still wasn't the Waltons, and I still cried under a cheap blanket, only this time it wasn't because I was disappointed.

thanks for sharing

Driving over Laurel Canyon with a used condom in my purse, I wondered where it all went wrong. Unable to pinpoint the specific moment when I had actually gone completely out of my mind and unable to deal with the fact that my brain was going about five hundred times faster than the cars in front of me, I speed-dialed Alice.

"Wake up. I'm in big trouble."

"What's up?" she mumbled in her morning voice.

"I'll tell you what's up. You know how sometimes when you're about to start your period but you haven't yet and then someone goes poking around up there, it can sometimes get a little funky? Not actual blood, but . . ."

"I guess. Do we really have to talk about sex right now?"

We had to and this is why:

I found a Viking a few months ago. And I guess it's important to mention that even though he's sexy in a dirty way (like all Vikings), my Viking is actually very clean. It's a product of his obsessive-compulsive disorder. Nothing too freaky, but he does love eights. Like when he turns the faucet off, he needs to make sure it's really turned off by turning the knob eight times. When he taps the water off his toothbrush, he needs to make sure the water's really tapped off by tapping it eight times. Stuff like that.

Now ordinarily the Viking comes to me. He had, however, recently crashed his motorcycle because, well, that's what Vikings do. I got the call last night. He was laid up on Vicodin and unable to drive. So I did what any red-blooded American girl would do. I donned my nurse's uniform and made a house call.

He wasn't lying either. His leg was a mess. Black, blue, bloated and pretty much scraped raw around the knee. He could barely walk although, as it turned out, the rest of him was working just fine. But even with his injury, the Viking was in high spirits. This was due to his soft, new, 1,000-thread-count sheets, which, by the way, were white as snow. The only thing the Viking likes more than eights are super clean, high-quality linens.

So after my eighth orgasm, the Viking, satisfied that he'd done his job properly, smeared Neosporin on his wounds, wrapped eight rolls of gauze around his leg and slipped into a pair of sweatpants. He walked me through the entire ritual in minute detail as he explained how it had all been carefully designed to keep any ghastly leg juice from marring his perfect new sheets. As for me, I barely had time to remind myself that all this nonsense is a small price to pay for Viking sex. I was asleep about eight seconds after he hit the bed.

This morning I woke up to the sound of a happy Viking singing in the shower. I smiled, content that everything was as it should be. Then I rolled over lazily and saw that everything was definitely *not* as it should be. I saw *it*, the funky stuff. Not bright red like blood, but clearly visible nonetheless. *Holy shit!* I sprang from the bed in a panic. *Dear God, please let that not be mine. Please let it be leg juice. It could be. His leg wasn't mummified during the act. Please, please, please let it be leg juice.*

And I was right on the verge of convincing myself that the origins of the funkiness were just maybe not definitely traceable back to me when I spotted a discarded condom mocking me from the carpet. I picked it up and examined it. It was funky. It was evidence.

What happened next is something of a blur. I think it went like this: I heard the Viking fumbling for a towel, I popped up like a jack-in-the-box, I yanked the comforter across the bed, and then, just before he entered the room, I shoved the used condom into my purse. There was not an ounce of thought involved, just fear in action. And it wasn't like I wasn't willing to confess my sin at some point; I just needed a little time to figure out exactly how to do it. But before I could come up with a plan, the Viking screamed, "Fuck. I got blood on the sheet." I turned to him. He was pointing at the bottom of the sheet. Not the spot I'd just hidden, but another spot. I looked. I saw nothing.

"It's right there," he said.

"What? *Where?*"

Honestly, my nose was jammed into the damn sheet and I still practically needed a magnifying glass to find the drop of blood, which was truly no larger than the head of a pin. Meanwhile, the Viking was foaming at the mouth, hobbling around naked on one leg in a desperate search for a toothbrush and bleach and cursing all the while. Needless to say, seeing him *totally freaking out* over a microscopic terra-cotta dot was not the kind of encouragement I needed to spill the beans regarding the real yet-to-be-discovered stain. I was dressed and out the door before he could count to eight.

"What the fuck is wrong with me? I'm tooling around town with a *used* condom! I was better off when the damn things were just perishing in my nightstand. What if I get pulled over and taken to jail for expired registration and they confiscate my purse and go through all my stuff? They'll find this thing for sure. They'll think I'm a hooker! *Good God, what if they call my mother?*"

"You're thirty-eight. I doubt they'll call your mother."

"They should! Jesus Christ, thirty-eight really is the new eighteen."

"Just throw the damn thing out the window," ordered Alice.

"You think I haven't already thought about that? *I can't!* I've got some agent-looking character in a BMW up my ass. I can just see this thing whizzing through the air, plunking itself down on his windshield like a Prada-seeking jellyfish. Then he'll saunter into the office and announce it in his staff meeting and the next thing you know every assistant in town will be "chatting" about it on iFilmPro and God knows what other websites. They'll probably expense a DNA test to figure out who . . ."

"You're a freak."

"Only because the Viking's a freak!"

"Uh-huh, and this is why two freaks should never sleep together," said Alice.

"Well, it's too late for that and I have the proof right here."

"Get over it. Sex is messy. Shit happens."

"I know that and you know that but . . ."

"*But what?* He's never had sex before?"

"I just don't think he'll see it that way."

"Fine. Call him and tell him to wash the sheet eight times. That should do the trick."

"It's not funny, Alice. And it's not even just about the sheet any-more. He's going to be looking for this stupid condom for days."

"As if," she replied. "He's probably already forgotten about it."

"*Are you kidding?* Forget that something unclean is lurking in his bedroom? That's exactly the kind of thing that would drive him to the brink of insanity."

"Dude, he was way beyond the brink when you met him."

"Oh, Christ. Knowing him, he'll probably call in a search party. And plus, even if he could forget, the wrapper is still there as a reminder. He'll be counting wrappers and condoms and see that that things don't match up and . . ."

"Why'd you leave the wrapper?" asked Alice, as if I were an idiot.

"I didn't do it on purpose!" I replied in defense. "It all happened so fast I didn't know what to do. I guess I should have taken that, too. I don't know what I was thinking. I wasn't thinking. Fuck me. What am I going to do?"

"Fuck him. It's just a piece of cotton."

"No, Alice, it's not just a piece of cotton. It's the only thing he's talked about since he bought the damn thing three days ago. It's his raison d'etre. This is a real problem, and I've got to fix it."

Then I had an epiphany.

"I'm going to buy him a new sheet," I announced.

"You know," said Alice, "the competition's stiff, but that may be the stupidest thing you've ever said in your life."

"I'm going to Bed Bath & Beyond right now," I countered.

"That's retarded."

"No, it's not."

"You don't even know if that's where he got it!"

"*What?* Haven't you been listening? I know everything about the goddamn sheet."

"Then you're an idiot. It'll cost you a hundred dollars."

"Two hundred," I shot back. I mean, really, what did she think this was? 1950?

"*What???*" screamed Alice.

"That's the whole point. If it were a cheap sheet it wouldn't matter. Oh, God. What a mess. Do you think it'll freak him out if I buy him a $200 sheet?"

"It'll freak *me* out. He's not even your boyfriend."

"I know that. If he were my boyfriend, I'd tell him to get over it. Do you think if I buy him the sheet he'll feel obligated to sleep with me again? Because I don't want *anyone ever* sleeping with me because they feel obligated. That's just gross. I know, maybe I'll mail him the sheet in a plain brown package, you know, anonymously."

"You've *completely* lost your mind. I'm going to Peet's. You want a latte? Actually, forget I said that. The last thing you need is coffee. Take a Valium. I'll see you later."

After hitting three Bed Bath & Beyonds only to find that they were all out of Viking sheets, I started to think that maybe that wasn't the best course of action. I went home and scrubbed the inside of my purse with a Brillo pad instead.

A week passed and I still hadn't heard from the Viking. Hardly unusual, but this time it bothered me. The stain had surely been discovered and since I hadn't received an accusatory call, I figured his leg must have taken the blame. I wondered if he'd cut it off in retribution? I wondered if he was sitting at home snorting Tide to make the pain go away? I wondered if he'd found a Bed Bath & Beyond in Arizona that had the damn sheet in stock and was currently hobbling across state lines on one leg? I wondered and wondered and wondered because, in the absence of a phone call, I didn't really *know* anything.

And I'm not talking about a phone call from me to him. I'm talking about a phone call from him to me. Here I was sleeping with someone who thought it was totally fine not to call me for a week or so at a time, and all along I'd been acting like it was totally fine with me, too, even though it was totally *not fine* with me.

Upon retrospectively realizing that I was not happy with our relationship and basically concluding that he didn't deserve me, I decided to IM him and find out what the hell actually happened to his precious sheet. What I found out was that he'd discovered the funk only moments after my departure and had, in fact, cursed his own battered leg. Upon hearing my confession and learning the "truth" (and I put it in quotation marks because really how could either of us know what the truth was in the absence of hidden cameras, which I don't think he had), he laughed his ass off. Once that was out of the way, mostly he was just surprised to learn that I'd spent a whole week worrying about it and insulted that I'd underestimated his laundering abilities. *Didn't I know him well enough to know that he could remove any stain from any thing?* Beyond that, he was incredibly relieved to hear that I hadn't flushed the condom down the toilet, as he'd suspected. Apparently, he'd been meaning to call me all week to tell me I shouldn't do that *ever again*. It's really, really bad for the pipes.

Afterward, I thought about everything that had transpired. Why had I given the sheet star billing in my story? How could I think a $200 sheet was more valuable than a night in bed with me? Did I really need someone ten years younger than me to inform me that I shouldn't throw balloons in the toilet? And how could I ever expect some Scandinavian jackass to call me *just to call me* when he wasn't even capable of remembering to call me about something that had been stuck under his own anal-retentive craw for the past week? I thought and I thought and I thought and once that happened things pretty much fizzled out with the Viking.

"Surprise, surprise," said Alice. "If you'd actually thought about what you were doing *before* you slept with him, you probably wouldn't have done it."

I thought about that too, but in truth I don't think it would have stopped me. I was looking for a Viking and there he was—big, blonde, reckless, and all over this cavewoman *in the beginning*. The morning after our first sleepover, we followed up with a hearty breakfast and a matinee of *Jackass: The Movie*. Then he gave some guy shit for checking out my ass. I thought I'd hit the jackpot. He was straight out of the cave—the kind of guy who might say, "Me Tarzan, you Jane"—except that if he'd swung by in a loincloth and called me Jane, I'm pretty sure I wouldn't have had sex with him. I can't explain it any better than that. I thought it was true in the abstract and I was right: I like Vikings. And I like neuroses, too. In fact, if you're not rearranging your sock drawer five times a day or blowing a gasket if everything isn't written in lowercase, I don't want anything to do with you. How could I ever possibly be OK with my own freaky self without the security blanket of someone else's freakiness to comfort me?

The interesting thing is that the guys who like me most—I mean, if I had to narrow it down to one group—are butchers. Butchers dig me. I'm not sure why, I only know it's true. Maybe I just look like something they could really sink their teeth into. And sure, grocery store butchers get it, but *real* butchers—men who have a passion for hacking up dead animals as opposed to those who are simply assigned to the meat department—they like me the best. It's as if they're bred to find me irresistible. And this Viking of mine, he was the son of a butcher. An anal-retentive Viking with butcher blood coursing through his veins, can you believe it? It was kind of perfect. And then it wasn't.

"Kind of perfect?" snickered Alice. "You need to call that shrink of yours and tell him he missed a spot."

"*Michael?* God no. He can never know about this. He'd be so disappointed. And that's not how therapy works anyway. You're allowed to fuck up, and then you get a grace period to figure it out on your own. You're not supposed to run to a psychiatrist every time you break a nail. As long as I learn something, it's OK. Michael doesn't need to know *everything*."

"You're delusional."

"All right, so the Viking wasn't perfect; he was a little unrefined and not really suitable for public outings, but we rarely went out in public. Plus, he was funny. Anyway, who cares? I think he's a jerk now."

"I have two words for you: *personal responsibility.*"

"*What?*" I screamed. "I'm the one who wanted to buy him a new sheet!"

"I'm not talking about the sheet, I'm talking about the relationship. If *you* put up with shit *you* don't like, then that's *your* issue."

"So you're calling me a doormat. That's nice."

"If the shoe fits . . ." said Alice.

"Jerks and doormats aren't mutually exclusive, you know."

"I know that."

"They're more like peanut butter and jelly."

"I'm just saying . . ."

"No, no. Take his side. I gotta go."

With the Viking no longer around to distract me, and Alice and I not speaking, I had plenty of alone time to reflect on my psychosis. So I started flipping through my mental files and soon discovered that I'd been taking preemptive blame for just about everything that occurred within a five-mile radius of me since 1964. Talk about a wake-up call. And I'm not just talking about little things like sheets either. One time when I was cooking a hot dog, my apartment building caught on fire. So what did I do? I ran down twenty-one floors of smoke-filled stairwell apologizing to anyone within earshot. Then, once I'd convinced every single tenant that it was my fault, a fireman appeared and announced that the cause of the fire was a smoldering cigar twenty-one floors beneath my apartment. And I've never smoked a cigar in my life. So what did I do? I apologized for misleading everyone.

Oh, and there were other incidents—incidents too numerous and too absurd to mention. I wondered how many metaphorical sheets I'd bought in my life. I wondered how many times I'd said *I'm sorry* in my life. I knew it was a lot and for sure more times than I'd accepted an apology because I simply wouldn't allow it. *No, no, it's fine. No need to apologize. Don't worry about me. I don't have feelings.* I soon began to realize that the reason a piece of cotton got star billing in my story was because the story was never about me. *Me? No, no, I'm not important enough to be the star.* As soon as an extra walked on set, I stepped back and adopted a supporting role. *Just tell me what you need and I'll do it.* I didn't matter. *No, no, as long as it works for you, I'm cool with it.* All that ever mattered was everyone else's happiness.

Ah-ha! So *that's* why I always found myself holding the stubby end of the stick! I knew instantly that everything had to change.

I called Alice to report my findings and she responded with her stock answer: "Great. So you're ready to come to an Al-Anon meeting with me?" It wasn't a bad idea per se; it's just that I'm afraid if I go to one of those meetings I'll end up using their lingo. They all do it. I don't know how anyone can think there's anything anonymous about it when they're all talking about *sharing* and how they're *showing up.* Things that people just don't say in the real world. But given that this was the first time Alice and I had spoken in four days, I figured it was best not to start out by insulting her second language. "No," I replied. "I actually came up with a different solution. I mean, going to an Al-Anon meeting is tantamount to admitting there's something wrong with me and at this point I'm pretty much fed up with taking blame so what I've decided is that I'm just never going to accept responsibility for anything ever again. Especially not where guys are concerned. From here on out, I'm the star of this show."

"*That's* what you called to tell me?" asked Alice, clearly not on the same page of the *me* handbook.

"Yeah, that, and that I'm never engaging in casual sex ever again. I gave it a shot, but I'm obviously not cut out for it. It's too stressful. Honestly, I don't know how you can sleep around like you do."

"I should've let you buy the sheet."

"Oh, come on. Is that really how you want to *show up?* What happened to *personal responsibility?*"

"I've got three words for you."

"Wait, let me guess. *Thanks for sharing?*"

"You're an asshole," replied Alice.

"I don't know, babe. You've got a contraction in there. I might have to call that three-and-a-half words."

"Delete my number from your speed dial right now."

"Sorry. No can do. But I'll tell you what, not because I did anything wrong, but just for old time's sake . . ."

"What?"

"I've got two-and-a-half words for you."

"Uh-huh."

"Alice . . ."

"Spit it out."

"I'm sorry."

"Cindy . . ."

"What?"

"Thanks for sharing."

the greek

I was driving to my local hardware store the other day and on the way I passed fifteen coffee houses, twenty-three nail places, ten hair salons, four full spas, twelve yoga studios, five Pilates studios, eight gyms, three doggie day cares, thirty-seven movie theaters, fifty-four restaurants and more stores than I could count. It was 2 P.M. on a Wednesday, but they were all full. And it wasn't even that far a drive. I was just too lazy to walk.

On top of that, the streets were teeming with people who looked like they had nowhere else to be but right where they were, spending money.

I know some people in Los Angeles wake up and go to an office every day because I used to be one of them, but when you drive down the streets here it's hard not to look around and say to yourself: *Doesn't anybody in this town have a job?* You meet people all the time who seem to be doing absolutely nothing and yet they're driving a brand-new Mercedes, eating at MR CHOW and wearing $275 jeans. After a while, you just stop wondering and accept the fact that yes, money *does* grow on trees.

I was working in Beverly Hills for about a year. That's right, I was back in the film industry. It was either that or *barista*—a word that nobody even knew until Starbucks took over the universe. That's how Hollywood keeps you in its clutches; it leaves you with no transferable skills. But in my defense, I didn't actually go for this job. All I did was answer my phone. Someone called and offered me a development executive position at a small production company, and I needed a paycheck, so I accepted. And the truth is that the whole experience was worthwhile because it made one thing clear to me: I love stories. I love reading scripts and doing notes and working with writers—maybe even enough to overlook all the other crap involved. But what I don't love, and what I'm done with, are bosses. Facing myself every morning is challenging enough. So now I'm thinking about getting certified to teach Pilates. That way I can be the boss, which according to *The Secret Language of Birthdays* is what I was meant to be, anyway. Or actually what I already am, seeing as I was born on *The Day of the Boss*.

Anyway, all of this is to say that my boss had Asperger's syndrome. I don't have the medical records to prove it; we just diagnosed him ourselves in the office. Someone had read an article in *Newsweek* about this particular strain of autism, and it seemed to fit, so we just shook on it. Maybe we didn't get it exactly right—autism covers a wide range of behavioral issues—but we were close. And my mother gets mad every time I say this, but I am 100 percent certain that I too would be at home on that very range.

Here's the deal: I'm a part-time recluse, a compulsive list-maker, *I love math,* and I rearrange my refrigerator once a week to make sure the sweets never touch the savories, all the labels are facing out, and the larger items are in the back, giving the whole thing a sort of stadium seating effect. But really, who can blame me? As Wordsworth said, "The world is too much with us." And he didn't even have basic cable, much less DirecTV. There's too much out there, and it's all going too fast. If I can trick myself into thinking my world makes sense by organizing stuff, if I can shut out the noise by holing away in my apartment for a month, if I can slow things down by doing yoga or hitting tennis balls or making some stupid list, I'm happy to do it. And I feel for anyone who can't.

The point is we weren't all cut out for a lifetime of overstimulation— I less so than some, my ex-boss less so than I. And while it was difficult to watch someone struggle with many of the things the rest of us take for granted, when you've got a broken record for a boss, it hardens you a bit. I'd go ask him what he thought of a certain director and instead of giving me an answer, he'd start listing the director's credits. I'd mention a certain movie and he'd start reciting his mental list of everyone involved, right down to the caterer. He'd ask me to do something, and then he'd call me seventeen times in the next half-hour to see if it had been done yet.

In addition to this, he had dubbed me "Madame Fonzarelli." For whatever reason he had it stuck in his brain that I was some present-day female Fonzie, and that my life was one fabulous date after the other. I asked him to please not use the word *date* around me as I hadn't been on one in ages, and yet every morning he'd see me and say, "Madame Fonzarelli, who'd you go out with *last night?*"

Often after a day at that office, you'd need a drink. On this particular occasion my coworker Donna and I went to a patio bar in Beverly Hills. It was a place neither of us had ever been, and it was packed with people sucking down half-price Happy Hour drinks. There were a bunch of guys who looked like they could have been a soccer team a few tables over. They weren't Vikings per se—they all had dark hair—but they did give off a Viking vibe; they were rowdy. One of them soon came over to our table and we learned that they were Greek. When our glasses were nearly empty, The Greek headed off to the bar to get more wine for us, and more ouzo for him.

Donna smiled at me and said, "So Madame Fonzarelli, what do you think?" I told her I didn't know. We agreed that he looked like he knew what to do with a woman, but all that dark hair gave me pause. Donna pointed out that I have dark hair, I pointed out that

I don't have it on my chest or back, and then The Greek returned. When Donna could no longer ignore the pleading cell phone calls from her nanny, we left, but not before The Greek asked me for my phone number, and I gave it to him.

I gave The Greek my phone number, not because he had a Viking vibe; I was still weighing that against the dark hair. I gave it to him because he actually *said* that he wanted to take me out on a date and *asked* for my phone number. That never happens. They never put themselves on the line; either they try to give you their phone number, or they try to disguise a date as a work thing—since everyone in Los Angeles works in the entertainment industry, it's easy—and then, after a few drinks, they pounce.

And it's not the pouncing that bothers me; it's the hiding behind the work façade that turns me off. After spending more time than I care to think about trying to convince men of their worth, I've concluded that you can't expect any man to be confident enough to maintain a healthy relationship with a woman if he doesn't have the confidence to ask that woman out on an actual date in the first place. Either that or he's just not interested enough, but either way you're headed for trouble. So yeah, I want be asked out on an actual date. And that's what The Greek did.

He called a few days later to firm up the details.

When I arrived at the designated location, the first thing The Greek wanted to know was why I hadn't let him pick me up. I said it was just easier this way, but he insisted there was more to it. Once pressed, I admitted that even if I hadn't been coming straight from work, it probably wouldn't have changed a thing; I knew nothing about him and therefore didn't really feel comfortable with him knowing where I lived. Well, talk about flip a lid. He looked like his head was about to explode. How dare I insult him! What was wrong with me? *Why didn't I trust him?*

The guy practically forced me to give him an answer he didn't
want to hear. It was entrapment, pure and simple.

Why I didn't leave at that point, I can't say. Was I attracted to
him? Was I amused by him? Was I trying to prolong the only *real
date* I'd been on in years, not knowing when lightning would
strike again? I have no idea. Instead, I asked him not to take it
personally, assuring him that I wouldn't give my address to *anyone* I'd just met, randomly, without a single mutual acquaintance
to vouch for him. But what I saw as sensible, he saw as offensive
and paranoid. So I said, "You know, The Boston Strangler *was*
invited into the homes of all his victims. Why? Because he
seemed trustworthy."

The Greek didn't like that very much, but we managed to get
past it, and a little while later I asked him what he did for a living.
It seemed like a reasonable question to me, given that he knew
what I did for a living and we had talked about it at length. He,
however, did not find it reasonable. In his mind, it made me a
gold-digger. *Why was it so important to me?* I told him it wasn't *so*
important to me, I was just curious. But he didn't buy it and he
wasn't budging.

"Look," I said, "I don't care if you're a garbage man, but now
that you've made such a big deal about *not* telling me, it's becoming a little more important."

He kept trying to make me feel bad about asking and I kept not
feeling bad. When I saw that we had reached an impasse, but I
still wasn't done with my Mai Tai, I decided to tell him a little
story.

"I used to live in San Francisco," I began. "My boyfriend and I
lived on the top floor of this apartment building, and we had some
friends who lived on the bottom floor. Our friends were extremely
social. They went to every hot new club and restaurant, and they
often had big dinner parties at their place. Along the way, they met

Andrew—super nice guy, always the life of the party, always brought a great bottle of wine to dinner. I think he had one of those vague jobs like "import/export." But mostly what he had was charm. He lived in Los Angeles, or maybe it was San Diego, I don't remember, but often traveled to San Francisco. In fact, my boyfriend's brother had even turned his apartment over to him once when he was away. *Why not?* Andrew seemed like a great guy. Then he started killing people."

"I don't believe it," said the Greek.

"Ever heard of Versace?" I replied.

The Greek never told me what he did for a living, but he did gaze deeply into my eyes and plant a passionate kiss on my lips once outside the restaurant. Then, as the valet was pulling up with my car, The Greek handed me a videotape. It was a movie he'd written, directed and starred in. He wanted me to help him get it into the right hands, and this bugged me more than anything else.

This is something I'd never experienced before moving to Los Angeles. Prior to living here, when a guy asked me out, I felt confident assuming that at least part of it was that he wanted to get into my pants. But here, it's not like that. Not necessarily. And while it can be both disappointing and annoying to realize that a guy is pursuing you for sex and sex alone, it is infuriatingly insulting to realize that he's actually pursuing you to further his career—in this case via film distribution—with an eye on fucking you along the way. I took the videotape and burned rubber.

Needless to say, viewing the tape was not my top priority. The Greek called to ask me out again before I'd ever watched it. I told him I was busy, and he responded by telling me that he was off to Turks & Caicos—a trip that was funded, I imagine, with money he'd picked off a tree.

While he was gone, I watched the movie. I don't remember

much about it, except that in one scene The Greek was completely naked and facing the camera—I believe this was the same scene in which he raped a girl, who, not for nothing, looked a little bit like me—and in another scene, he delivered a monologue about how he preferred fake tits to big, floppy, real ones.

Now, I know it was just a movie, but you have to wonder about any man who feels it's appropriate to hand something like that over on a first date, especially when handing it to a woman with big, real breasts.

Of course, my dear friend Nigel insists that my breasts aren't big, but they are Ds so I'm pretty sure Nigel has either been living in Los Angeles too long, watching too much porn or both. And I've spent way too much time being self-conscious about having big boobs to now start feeling self-conscious about having boobs that aren't big enough.

Rack size notwithstanding, The Greek called a few times after that, but I let him go to voice mail.

A month later, Donna came into my office and told me that he'd called her. What should she do? I handed her the video and told her to do whatever she wanted, but to leave me out of it.

After numerous calls, Donna agreed to meet with The Greek to discuss his film, and I made sure I was out of the office when it happened. Donna reported back after their meeting. Apparently, he'd started out talking about work stuff, but soon switched the subject to me, because, well, that's how they do things in Hollywood. The Greek didn't understand what went wrong, but like I told Donna, we've all got our own mysteries to solve.

I saw The Greek from afar a few times after that, as I was driving past Starbucks. He was always sitting out front, talking on his cell phone. He did have a certain animal magnetism, I'll give him that much. But the Starbucks setting did nothing to capitalize on it.

Then one day I was in Beverly Hills with Alice. We'd just finished a post-yoga lunch and were doing a little shopping before heading off to get our nails done when Alice turned to me and said, "I wonder what a guy like that does for a living?" "Who?" I asked. She pointed over to Barneys. The Greek was exiting with two enormous shopping bags. He looked like a drug lord, but seeing as I'd have had to stalk him all the way to Turks & Caicos to prove it, instead, I just shrugged.

the most beautiful girl
in the world

Ah, France. Where the men are men, the women are women and the senior citizens still have wrinkles. Not like Hollywood, where every other person has their face tightened and lifted, some to the point of looking Asian, but not really. Like they're from some country in the Far East that has yet to be discovered.

Personally, I find it extremely rude when someone who used to have round eyes shows up for lunch, without any warning whatsoever, looking Chinese-*ish*. I'll be there scoping the place out for a familiar face, when suddenly a faux Asian is standing before me straining to open her mouth enough to announce herself. And even then it takes a few moments to identify someone when operating solely on voice recognition, a few *extremely uncomfortable moments* during which an unspoken dialogue is occurring with her saying, "What the hell are you looking at?" and me saying, "What the hell did you do to your face?"

Of course, you can't actually say anything out loud because it's incumbent on the victim of said surprise attack to yield to the ruse. Although that's not even true, because you are supposed to say *something*; you're supposed to say they look great then pretend like you can't quite put a finger on what's different, thus perpetuating their misguided belief that no one actually notices that instead of turning back the hands of time, they've switched nationalities. But I usually just sit there with my mouth agape.

I'm assuming these people are merely casualties of an imperfect science. And to be fair, you can't really expect a plastic surgeon to get it right every time. I think a face-lift takes three or four hours to perform. That is an awfully long time, and I don't know about anyone else, but around 2:00 P.M. every day, I start to get a little punchy.

But who knows? Maybe they aren't casualties, maybe that's the look they were going for. Los Angeles has a rather large Asian community, and from what I can tell most other cultures are kinder to their senior citizens than we are, so maybe they're just doing a little prep work before making their way to Chinatown in the hope of being mistakenly taken in by some family that might actually treat them with respect. I know I'm moving to France when I get old so I can still get invited to *real* parties, as opposed to some annual family reunion where they wheel you out just to lift everyone else's spirits. *Look, Great-great Aunt Sally's still alive! That means I've got sixty years left! That means I'm nowhere near middle-aged! Hurray for me!* And I won't even need plastic surgery to do it. All I'll need is a plane ticket. I'm counting on socialism to pick up the tab for my housing and medical needs from there.

It's all so strange. Everyone wants to live forever, but no one wants to *look like* they've been alive forever. Isn't that "having your cake and eating it too"? And aren't we taught as children that that doesn't work? I've already decided that I'm never saying *never* again because every time I utter the words it's as if I'm daring myself to do something and I can't resist the challenge; knives are definitely out, but I could break down and squirt something into this wrinkle I've got on my forehead at some point.

Or perhaps I should call it *that wrinkle* and follow it up with a track off my Halloween Sound Effects CD, since I hardly even noticed the damn thing until Erica beseeched me to *Please shoot some Restalyn into that wrinkle . . . before it's too late!!!* Then again,

she is a facialist and I do live in a town where people start shooting Restalyn, Botox and whatever else is handy into their faces as
soon as they've gotten puberty out of the way. And they call it
"maintenance."

Since my last visit to Erica, I haven't done anything with *that
wrinkle* other than stare at it endlessly, nor have I really been
tempted to. I read somewhere once that "Truth comes as a con-
queror to those who have lost the art of receiving it as a friend."
So why not be friendly?

As far as I'm concerned, a life well lived is the greatest defense
against the fear of aging, as well as the fear of dying. It keeps your
thoughts in the present, it satisfies the soul, and it produces a
twinkle in the eye that I find more youthful, more beautiful, and
a hell of a lot sexier than terrified eyes looking out from a face
eerily reminiscent of *The Scream*. But again, maybe that's just me.
I'd rather laugh than have a face free of laugh lines. And I'd rather
look at my laugh lines as a souvenir of a happy life than see them
as something I need to hide from the world in order to fit some
ridiculously narrow definition of beauty.

"You want a broader definition of beauty?" asked Tomas. "Then
move to Europe."

Once again, Tomas was insisting that I'd do much better there,
as Europeans would be more inclined to embrace "my kind." I
don't know why he was pushing so hard to get rid of me because
every time I leave for more than thirty-six hours, I get an e-mail
from him begging me to come home. But I'm sure that when I do
manage to secure my Barbie dream house on the beach in Biarritz,
it won't be long before he's knocking on my door looking to hit me
up for some Lillet.

Still, it wasn't a bad idea. My best relationship was with a
Frenchman, I'm a total Francophile, and I knew I couldn't pos-

sibly do any worse with men in France than I was doing right here. Tomas and I compromised; I took a vacation. He promised to take care of Frankie, and I promised I'd bring him back an au pair.

As luck would have it, I still had girlfriends with big honkin' expense accounts. Lauren and Rachel were heading to Paris, compliments of the magazine world, and I figured the magazine world owed me one for having repeatedly suckered me into paying for page after page of advertisements that someone else paid them to sell to me. So I tagged along.

And there I was, loving life, feeling fabulous and clinking champagne glasses with Lauren at the Ritz, when this guy walked into the bar. I dove under the table. "*Holy shit. Hide me!*"

Here I had an entire ocean separating me from the scene of the crime, and this character's waltzing into the Ritz during *my vacation* like he owns the place. That cheeky little bastard! Didn't anyone tell him that once I've embarrassed myself with a man he's supposed to just *die*, or at the very least go blind?

But there he was, not a German shepherd in sight.

"We've got to get out of here *immediately*," I whispered into Lauren's kneecap.

"Why? What happened?" she belted out as she flipped around in her chair and began scanning the crowd.

It freaked me out to no end. "Stop looking!" I whisper-screamed. "I slept with that guy."

Lauren's eyes lit up. "Which one?"

I yanked at her skirt hem with all my might. "Just sign the damn check and stop staring."

But she didn't. She took her sweet time paying the bill, leaving me to sweat it out under the table for a good fifteen minutes. Then and only then did she make a halfhearted attempt to provide cover as I slunk toward the nearest exit. I'm not sure, though. He may have seen me.

Once outside, Lauren tried to hit me up for details, but given that the details in question comprised what was quite possibly the most shameful episode in my entire life, and given that I'd planned to take the whole sordid affair with me to my grave, I pleaded the fifth and we headed off to meet Rachel at this hammam I'd read about in some fancy travel magazine. It was supposed to be an authentic Turkish hammam, and it was supposed to be *fabulous*. It was probably the grossest place I've ever been in my life, and I've been in Port-a-Potties on Bourbon Street at the end of Mardi Gras day.

Lauren took one look and bolted, but Rachel and I didn't want to seem like the kind of Americans who insist on asking for ice cubes in Europe because *that's how you drink a Coke back home*. Instead, we paid our money, we went in, and it got *much, much* worse.

"*Holy hammamas!*" I whispered to Rachel. "So this is where Turkish women go to die."

The place was crammed full of 'em—naked, wrinkly and old as the hills. It was a sight I never needed to see, and it made me fear aging more than shark attack. But as bad as it looked, it was nothing compared to the stench. I started to gag. Rachel pinched her nose, turned to me in horror and whispered, "Is *that* going to happen to us?"

I wanted to tell her that it didn't matter as long as she still had a twinkle in her eye. I wanted to tell her that daily exercise and a nutritious diet, including lots of dark, leafy greens, berries, and assorted fish—high in omega-3s, but low in mercury—would help ensure a better tomorrow. But more than anything, I wanted to wash my feet. "I'm pretty sure we won't be Turkish," I whispered back. "Come with me."

Unlike silly American spas, authentic Turkish hammams in Paris don't offer shower sandals. All they'd given us was one towel each and that towel was about the size and thickness of a one-ply paper napkin, like the kind you might get at a fast food joint. The floor was filthy and we were barefoot. Some of these women had flip-flop–looking things on their feet and some of them didn't. I half-expected those who'd brought their own to begin whirling like dervishes in an ecstatic self-congratulatory fit.

Rachel and I had only the $400 Accessoire sandals we'd just bought and worn out of the store, and there was no way in hell they were ever touching this floor. I worried about their safety even back in their cubbyhole behind the front desk.

My plan was to go to the bathroom, wash my feet and then take a huge flying leap from there to the holding slab where all the spooky Turkish women were awaiting their massages. Upon landing, I'd nuzzle between them, close my eyes and pray for it to all be over as quickly as possible.

The bathroom was not a place to clean anything. It was a large room with holes in the floor. The holes served as toilets. Not everybody was a good aim and apparently not everyone agreed with my policy of only doing number two in one's own home. There was a spigot at the far end of the room, and a substance that looked like very weak tea flowed from it. I imagine that was the place one might "wash" one's feet if one had the fortitude to walk through the minefield. I, however, did not.

Crestfallen, Rachel and I returned to the main room. Turkish sea lions were beached atop marble holding slabs on both sides; massage tables huddled together in the middle of the room, fearing for their lives. As we approached, the sea lions, instead of moving over to make room for us, closed the gap, daring us to come ashore. "They hate us," said Rachel, completely abandoning the whisper. "They hate us because we have bikini waxes, something they've obviously never heard of." I nodded in solemn agreement.

The whole thing was extremely unsettling. I felt like I was in a scene from some female version of *Midnight Express,* but a scene that had been left on the cutting room floor after being deemed too gratuitously gruesome. And all this time I'd thought Turkish women were beautiful! Every Turkish woman I'd ever seen had made me feel like a gorgon in comparison! But not this batch.

We should have made a break for it then. We were really taking that "when in Rome" stuff too far. At least the guy in *Midnight Express* had a reason for staying. *He was a prisoner!* We were just stupid.

Rachel and I held our "towels" over our Brazilian waxes and walked over to the other side, where we found a woman who was either dead or close to it. She was approximately the size of a small mosque. After numerous attempts, we finally shoved her over. Rachel carefully placed her towel on the slab, I helped her up, and then I placed my towel next to Rachel's. "Hold my hand," I said. "I don't know what I'm standing in, but it's super slippery." Rachel took my hand; I hopped up and joined her. "This is complete bullshit," I said. "I'm writing a letter to that magazine the minute I get home."

I was staring at the ceiling dreaming up hate mail when Rachel turned to me with imploring eyes. "Please tell me a story, *anything* to take my mind off this." I stared at the ceiling some more. I thought about the guy at the Ritz. I looked around the hammam. I knew nothing was as bad as this.

"All right," I said. "When I first moved to Los Angeles, there was this guy. He came into the office a few times and according to my boss he thought I was the most beautiful girl in the world."

"Smart man. Who was he?"

"Just a guy. That's all I'm telling you. Anyway, I'd never really thought about him much, but suddenly here I was *the most beautiful girl in the world*."

"This is right after you escaped that jerk in San Diego, right?"

"Exactly," I replied. "And that's key to the story. I'd just emerged from hell where no one had said anything nice to me for two solid years. I was highly susceptible to flattery and a complete basket case to boot. So I went out with this guy, and I slept with him *that night*."

"*You?*"

It killed me to do so, but honesty compelled me to confirm with a nod of the head.

"You must have really liked him."

"*Liked him*? I have no idea. But I was in a very fragile state, he thought I was the most beautiful girl in the world, and I guess I figured he deserved a reward for that. Don't ask too many questions. It's painful enough as is."

"Very well. Continue."

"So San Diego was awful and I was coming off a nervous breakdown. I wasn't hallucinating or anything anymore, but in place of that I had this new problem: My feet stank."

Rachel lowered her head toward my feet and sniffed. "They just smell like Turkish turds to me."

"Thanks," I said. "But at the time, for about six months maybe, they were really sweaty and really stinky. So I had sex with this guy, at least I think I did, although I might have made that up somewhere along the line just so I could punctuate my humiliation with a big, fat exclamation point. I don't remember anything about the act itself. All I really remember is being naked in his bathroom frantically trying to wash the stink off my feet. And it worked. My feet smelled like soap. But then there was the issue of my shoes, which most definitely did *not* smell like soap. I was in a complete panic, desperately trying to find a place to hide them, but he had a very poorly designed bathroom with zero storage space. I'm telling you, I would have flushed them down the toilet if I could have. I would have eaten them. *Anything* to make them go away. I was on the verge of tears when I finally stuffed them with toilet paper, turned them upside down and shoved them under the bath mat."

"That's it?" said Rachel.

"Yeah, that was it. He never called me after that. He said he was going to, but he never did."

Rachel thought it over. "Maybe it wasn't your feet. Maybe he just sensed your desperation."

"Maybe. He would've had to have been dead not to."

"Or maybe it wasn't *just* your feet. Maybe . . ."

I shook my head. "Trust me, darling, I checked. I checked the minute my feet started stinking and I have continued to check periodically just because, why not? I can assure you it both smelled *and tasted* like a fruit smoothie. I was on a big pineapple kick at the time."

"Does it really work that way?"

"Totally. That's why French women sometimes put rose water in their tea."

"Wow. They know all the tricks."

"I know, but come on, these are the people who made perfume an everyday thing. And I'll tell you something else, I hate when Americans toss on perfume and refer to it as a French bath. *The French bathe.* It's just that after they do, they often follow it up with a cigarette. Perfume is used to cover up the smoke smell."

"Is that true?" asked Rachel, somewhat dubious.

"I don't know, but the word comes from the Latin *per fume,* and that does mean "through smoke." Either way, I'm 100 percent certain my problem was confined to my feet. It was a weird nerve thing, but it was awful. And you know me, after that I was convinced he was telling everyone in Hollywood my feet stank. I was afraid to go out. I just sat in my apartment soaking those stinkers in Woolite for the next three months. I even considered moving back home."

"And you never saw him again?"

"Oh no, I forgot that part. I saw him about an hour ago, at the hotel. He probably pointed me out as I was leaving and announced that I had stinky feet. I wonder if he speaks French."

"I wonder if the French would even care."

"I wonder if the Turks would even notice."

At this point, it was pretty clear that Rachel and I were being ignored. New sea lions were wading in and being massaged while we were being passed over. Rachel didn't like it one bit. "It's not like I want their stupid massage," she said. "I just think it's wrong. We have to say something."

With that, Rachel stomped over to the biggest, meanest Turk in the lot. Words were exchanged—in what language I don't know—then Rachel signaled me over. She got atop one massage table and I was directed to another. I looked at the table; a white sheet covered it. A bloodstain the size of a grapefruit screamed from the center of the sheet, obviously the mark of a Turkish vagina, although I would have sworn Rachel and I were the only two people present young enough to still menstruate.

I wanted to run, but I was far too worldly for that. Instead, I took a deep breath, tossed my "towel" over the stain, got on the table, closed my eyes and pretended to be back in Los Angeles, at Burke Williams, which for all the bitching I've done about the place suddenly seemed like heaven on earth. Then my masseuse coughed up something that looked like it came from her bowels, spat it on the floor and started rubbing her hands together with great fury.

I tried to think happy thoughts, but my mind was having none of it.

The massage began at my feet, and as the pumeling continued up my legs, my brain started to fill with one giant picture of the slime being scooped up off that godforsaken floor and smeared all over my body. I tried to hang tough, but my prissy American upbringing got the better of me. Tears leaked down my cheeks, I heard the Turks cackle, and I just thought, *Fuck it, I am an American, and this has got to be breaching at least one of our amendments.*

My eyes shot open in time to see two Sasquatch-sized mitts coming in for a landing on my freshly scrubbed face—my *beautiful* freshly scrubbed face. A blood-curdling scream flew from my mouth as I leapt out of reach; Rachel was off her table and at my side with vampire speed. We hauled ass to the front desk in our birthday suits, grabbed our clothes, threw them on, dashed outside sandals in hand, and ran smack into *him*.

I started to hyperventilate. Rachel got the picture. Of course, she also knew him, because she knows *everyone*. And of course, she had to be polite, because she went to Chapin.

So with my eyes glued to my toes, Rachel said hello and proceeded to "introduce" me. Then he and I looked at each other and smiled the creepy smiles of two people who slept together (?) over a decade ago and then didn't, leaving one of us to wonder why it ended, and now, seeing him again, why on earth it ever happened in the first place.

After a few moments, he sniffed the air around us. "What's that smell?" he asked. But before I could leap in with a detailed explanation as to where we'd been, what we'd been through and what he was and wasn't smelling, Rachel sniffed right back at him and said, "Oh, that? That's just my feet."

I stood speechless, a deer in the headlights. Should I laugh? Should I cry? Should I make a mad dash for the nearest Métro station? I didn't know what to do. So I took Rachel by the arm and oh so rudely began pulling her down the street. Eventually we made our way back to the Ritz and headed off to our respective rooms.

What Rachel did after that I couldn't say, but I know exactly what I did. I rang room service, ordered up a pineapple and slipped into a bubble bath. And there I sat, cursing the Turks, eating the hospitality fruit, and wondering why what some guy I probably never even liked, thought, said or smelled, still mattered to me now, over a decade later.

The whole thing seemed eerily reminiscent of that used condom episode, but I knew there had to be a difference because I'd run into the Viking numerous times since then and every time we saw each other we'd both burst out laughing. Was it because I actually liked the Viking? Was it because, in that instance, I had befriended the truth with my timely confession, thereby robbing it of its power? Was it because this other character was now worth about a billion bucks? I didn't know, I only knew that I couldn't leave the bathtub until I figured it out.

I thought about calling Michael to get his take on it, but I'd already spent $50 on a room service pineapple, I didn't know if Lauren could get away with expensing a pineapple, I couldn't find her to ask her, steak frites was sounding better by the minute, and, well, it seemed a tad imprudent to spend *anyone's* money just to hear a psychiatrist laugh at me from across the Atlantic. So I made a bubble beard and stroked it, thinking that might help.

It was a few hours later and with pruned skin that I came to the conclusion that *he* had simply set the bar too high. If he'd thought I was only marginally good-looking, none of this would have ever happened. But because he thought I was *the most beautiful girl in the world,* I'd not only been tricked into getting naked with him, I'd also been set up to fail.

The Viking never resorted to flattery, nor did he care about beauty—availability was his number-one requirement—but *this guy*, he had awakened every sick little perfectionist cell in my body with his stupid subjective compliment. No wonder stinky feet felt like such a monstrous faux pas. Flaws weren't an option, not even temporary ones.

"Christ," I said to myself, "carrying a title sounds a little too much like work, if you ask me."

My heart went out to kings and queens everywhere.

men are the new women

John is the last real man in Hollywood. Or maybe he's the first, I'm not sure. I don't know him very well, which probably helps, but as far as I'm concerned, he's everything a man should be. Unfortunately, he's also married.

I ran into John the other day at The Grove. After far too brief a hello kiss, he asked me if I was seeing anyone. I told him I wasn't. "I don't get it," he replied, as if waiting for some sort of punch line. I told him I didn't get it either. I told him I was beginning to question everything I once believed to be true about men. I told him that I thought men used to be the way I imagined, but that something had changed and I'd obviously not gotten the memo.

John started laughing, "Oh yeah, you didn't hear? Men are the new women."

He told me I had to deal with it, but until I know for sure that Vikings are extinct, I just can't. I don't want to. As a woman, I consider it my birthright to be manhandled.

"Not anymore," said John. "You guys changed the rules."

Apparently, what happened is this: First women became men, and then men, fearing that they were becoming obsolete, became women. It makes perfect sense if you think about it. And believe me, when you're lying in bed alone night after night, you have plenty of time to think about it.

My mom and I went to Trader Joe's the last time she visited me in L.A. We were loading my car with groceries when her eagle eye detected that my wiper blades were not up to snuff. She closed in on one of the blades and poked at it. It crumbled at her touch.

"Is this how people live out here?" she asked sharply.

I tried to defend myself, explaining that in a place where it only rains one month out of the year it's easy to let something like wiper blades slide. You change them, they bake in the sun for eleven months, and then when you finally need them, well, sometimes they're sort of petrified.

Being that my mother lives in New Orleans, she insisted that you just never know what the weather's going to do. The wiper blades needed to be changed immediately.

"Fine," I said.

She wanted to go to Pep Boys, but I didn't know where the closest one was. "Oh, for Christ's sake," she said, as she grabbed the first man she saw and asked him where she could find a Pep Boys.

He didn't have a clue.

Then she asked two more guys. They didn't know either.

My mother was positively mystified. "What's wrong with men your age?" I answered with a shrug.

But then it dawned on me: No guys my age knew where to find an auto parts store because no guys my age knew what to do with auto parts. "They don't know how to fix cars!" I blurted out as if just solving a puzzle on *Wheel of Fortune*. "They're too busy checking themselves out in the mirror. They're slathering product in their hair. They're getting manicures. They're reading fashion magazines, if you can believe that one!" But my excitement was quickly overshadowed when I remembered that I don't want a man who takes longer to get ready than I do. I want a man who knows how to change a flat tire. Sure, I can do it. I just don't want to do it. I'm a girl.

I have friends who think it's about time men start holding themselves up to the same absurd physical standards that women have been holding themselves up to for years. And you know what? They're out of their minds. When the image-obsessed portion of the population shoots from 50 percent to 100 percent, that ain't progress. I've been sitting here like a moron wondering when women were finally going to lighten up on themselves, and instead I've got to deal with a bunch of men acting like freaks, too?

One thing that's been forgotten, however, is the part about how women used to cook, raise the children, make a home. Now nobody does it. I guess a cozy nest just isn't as sexy as a million dollar bonus, but what I can't figure out is how the women's movement ever got labeled *feminism* when it's done so very little to elevate the value of traditional female roles and so very much to elevate the value of traditional male roles. It's turned thankless jobs into worthless jobs. That's not feminism, that's masculinism. And those thankless jobs not only had value, they had a very important purpose.

I was watching this show about lions recently. It was the usual setup: a big manly lion, a motherly lioness, a few cubs. This is great, I thought, these cats know how to do things right. That lioness doesn't care that her mate's out there on the Serengeti getting all the glory; she's happy to stay in the den with her litter.

Then something weird happened. The lioness split. What the hell's she doing? I wondered. This can't be right. She wouldn't leave her cubs alone and open to hyena attack. Could it be that she was going next door to grab a chimp to watch over them?

"No!" I screamed at the television. "Don't do it!"

But the lioness just kept slinking along, all slow and sexy. In fact, she slunk right up to her lion, who was standing guard protecting their family, and gave him a little purr. They nuzzled a bit, and then she continued out into the wild where, get this, *she* took down a gazelle.

I couldn't help but laugh. Oh, this is never going to work, I thought. She's going to come back with some fresh meat, he's going to feel emasculated, she's going to start bitching about the inequality of their relationship, the cubs are going to start crying, all hell's going to break loose and that goofball in the pith helmet's going to lose a leg or something. He's standing way too close. Somebody should have told that poor fool that the post-fem days are upon us. We *can't* just get along.

But the lioness returned, and to my great surprise, everyone feasted on gazelle, the cubs went to sleep, and then, the lion, in an explosion of confidence and virility, let out this crazy roar and took that multitasking mate of his from behind. Talk about getting his share! I was dumbfounded. How could this be? Why weren't they throwing things at each other or at least engaging in passive-aggressive behavior? What was the key to their happiness and where could I make a copy?

The whole thing felt so foreign that I wondered if I wasn't watching IFC, but no, it was Animal Planet. This was a nature documentary. This was what happens when the survival of your species actually takes precedence over who's getting credit for what. This was what happens when male and female roles actually are valued equally. It wasn't an outdated propaganda film; this was the stuff that *Born Free* was based on. It's just that out here, in the civilized world, the laws of nature no longer apply. They've been overturned.

The other day, Alice and I were driving down the street when I spotted a strip joint. It was an all-nude strip joint. The sign outside advertised a FREE LUNCH BUFFET. But there were only two cars in the lot, even though it was lunchtime. I slammed on the brakes and said, "Get your cell phone. Take a picture. This is priceless." I mean, come on, the girls are totally naked, they're giving away free grub, and they could only pull in two customers? I'm no fan of strip joints, but there's something very wrong with that.

Alice's theory was that, at least in Hollywood, men are like well-fed tigers. Women are so easy to come by that men can bask in the sun all day long, licking their paws. Forget about stalking. That meat's available 24/7.

"I'm not so sure it works that way with real tigers," I said, "but I get your point. The question is why is it available 24/7?"

"I don't know," said Alice. "Because women are the new sluts?"

"Exactly," I replied. "And why buy the cow if you get the milk for free?"

Alice looked at me like I was my mother and said, "Uh, maybe the cows aren't for sale."

I laughed heartily. "Oh, these cows are for sale," I said. "But let's pretend they're not. Still, what's the point of producing so much milk that everyone's refrigerators are jam-packed and you can't even give it away for free anymore?"

"I don't know, because then the government will buy it?"

"It's not funny, Alice. You can't de-ball a man then stick a vagina in his face and expect him to know what to do with it. You can't even expect him to care. Why should he? The market's been flooded. Women have devalued their own stock. It's so counterintuitive it makes my head spin."

"Did you just say *vagina*?" giggled Alice.

"That's right. I said *vagina* because, hey, guess what, that's what it is. Nobody giggles when you call a tree a tree, but everyone's so uncomfortable with their sexuality that they have to come up with a hundred other names for their genitalia in an effort to distance themselves from . . ."

"Did you just say *genitalia*?"

"Bite me."

"All right, all right. I'm being serious. Do you really call it a *vagina* when you're with a guy?"

Exasperated, I turned to Alice. "Look, you find me a man I can have a mature relationship with, and I'll call it his little pink football if that's what turns him on. You're missing the point."

"There's a point?"

"Yeah there's a point, and the point is everything's all out of whack. Feminism gave women carte blanche to sleep around because men do it, but guess what, men also beat each other to a pulp, and I still don't want to have my face smashed in."

Alice responded with pity. "God. I had no idea you were so repressed."

"Repressed? I'm the opposite of repressed; I'm desperate to find a man who'll suggest we do something that makes me blush. And you better believe I'll say yes. I just want it to be the right man, a good man. True sexual freedom isn't achieved by performing wacky physical acts with every Tom, Dick and Harry; it's a product of intimacy. It's about sharing something with someone you love, someone who makes you feel comfortable enough and safe enough to try new things, things you wouldn't do with every other guy in town. That's what makes it special."

"Really? What kind of new things?"

"Anything!" I screamed.

Then we just sat there staring at the all-nude strip joint for a few minutes.

Breaking the silence, I said, "I once heard a man say something. He said, 'Sleep with a different woman every night and you get the same thing, but sleep with the same woman every night and you get something different.'"

"That's pretty cool," Alice replied.

"I know. But he was already taken. So getting back to the point: I don't care if other women sleep around—whatever floats your boat—I just don't want to be punished for it." Then I pointed to the strip joint's empty parking lot, adding, "And when I see something like this, it really concerns me."

Just then, a bald-headed accountant-looking character walked out of the strip joint, by my count, leaving only one customer inside. He smiled at us. Alice smiled at me.

"You want a man who still understands the value of pussy?" she asked. "There he is. Go get him."

"Hardy, har, har," I replied. "I think not."

"Come on, I thought you decided Vikingism was a state of mind. Give him a spin. He might surprise you."

"I'm not giving him anything. He looks like a pedophile. And I don't want some guy who goes to a strip joint to eat a free lunch buffet anyway; I want a guy who comes to my house at lunchtime to eat something else entirely. But it's cool, laugh all you want, laugh your ass right to extinction, because that's what's happening. Just because we've figured out a way to get by on our own doesn't mean we aren't supposed to be together. Mark my words: Human beings are the new wooly mammoths."

Lying in bed alone that night, I began to wonder if I wasn't just a victim of my own goofy generation—a woman longing for a traditional male-female relationship caught in the cross fire of gender role confusion. In some ways, it seemed to make a lot of sense. I didn't like fiddling with that tire pressure gauge, but I did like having the car door opened for me. I didn't like working in a competitive environment, but I did like doing my own laundry. I didn't like Martha Stewart, but I did like *Martha Stewart Living*.

But then when I thought about the reality of a traditional relationship, I wasn't so sure. I did want a man to hold me at night, but did I really want to pick up after him during the day? I did like kids, but did I really want the E-cup boobs that a pregnancy would surely inflict upon me? I did like to cook, but did I really want someone looking to me for a square meal every night? I mean, sometimes I prefer to eat nothing but smoked salmon and chocolate mousse for days on end. And what about money? Could I ever really swallow the idea that everything my husband earned was half mine? Could he? Or would I have to go through life feeling like a twelve-year-old always begging for an advance on my allowance?

That money thing really bothered me, and it made me wonder. Why did my mother brainwash me into believing that I didn't need a man but I did need to make my own money, only to pick up the phone years later and demand grandchildren? What did she expect me to do now—buy them? Was she subconsciously pressuring me to have it all, perhaps without even knowing what confusion she was creating? And if so, was I responding by having nothing simply to defy her?

I had no idea. I only knew that living in a world where anything's possible confused the shit out of me. Say what you will about the 1950s, at least men and women had clearly defined roles. But was I given a role? No, indeed not. Instead, I got slipped a little mickey called freedom. Sure, I've got rights and opportunities that women didn't have before, but freedom is also intoxicating. And now that I was plastered, they were telling me to just choose my role in this world. How was that supposed to work? I can barely walk a straight line.

To top it all off, it was becoming increasingly clear that Vikings were inherently problematic. I'd just seen *Jackass: The Movie* again, and while I did find it wildly amusing, I didn't have to wonder long before concluding that a daily dose of shenanigans like that would get old, fast. What would happen when I wanted my man to make love to me gently? What would happen when I wanted to go someplace where they expect you to eat with utensils? What would happen when he came home, not with greenbacks, but with some kind of weird booty? I can't barter worth a damn.

No, insisting on a Viking was a great way to keep people from trying to set me up with any old Tom, Dick or Harry, but no matter how hard I tried, I knew in my heart of hearts that a Viking wasn't the answer. I didn't want a Viking; I wanted, I don't know, the male version of me? Me but other than me? Me but better than me? Maybe he'd be big, maybe not. Maybe he'd be blond, maybe not. Maybe he'd be reckless, maybe not. Who knows? Maybe he'd even slather product in his hair and get the occasional manicure. It was hard to say exactly what I wanted in a man, but I couldn't shake this lingering romantic notion that I'd know him when I met him, and that the fog of our combined confusion and doubt would then magically dissipate, allowing us to come together, find our places in each other's lives and figure out a way to make it work.

But then I thought about all those books about success and how they always talk about having a plan and goal. I'd never had a plan in my life. All I had were vague ideas and a dwindling trust in my own instincts—two things not often called for in any recipe for success I'd ever seen. And even if I could somehow pull it together with my meager ingredients, did the right man for me even exist? I suddenly wondered if I wasn't like that final dodo bird, wandering around aimlessly in search of her mate until the day she died, never realizing she was the last of her kind.

Filled with despair, I speed-dialed Alice.

"What now?" she answered, somewhat grumpily I might add.

"What are you doing?"

"I'm in bed. And I'm tired. So if this is about how all the fish in some lake in England are turning into hermaphrodites because of the hormone levels in the water, I'm not interested."

"It's not," I assured her, adding, "If you don't care about the environment, that's your business. This is about dodo birds. I was thinking about the last dodo bird and . . ."

"Oh, God. Don't even say it."

"Say what? You don't know what I'm going to say."

"Oh yes I do. You're going to say you're the last of a dying breed and that's why you're still single."

"How'd you know that?"

Alice let out a long sigh. "Because dodo, there's a Dave Matthews song about a dodo bird that I've listened to at *your* house."

"That song's not about me."

"Yeah, I know that. But I also know how your brain works."

She does this a lot, and it always amazes me. "Well, good call. I'm impressed. I wondered where I came up with that dodo analogy."

"You know I love you so don't take this the wrong way, but please, get over yourself. You're not that special."

"Alrighty. Then I'll just thank you for your support and be on my merry way."

"What do you want from me!?! It's almost midnight."

"I don't want anything from you, but what I wish for you is a nice long soak in a lake, preferably an English lake, and after that, may I suggest a dinner of fish and chips at the nearest pub?"

Alice sighed yet again. "Your perfect man is out there somewhere. I promise."

"Really? The male version of me?" I asked excitedly.

"The male version of you? What does that mean? A mass of contradiction and neuroses, but with a cock?"

"I was thinking more along the lines of a penis."

"Oh God, I hope not. But if that's what you want . . ."

"It's because of birth control pills, you know."

"What is?"

"The feminization of fish."

"Nuh-uh. No way. No fish talk."

"But it's true. And the water we drink and bathe in is chock full of hormones, too. So maybe there's some actual scientific basis for what John was saying, maybe he's right, maybe men really are . . ."

"I'm hanging up in five seconds."

". . . the new women. And maybe I was wrong about feminism too, maybe they had a plan and a goal . . ."

"Two seconds."

". . . maybe they knew it would look like masculinism in the short-term, but that ultimately . . ."

"I'm hanging up now."

"But I don't want to live on a penis-free planet!"

"Good-night."

this is pilates

Well, the verdict's in. I need to lighten up. Orna told me. I think it's worth mentioning that the context was Pilates, and the verdict was delivered by a woman with two years of mandatory military service under her belt.

Israeli women are not light. I learned that much from Leora.

I met Leora when I first started doing Pilates years ago. At the time, I was just another student, as was Leora. I was a bit awed by her, too. Wildly successful and super elegant; she put the *fem* back in *feminism* for me. Oh, how I worshiped Leora *when she wasn't pulling her commando crap on me*. Like the day I was lying on the Reformer peacefully doing my footwork and made the mistake of mentioning that I'd seen a cute guy at Bristol Farms . . .

"*Which* Bristol Farms?" demanded Leora.

"The one in Beverly Hills."

"What time was it?"

"I don't know, probably around 6 P.M."

When Leora leapt off her Reformer like a ninja, pounced on me, twisted my arm around my back and rammed my nose into the mat, it struck me that maybe that wasn't the right answer.

Leora is yet another married friend who falls into the subset of friends who want to use me as their vessel of vicarious living. That said, my reluctance to sleep with a different guy every night has been a major disappointment to Leora, who sees it as nothing more than insolence—a rude, childish refusal to give her anything juicy to sink her fangs into. I told her that it had nothing to do with her; I simply wasn't interested in getting naked with every clown in California so he could tell every other clown, not to mention me having to endure it.

And I had to say all that while hanging upside down on the Cadillac! But Leora's ruthless. She walked over just as regal as could be, poked me in the ribs with a weighted pole, and sneered, "You think you're so special."

I insisted that I didn't think I was *so* special, I just thought I was special enough to hold out for someone special, instead of dropping my pants every time the circus comes to town, adding that perhaps it may seem like I think I'm *so* special due to the fact that circus never actually leaves this town. Plus, I'm pretty sure I've already filled my stupid sex quota.

"You're just a prude," snickered Leora.

"*Excuse me?*"

She glared down at me. "Prude!"

"Just because I'm not a total slut, doesn't mean I'm a prude. In fact, some of the sluttiest women I know have barely made it past missionary position. I hate to break it to you, but I've done a lot of things you've never done. *A lot.*"

Suddenly Leora's eyes lit up like miniature hand grenades exploding in the Israeli sky. "Oh yeah, like what?"

"None of your beeswax," I replied, as I hoisted myself back upright.

It took forever, but once Leora had exhausted her library of psychological warfare techniques and saw that I *still* wasn't going to give in and sleep around simply for her amusement, and once she had accepted the fact that I wasn't interested in anything other than a serious relationship, she began monitoring my every social move to ensure that I didn't screw it up. But in Leora's eyes, I always did. If I told her that I walked outside to pick up the newspaper, she'd find something wrong with the way I'd done it.

"What were you wearing?" she'd demand.

"What was I *wearing*? The sun wasn't even up. I was wearing pajamas."

"What *kind* of pajamas?"

"What does it matter? No one else was around. Even the homeless people were still under their blankets."

"It *matters*. Don't talk to me about the homeless, I want to know what kind of pajamas you were wearing!"

"Jesus, woman. Flannel. Flannel pajamas with cowboys on them, three buttons were buttoned, the top and bottom buttons remained unbuttoned. My hair was in a ponytail. Oh, and I was barefoot."

Leora would just hang her shaking head. "And you expect to find a man like *that?*"

So, like I was saying, it was with my nose rammed into the mat, and my humerus under threat of dislocation that I screamed, "It could have been 6:30 P.M. I'm not sure." Leora continued to increase the pressure on my arm and I continued to squirm, until Brenda, the owner, walked in and, probably fearing a lawsuit, said, "Leora, let her go."

I jumped out of Leora's reach while massaging my rotator cuff and screamed, "What did I do wrong *this* time?"

As it turned out, I had seen this guy at the *right* grocery store, but at the *wrong* time. I knew it infuriated Leora every time I said I didn't care about money and that she considered anything less than a salary of a million a year unacceptable, but I thought I was in the clear by saying that I'd seen him at Bristol Farms, where everything is wildly overpriced. I reminded Leora that this is Los Angeles, where hardly anyone goes to an actual job and yet everyone magically has money. The guy could have been a pauper or he could have been a zillionaire, you just can't tell, except that if he were a pauper, he would have been at The $1 Store, where he would have been able to get more than a single grain of rice for his dollar, and I would have never seen him. I thought I was safe, and believe me, I thought about it.

What I hadn't realized was that it was not simply money, but also a strong work ethic that any potential mate must possess. According to Leora, I wasn't supposed to even look at a man who dared cross the Bristol Farms threshold before 8:00 P.M. Anything earlier than that was a sure-fire sign of laziness, which, like just about everything else, I would consider unacceptable if I had half a brain in my head.

I told Leora that if she had paid attention she might have picked up on an essential element of the story—which wasn't even a whole story but one stupid sentence—which was that I, who have no money, was also shopping at Bristol Farms, clearly illustrating that I do *not* have half a brain in my head. Then I got back on the Reformer and started doing arm curls.

Leora hopped onto her Reformer instantly. "How many springs do you have it on?" she demanded.

"One, Leora. You're only ever supposed to do them on one."

Leora put hers on two. Her form sucked.

"If you put it on one, it would be easier to isolate the muscles," I said.

"I do it on two," she insisted.

"Fine. Do it on two, but you're not doing it right."

"I can handle two."

———

Leora kept doing it on two, and I kept doing it on one, as I watched the veins in her neck bulge like giant blue pythons desperately trying to break free of a nude stocking, knowing full well that if she were doing it *right*, that would not be happening. Her power-house was not properly engaged. Her feet were not in line with her knees. Her shoulders were hiked up, practically piercing her eardrums, as she strained to lift her arms. She wasn't even doing curls; her arms were almost totally straight. It taunted every OCD cell in my body and I wanted nothing more than to bash her brains in with a Magic Circle.

But I controlled myself. I controlled myself because when Joseph Pilates created Pilates, he didn't call it Pilates, he called it *Contrology*. We were supposed to be using our minds to *control* our bodies. Pilates is all about form. And it infuriated me that Leora's flagrant disrespect for the laws of Pilates was threatening to undermine my own mind control.

I glanced at the clock. I'd been working out for forty-three minutes. It made perfect sense. According to Pilates, it's *impossible* to maintain a satisfactory level of mind control for more than forty-five minutes. I was on the tail end. My mind was weak. I abandoned the Reformer to begin my cooldown.

Lying on the mat, I gazed at the water dispenser and began to fantasize about Uncle Joe materializing out of the spigot like a big, mean genie. Joseph Pilates: the only thing less light than an Israeli woman. The man had zero tolerance for anyone who didn't see things *exactly* his way. And talk about opinionated! From child rearing to soap to furniture to masturbation, which he proclaimed "the curse of mankind," the guy had something to say. He also had some completely revolutionary designs for chairs and beds that I'm convinced were never taken seriously because he probably approached every manufacturer in his underwear. It's hard to find a picture of the guy with clothes on. He didn't really believe in those either.

But I didn't care, because we did see exercise exactly the same way. Pilates rocks! As long as Uncle Joe and I stayed on subject, everything would be groovy. He'd seep out of that water spigot in a plume of mist, look around the studio, see me lying on the mat in perfect form, and smile proudly. Then his eyes would land on Leora.

Ha! He'd grab a Thera-Band and fly over to her Reformer in a rage, snapping that rubber cattail in the air, and picking up where I'd left off. Her ass was grass. She wouldn't dare contradict him. How could she? His last name was Pilates.

Uncle Joe never came, and I finally got sick of Leora claiming that she'd won at the end of every session. I switched studios. And it was at my new studio that I went through training to become a Pilates instructor. Why not? I loved it, I got to be my own boss, and it was the only job I knew of that practically begged you to be anal. Nobody cared about precision and alignment in the movie business, or, I don't know, maybe stunt people did, but nevertheless, I kissed the film industry good-bye, and moved on to what I *thought* would be a kinder, gentler life as a Pilates instructor.

Then I met Orna, another Israeli. Apparently, there's one at every studio. She was Leora's sister-in-arms, unless of course they were to be pitted against each other in a gladiator fight, in which case their competitive nature would take over and I'd probably bet on Orna. Leora's a femme fatale; Orna's just plain fatal. But again, super nice *until* the flashbacks start kicking in.

It happened just the other day, as I was perched atop a Wunda Chair. All I did was ask Orna to check my form. But before the question was even out of my mouth, she let loose with a cackle and shot back in her thick Israeli accent, "Lighten up. Stop worrying about form. *Just do it.*"

You can take the girl out of the army, but you can't take the army out of the girl.

The thing is, I'm sick of working in competitive, bully-filled environments, and I'm sick of Israeli women berating me on my own turf, too. Is a little studio camaraderie really that much to ask for? Not to mention the fact that I didn't want to *just do it;* I wanted to do it *right*, otherwise I never would have asked her check my goddamn form in the first place. But I did, and she didn't. And that's when I glanced at the clock, saw that I'd been working out for fifty minutes—meaning that technically the rules of Pilates no longer applied—jumped off my Wunda Chair, grabbed a Spine Corrector, hurled it at Orna and screamed, "Listen sarge, *this is Pilates!* Nobody gives a shit how many Uzis you can lug through a minefield, but you better fucking believe that *form matters!*"

I mean, really, if she had half a brain in her head, she'd know that.

klimax

I was seeing a guy who had just enrolled in this class, Girls 101 or something like that, which basically taught common sense. Things like, if your girlfriend's having her period, don't scream at her about being "on the rag." Be nice to her and offer to cook dinner instead.

Of course, at the time, I thought it was the greatest thing ever. I thought I was the luckiest girl in the world to have someone so sweet, so evolved, that he actually wanted to understand me and *cared* how I felt. I mean, really, this is what it had come to. But in his defense, at least he was man enough to admit that he was lost. At least he wasn't afraid to take that first step and ask someone for directions.

So one night he was going down on me when suddenly he stopped, pulled his head up and informed me that I gave him a complex. I wanted to tell him that there's a little thing called *personal responsibility*, and that I couldn't just give him a complex without him first signing the permission slip, but given the circumstances, I thought it not in my best interest to pick a fight. I remained silent as he recounted my offense. Apparently, I'd inflicted this complex upon him the first night we were together, when I told him about my neighbors.

I used to have these neighbors who had exactly the same sex for exactly the same length of time at exactly the same hour every day. I'd told my boyfriend about them, and about how sometimes

I would lie in bed at night and try to lip-sync the woman's moans, which were exactly the same every time. I thought it was hilarious. But my boyfriend, I now learned, had been tortured by the story for months, wondering whether I was judging him the same way.

Hoping to restore his confidence, I assured him that I knew the difference between my neighbors and me, and that I was very happy with what he was doing. "You should just continue."

A few moments later, he resurfaced and gleefully announced, "I'm doing the ABCs." In Girls 101, they'd been taught that if they didn't know what else to do down there, they should do the ABCs. It's a fine idea, I suppose. Telling me, however, was not. Shortly thereafter I completely lost the ability to have an orgasm during oral sex, because every time he went down on me, my brain was transformed into a giant movie screen and projected onto that screen was the image of a five-year-old boy, sitting at a very small desk with a very fat pencil, nervously attempting to recreate the alphabet. It wasn't sexy; it was creepy. And I'm way past faking it.

At first, it was easy enough to deal with. He'd go down on me, I'd quickly move us on to other things, and that was that. It wasn't ideal, but at least it got me out of kindergarten. Unfortunately, as soon as he caught on to the fact that I didn't want him going down on me, going down on me was *all he wanted to do*. This, I think, is a major difference between men and women. Most women I know would be perfectly happy to never give another blow job again as long as they live. Sure, I know a few super competitive women— three of them to be exact—who go down on every man within reach, pride themselves on giving the *best blow job ever* and brag about it at parties, but they are definitely not the majority. So I always respond in kind. "That's incredible!" I belt out enthusiastically. "I'm the best at getting face!" *Getting face?* "Yeah. It's when a guy goes down on *you*. Put your trophy aside sometime and give it a whirl. It's *the best!* Your hair doesn't get glued to your cheek or anything!"

And, just for the record, I really don't know how all three of them can give the *best blow job ever*. They can yap about it all they want, but it's hard for me to be impressed, given that they really have no way of knowing what the hell they're talking about and I certainly don't have what it takes to properly resolve the debate. I guess they're just skipping along based on what they've been told. The thing is, and I don't want to alarm anyone here, some men are actually capable of *lying*. Dangle a blow job in front of their face, and they'll agree to pretty much anything.

Case in point: I was at this diner eavesdropping on a young couple in the booth behind me. They were negotiating. She wanted a Rottweiler puppy; he did not. She was offering up all kinds of incentives—backrubs for a year, car washes every Sunday, unlimited football privileges—and he wasn't budging. He insisted that he didn't want a dog, and nothing she said was going to change his mind. Then she landed on the golden carrot. "I'll give you ten blow jobs!" she blurted out. His ears perked up. Now she was talking. He wanted twenty. She thought that was outrageous. I think they finally settled on sixteen. All I know for sure is that *blow job* was the magic word. Once she said that, a deal was in the works.

She's not alone, either. I know women who've gotten jewelry, cars and fabulous vacations in exchange for blow jobs. *A veiled form of prostitution?* Perhaps, but for a lot of women, unless there's something in it for them, they just aren't that interested. They may give it a halfhearted go, but if they don't get results in the first three minutes, they're out of there. If they had their head pulled up, they'd never go back.

———

Men, apparently, are different. I knew this guy once—nice, smart, super good-looking. He was constantly pestering me to let him come over and go down on me, claiming all the while that he was the best. But I'd been down that road before, and I was certain he'd want something in return. They always do. They tell you they just want to go down on you, but ultimately they all try to lure you into reciprocating, then stomp their feet like children when you remind them that *that* wasn't part of the deal. What ever happened to honor? I thought a man's word was supposed to mean something.

This guy swore his did, so after about a year, I gave in. He came to my office, I locked the door and down he went. Afterwards, he smiled smugly, not unlike a Boy Scout who'd just won the Pinewood Derby. "So how was it?" he asked.

"Pretty good," I replied.

"*Pretty good?*" he snorted, as if I were some silly seventeen-year-old who had nothing at all to compare it to. I mean, really, *as if*.

"Yeah," I said. "Pretty good, and definitely the best thing that's ever happened in this office." Then I told him he had to skedaddle because I had a conference call.

Two days later he's ringing my phone off the hook, begging me to let him come back, assuring me that he'd do a better job next time. I told him to let it go. Who cares if it wasn't *the best?* No matter how good it was, it couldn't have been the best because I wasn't in love with him and he wasn't in love with me and outside of that it's all, I don't know, *performance art?* But he wouldn't hear it. He just kept calling and calling and calling.

What it all means, I couldn't tell you. I probably couldn't pass a Boys 101 class if my life depended on it. I've accepted the fact that men, as a group, will baffle me until the day I die. That's why I prefer to deal with only a select few, and with a good year or so between each to sit back and scratch my head in wonder. I'm not often intrigued enough to invite a man into my bedroom, but when I am, I prefer to make the most of it. I'm not trying to win an award; I'm just hoping to have a mutually satisfying experience. I thought that was the whole point. But sometimes I wonder if I'm the only one who feels that way.

I know women who've blown away, simply to fool a man into thinking he's hit the jackpot, then, once the knot was tied, they act as if they've filled their quota and never need to do it again. I've got one married friend—a guy—who tells me his wife hasn't gone down on him in three years. I've got another married friend who tells me she enters blow job reminders into her BlackBerry; they pop up, she goes down—and this is someone who used to tell every guy within earshot that she *loved* giving blow jobs. One divorced friend told me she thought blow jobs existed on a rainbow scale. You meet someone, you grow attached to them, you desire to please them more and more, then you reach the apex of the rainbow and the downward slide begins; you start to become complacent in your relationship, life gets in the way and pleasing your partner takes a backseat. As they say, relationships are all about compromise, and as she said, when you start talking about compromise, you're talking about negotiation, and when you're talking about negotiation, blow jobs take on a whole new meaning. *You want a blow job? Great, I want you to take out the garbage, mow the lawn and watch the kids.* So maybe that's why so many men act as if there's just been a dinosaur sighting at the mention of a blow job.

I was discussing all this with Nigel who demanded that I tell him exactly *why* women didn't like giving blow jobs. How the hell am I supposed to know? Just trying to understand myself is a full-time job. And it's not just women, anyway. I read something the other day that said 40 percent of both women *and men* not only didn't like performing oral sex; they flat-out didn't do it. I guess some people are just grossed out by it. And who am I to judge? I'm grossed out by licorice. But Nigel wouldn't let it go, so I told him that if I had to guess, I'd say it probably just seemed a little too much like work when compared to something like say, intercourse, which, especially when you're talking missionary position, requires virtually nothing but passive acceptance on the woman's part. It won't be the best sex a guy's ever had, but if he's just looking to get off, it'll work.

The truth is women don't have to perform oral sex. It's a bonus. Even the Rottweiler girl understood that and she was barely legal. Let's boil it down to biology. Let's just talk about sex. And let's exclude the picture-perfect people and take away all the fancy trappings, both of which exist in excess in Hollywood, thus rendering it a brothel with a gaudy neon LOVE FOR SALE sign that never dims. Let's send an average woman and an average man out for the night in, say, Arizona, with nothing but themselves as bait and strict orders to seal the deal, and I assure you that woman is going to have way more men to choose from than her male counterpart. Plus, she can probably land a guy who's out of her league. I'm not saying he's going to love her forever, I'm not saying he's going to call her the next day, I'm not even saying he's going to spend the night. He could hate himself for doing it *while he's doing it*. But if you're just talking about sex, it's not that difficult to do what needs to be done to awaken a man's animal instincts and get him to go along for the ride, at least once. Even if he's resistant at first, chances are, with a little finesse, or maybe by shoving your hand down his pants, you can get him there. Why? Because he's been programmed to spread his seed. It's in his DNA. That's just how it is. Unfortunately for men, the same doesn't apply in the reverse. And only a very foolish woman would overlook this simple truth, a truth that men are keenly aware of.

So if you want to *really* break it down, by merely agreeing to a sexual encounter, a woman is now in the driver's seat. I don't care what she had to do to get the man there, he's there now, he's got sex on the brain, he's semi-erect, and this, ladies, is the moment to get face. After that, you're square. If he then wants something, and he will, you exchange it for more face time. Or don't get any face time. I don't care. Get whatever you want. Just know that once you're naked, you're in the position to ask for anything you desire. After that, it's his turn, and most likely, once a man realizes that you understand the game, he's going to go straight for penetration.

My advice to men in search of blow jobs? Take away their value. Act like you don't care. Or better yet, do it the Hollywood way: Create the illusion of demand where there is none and start a bidding war. Everybody knows people want what they can't have. Act like going down on you isn't even an option. And if that's too big a stretch, then just leap right in. Don't go straight for penetration; choose oral sex. Like I told Nigel, it's the win-win solution, because any woman with half a brain is still going to want to have intercourse after that. If you're sleeping with quarter-brainers, well, you've made your bed.

The funny thing is a lot of the guys I've talked to have said that, technically speaking, most of the blow jobs they've received haven't been all that great. And I'm not surprised. Going down on a guy can be a little awkward. There are so many odd-sized movable parts to fiddle with and unless he's got a bullhorn and some of those orange glow sticks they use for landing aircrafts, it can be very difficult to know if you're getting it right. And if he does have a bullhorn and glow sticks, it's next to impossible to focus on the job at hand, anyway.

So I ask you, if a woman doesn't have a genuine desire to go down on a man, why would she choose to fumble around and feel like a novice when it's so much easier to lie back and feel like a pro? And even if she does have a genuine desire to do it, she still knows she's giving away something that could be traded. So if a man's not treating it, and her, like a gift, then why give it away? Maybe that's the real problem—that men and women, for the most part, simply don't treat each other like the gifts they are, opting instead to abuse, manipulate, suspect, neglect, fear and/or just barely tolerate the opposite sex as if they're nothing more than a necessary evil.

Even the type A's who appear to be "gifting" with abandon aren't just giving it away for nothing. They're getting bragging rights in return. And it's not like I really care who anyone's going down on, but when grown women (and men) are running around telling everyone in town that they're *the best,* you've got to wonder if maybe, just maybe, they didn't get the validation they needed at home.

Or I don't know, maybe they did get the validation they needed at home; maybe they've just gotten messed up since then. I mean the world *is* out to get us. I open the *L.A. Weekly* and half the pages are filled with ads for liposuction, vaginal rejuvenation, breast implants, you name it. My own mother called me the other day to interrogate me about laser hair removal and, get this, *anal bleaching.* She'd heard about it on *Dr. 90210.* I told her what I knew about laser hair removal, but as far as I'm concerned, anyone who gets their anus bleached has too much time on their hands and nothing but rocks in their head. There's not much more to say on the subject.

But maybe that, too, is part of the equation, maybe some women are simply avoiding blow jobs because they fear reciprocity and the shameful reveal that their vaginas don't look *exactly* like Miss January's. It seems strange to me, but these are strange times. I get five e-mails a day about some potion or other that's supposed to increase penis size and prolong erections. I'm convinced my little brother's behind it; it's exactly the kind of thing he'd do. But really, all it does is confirm for me that we live in a society hell-bent on convincing us that we have to spend every dollar we make "improving" ourselves. Talk about creating paranoia.

And it all happened so fast. Back in the '70s the only thing you needed to have sex was a van; now we're being told that it actually requires pills, creams and a series of surgical procedures. What a rip-off! Those hippies didn't even shave before slipping off their bell-bottoms! But anyone can have a nice day when they're sucking on a bong and staring at blacklight posters; it's not quite as easy when you're spending 90 percent of your time examining yourself in a fun-house mirror then comparing what you see against a bunch of Photoshopped images. So it's really no wonder everyone's both desperate for validation and terrified to simply be themselves and get the only validation that really counts, the kind that says *you're OK just the way you are.*

So what happens instead? Everyone consumes themselves with constructing elaborate façades, getting those façades validated, then wondering why we still feel like crap. *Duh.* It's because *you* were never validated. It's a no-brainer. But nobody listens to me.

And why should they? I'm living proof that following my guidelines doesn't cause anything but trouble. Had I screamed Daddy and declared that Mr. Alphabet was *the best,* he'd have probably grabbed his blue ribbon and trotted happily away. But I couldn't do that. That wouldn't have been genuine. So instead, there I was night after night, lying in bed, staring at the ceiling, doing the ABCs in my head. Sometimes I'd even purposely go off course and think about something else, like whether I wanted Indian or Thai for lunch the next day. Then I'd tune back in to see if I could figure out which letter we were on.

When he got to Z, I'd pretend not to know, he'd look at me expectantly, and I'd just mumble something about him being inside me. No go. He wasn't budging, and I wasn't climaxing. It was a standoff. The only time his head ever moved from between my legs was when I had to go to work, at which time he would point out that he wasn't done, and therefore hadn't failed me. We were just taking a break. It was kind of like the Tour de France, where they have established starts and finishes, adding up all your times so you can grab a few hours' sleep here and there.

Then one night he caught me lip-syncing the alphabet.

"What are you doing?" he demanded.

"Nothing," I replied.

"It's no wonder you can't have an orgasm if you're talking to yourself the whole time."

"Excuse me," I said. "But I *can* have an orgasm."

"Then why haven't you had one in three months?"

"Can we just have sex like old people? I *promise* I'll have an orgasm."

"No. Not until you have one *this way.*"

Then he disappeared back under the sheets like a kid donning a ghost costume. The added visual was more than I could bear and frankly, I was beginning to worry. I mean, how many licks *does it take* to get to the center of a Tootsie Pop? And how many more licks does it take until that sucker disappears forever?

I didn't know; I only knew that the masquerade had to end.

"You may as well just come up," I said. "It's not going to happen."

"*Why not?!*" he pleaded.

"Because you're making a *J*," I sighed. "You're making the letter

J, and I can't really get into it when I know you're just working your way through the alphabet. It's too impersonal."

Well that did it. The sheet went flying, and he started ranting and raving, insisting that he wasn't making a *J* and that I'd gotten it all wrong. I leaned back against the headboard with resolve. After remaining silent through hundreds of *J's*, I knew exactly what a *J* felt like.

He insisted that it could have been a *U*. "Sure," I said. "It could have been, because that too is part of the alphabet, but it wasn't. It was a *J*."

After about forty-five minutes of arguing, he finally relented. Folding his arms in a huff, he said, "Fine, it was a *J*."

"No shit," I replied.

He wasn't a very good sport about losing the argument and accused me of judging him all along, just like I'd judged my neighbors. I insisted that I'd only started judging him once I knew he was repeating an easy-to-follow pattern. As far as I was concerned, he'd sabotaged himself by broadcasting his neighborly technique, but he saw it differently, claiming that I was trying to sabotage our relationship by not complaining in a more timely fashion.

"That's ridiculous," I replied. "If I wanted to break up with you, I'd just break up with you. I assumed you'd figure out that the alphabet wasn't working and move on, but *obviously* I was wrong."

"Of course you were wrong," he screamed. "How could I get bored with the alphabet? *I'm a writer!*"

"*Oh really?*" I replied. "Because you haven't written anything other than the alphabet in a *long, long time*."

"Oh, so that's why you want to break up with me?"

"I don't want to break up with you! Can't you just come up with something a little more original?"

"Obviously not," he screamed back. "If I could, I'd be writing."

"So, what? You're just using me so you don't forget the alphabet? I've got an idea: Why don't you move to China or someplace where they use a *different* alphabet."

"Because I don't want to move to China!"

"Then go to Chinatown."

"No! I don't want to go to Chinatown or Koreatown or any other town!"

I stared back at him, exasperated. "So what *do* you want?"

"I want to not fight."

"Fine, but you started it."

"*I* started it?"

"Yeah, with the letter *J*. And I don't know how you can be mad at me for being too preoccupied with the alphabet to lose myself, when you're the one who engraved it in my brain three months ago and haven't mixed it up once since then! It's totally unfair."

"Well, if you didn't like the alphabet then why didn't you just tell me?"

"I did tell you. I told you through *actions*. I lit up for *I*'s and lay dormant for *U*'s. Aren't men supposed to be nonverbal communicators? You should have picked up the damn signal."

"Well I didn't, and you knew it! So why didn't you just *say* something?"

"*Why?* Because I didn't want you stuck in limbo."

"*Limbo?*"

"That's right, limbo. It seemed pretty clear that you weren't confident enough in your own technique or comfortable enough to improvise, and I was afraid that if I took the alphabet away from you you'd just be all adrift in the sheets like some bewildered spirit."

He started laughing. "You really thought that?"

I nodded.

"*Really?*"

I nodded again.

"That's ridiculous," he said. "I don't need the alphabet. I just thought it was funny."

"Really?"

He nodded.

"All right. Then let's just have sex."

"OK, but first I want you to come this way."

At this point it was evident that I was never going to get what I wanted unless I complied with his demands. So I turned my frown upside down and tried to play nice.

"You know you don't have to have a plan," I said. "It's not a test. It's supposed to be fun. They must have mentioned that in class."

"I know," he replied.

Then I said something about how I'd be happier if he just relaxed, assuring him that I'd let him know what felt good. I mean, really, *fumble around*. It's OK. Another person's body is supposed to be a mystery that reveals itself over time; sex is supposed to get better and better as two people become more in tune with each other. I don't care if a man doesn't take me to the pinnacle of Mount Ecstasy and make me speak in tongues on day 1. In fact, I'd prefer if he didn't. There's nowhere to go from there but down, and any man who's that skilled is out of my league anyway. I'm either going to transfer back to the beginner class to avoid any potential embarrassment or make myself crazy wondering how many women he had to plow through in order to figure it all out. Who needs that? I just want a man who feels secure enough with himself, and has enough faith in me, that he's at least willing to try to throw everything else out the window long enough to take me in his arms and make love to me like he means it. *Sign me up!* I know it's possible. If Dave Matthews is singing about taking his woman to bed and loving her "like the end is near" then he can't be the only guy who's ever felt that way.

And OK, sure, Dave could simply be messing with me. That too is possible. Maybe he and Barry White really have conspired against me, engaging in some secret handshake as they set out to fill my head with artificial auditory visions of some mind-altering lyrical love impossible to ever experience in real life. But it seems highly unlikely.

Of course, if it were just Barry, I might believe it was all an evil scheme. I know he's a liar, because back in the day, when my Barry White obsession was at an all-time high, I tracked down his muse. Not at her house, on the Internet. I figured a picture would help me make sense of the spell she put on her man. Her name was Glodean and she was pretty enough, but as I was checking her out what really struck me were her fingernails. You see, in one of Barry's songs, he sings about making her toenails curl. But let me tell you something, that woman had the longest nails I've ever seen outside of *The Guinness Book of World Records.* So if her toenails were anything like her fingernails, and I suspect they were, Barry didn't have to do squat to make them curl. In fact, I can almost guarantee that those babies were coiling around her ankles long before she and Barry ever met.

But liar or not, it doesn't even matter because by all accounts those two were about as loved up as any two people could be. Barry may have stretched the truth in a song or two, but he and Glo definitely had a soul connection. And Glodean's toenails, while nothing I would want on my own feet, apparently didn't interfere with that connection in the least. So I'm not buying the conspiracy theory.

Regardless, Alphabet Man was too busy repositioning the sheet to listen to a word I said. Talk about disconnected.

So I took his hand and tried to *connect.* "You know I'm on your side, right? There's no need for performance anxiety because there's no need to perform. I just want you to be here with me."

"Thanks, that takes a lot of pressure off," he said at light speed, eager to return to his post.

Unconvinced, I looked him straight in the eye. "No alphabet?"

"No alphabet," he promised.

"All right. Carry on."

I kissed him, he kissed his way back into position and I dropped my head onto the pillow, believing the problem to be solved. A few moments later, my eyes shot open. Something very familiar was happening down there. It wasn't an *A*, but . . . What the hell was it? Suddenly it hit me. It was a *4*! *Oh my God,* I thought, *numbers are infinite!* *5*. It was time to break my own rules. *6*. So I grabbed his head. *7*. I started moaning. *8*. I wiggled my hips around. *9*. I threw in an "Oh, baby" or two, not terribly original but it seemed fitting, and what do you know? Before he got to the double digits, I was klimaxing like krazy.

Then he left feeling like a winner and I called Alice to unload.

"And that's klimax with a *K*, in case you were wondering," I said.

"Yeah, I figured as much," responded Alice, "like that fake crab meat they call *krab*."

"Exactly."

"But does that really work? Can you really fake an orgasm when he's, you know . . ."

"Oh my God, did you miss the whole story? He wasn't tuning in! It's easy to trick someone when they're not there."

"I guess that's true. Mostly I just can't believe you kept your mouth shut for three whole months. I thought you two were swinging from the chandeliers all this time."

"Hardly. I was just biting my tongue, hoping things would improve so I could torture you with *true* stories of my hot sex life."

"That I believe."

"I still can't get over it. I mean, who knew oral sex could feel like one big time-out?"

"I certainly didn't," replied Alice.

"Well, trust me, it can. I'm never letting anyone go down on me again. From here on out, I'm going straight for penetration."

"You did get that eventually, didn't you?"

"Nope."

"*What?*"

"There was nothing I could do about it. It was his turn to pick."

"*And he didn't want to?*"

"No. Or I don't know, maybe he wanted to but was just too exhausted. Maybe he doesn't like girls on top. Don't ask me. Guys are weird."

"So he went for the blow job, huh?"

"No. He just went," I said matter-of-factly.

"*Home?*"

"I don't know where the hell he went. I didn't follow him."

"He didn't want *anything* in return?"

"Are you kidding? He told me he'd be back tomorrow to start collecting on his three months' worth of blow jobs."

"Wow. That's genius," said Alice. "I wish I could have seen your face."

"Yeah, well, at least my face still moves. He looked like he'd had a stroke after all that tongue twisting."

"That's funny."

"Not really, because now I do want to break up with him, and he's going to think it's because I don't want to pay up, but it's not. It's not even about the ABCs. But I know that no matter what I tell him he's still going to think it's about sex because it's easier to blame the symptom than address the actual problem."

"You can't worry about what he thinks."

I sighed. "I know, but I will. It's what I do."

Still mourning the loss of an orgasm that never was, I hung up the phone feeling duped and dismayed. It seems you can't count on anything anymore. Maybe that's why women don't like giving blow jobs. Maybe they're just afraid they'll be blowing their one chance to end the night with a bang.

something shiny

"You lay a lot of eggs," she said, "but none of them ever hatch."

Maybe there was *some* truth to that, but coming from my own hen it seemed unduly harsh.

"*Really?*" I replied. "You think so?"

"Yeah, I think so. And don't look to me for the answer either. You've always been like this. You wanted to take ballet, so I enrolled you in ballet. Then as soon as you got there you wanted to go to art classes, so I enrolled you in that. Then as soon as you got there you wanted to take tennis lessons, so I enrolled you in that. And no matter where you were, all you ever *really* wanted to do was talk. Not five minutes after you were born I heard you say to the doctor, "You know what?" And you haven't shut up since. So don't ask me why your eggs aren't hatching. Talk it over with yourself. I'm sure you'll come up with something."

"Well, I think the answer's obvious, Mom. If I was already speaking the day I was born, I was probably just too advanced. Kids need to be *challenged*."

"Mmmmhmmmm," she replied, dismissively.

"Why are you picking on me?" I demanded.

"I'm not picking on you. I'm just making an observation. Don't be so sensitive."

"But I don't even know what prompted the observation. We

138

weren't talking about food *or* animals. We were talking about knitting. What's that got to do with unhatched eggs?"

After a little chuckle, she said, "You'll figure it out."

I hung up the phone, fully annoyed. Why did *I* have to figure everything out? Was this her grown-up equivalent of "Look it up in the dictionary"? All my life I'd only ever heard the woman say three things. Scratch that, four. If I didn't know what a word meant, she wouldn't just fork over the damn definition; she'd tell me to "Look it up in the dictionary." If I was bored, she wouldn't call in a troupe of puppeteers; she'd tell me to "Go read a book." If I was hungry, she wouldn't whip out a notepad and take my order, she'd tell me to "Eat a banana." And if we didn't have any bananas, you know what I got? Not the overflowing platter of fried chicken and biscuits that I actually wanted her to serve me, but a casual "If you can read, you can cook." *What a gyp!* Our relationship bore no resemblance whatsoever to the Eloise-Nanny model I aspired to. And kids aren't supposed to be frying chicken, anyway. *Maybe* a grilled cheese sandwich, *but fried chicken???* God have mercy! Couldn't *she* have figured out that an eight-year-old has no business hovering over a vat of 500-degree peanut oil? I only had to plop one drumstick in to figure that much out.

My blood was threatening to boil when I picked up the scarf I'd been working on for the last six months and resumed knitting. The calming effects of repetitive motion soon brought me down to a slow simmer. With my mother out of the way and unable to benefit from my confession, I silently acknowledged that I had indeed laid a large number of eggs, although I didn't have the foggiest clue why they weren't hatching, or why my mother felt compelled to rub my nose in it. I *wanted* them to hatch. That much was obvious. Otherwise, why would I waste my precious time laying them? Completely perplexed by the questions at hand,

I tossed the scarf aside, grabbed my handy *L.A. Weekly* and checked out the film section.

I was on my way to the movies when Pauline called and invited me over for dinner. She wanted me to meet her boyfriend's kids. I turned around and headed over.

The kids were eleven and fourteen and they were *absolutely fascinating*. Brad, the eldest, spoke fluent German (although his parents didn't speak a word of it), had a passion for both science fiction and Italian cooking, would be going to summer camp in Tuscany to hone his skills *and* he already knew he wanted to be a nuclear physicist and had enrolled in advanced classes to make it happen sooner.

At first I wondered if all rich people just instantly knew what they wanted out of life, but then I remembered my friend Robert who's about a hundred years old, had super wealthy parents who finally cut him off at the age of forty, and still didn't have a clue.

I turned to Mia for some sign of the familiar. She'd been doing pirouettes around the dining room table throughout dinner and hadn't so much as touched a leaf of lettuce. She had only one interest: ballet. She had been studying her art since the age of three and currently danced four hours a day on school days and eight hours a day on weekends. She had just been accepted into a special ballet camp in New York, where she would be dancing forty-eight hours a week with one day off, a day on which I imagined all the fledging ballerinas sitting around in a hot tub massaging each other's legs.

Intense feelings of inadequacy began surging through my body. I was certain everyone was aware of it, and I desperately needed to redirect the unwanted attention. So I said, "Hey, Mia. Can I bum a cigarette?" Her father, Darren, looked at me like I was out of my mind, but I didn't care. I had my own shit to deal with. Mia just giggled, claiming that she didn't smoke. But I was all over it, instantly topping her with a snide cackle. "*And you call yourself a ballerina?*"

Where did kids like this come from? I looked at Darren, but that certainly wasn't bringing me any closer to an answer. And Pauline wasn't even related to them. If I could just meet their mother, I thought, maybe then I could solve the mystery. But I knew a request like that would be met with a refusal at best. So I ordered Brad and Mia to lift their shirts and show me their belly buttons instead, pissing Daddy off in the process.

"What are you doing to my kids?" he demanded.

"Nothing," I replied. "I saw this movie once with aliens and they had two belly buttons."

Brad had seen it, too, but he and Mia only had one belly button each. While not the kind of evidence that would hold up in a court of law, it was the best I could do in a pinch and it did bring me a smidge closer to accepting the fact that these children were actually human. I drained the remaining two-thirds of a bottle of Pinot Noir into my glass and starting chugging. How could they be like that, and I be like *this?* It just wasn't fair.

I already knew it was verboten to voice anything even remotely resembling a suggestion that my mother might have something to do with it, but I could still secretly think it. She could dig through my purse, but she couldn't dig through my mind. That's where God drew the line, making it clear that He was on my side.

So I wondered. Had I really wanted to quit ballet, or did she just decide that it was too far a drive? Had I really wanted to quit art classes, or did she just think the teacher was a pervert? Had I really wanted to quit tennis lessons, or was she just sick of buying balls? I love tennis now and often wish that I'd started playing much earlier, back when my mother was in charge.

How could she not have noticed my incredible forehand? My love of tennis skirts? That boxful of blue ribbons I'd been awarded for my record-breaking leaps in *high jump* competitions statewide? And forget about the box; according to her, she was in the bleachers witnessing it all in real time. But was she? And if so, didn't she know that high jump was a dead-end sport? Why couldn't she just put two and two together and see that I was clearly born to scissor-kick over a net victory after victory? Two eyes and a thimbleful of imagination is all it would have taken to figure that out, and I know she's got 'em, because she used them often enough to draw conclusions about all the *bad* things I was doing, usually coming down eerily close to the head of the nail.

And sure, that was her job, but it was only *part* of her job. Another part of a mother's job is this thing called nurturing. That's what your supposed to do with the good stuff. So why didn't she nurture what I'm certain must have been at least the germ of a passion? And even if I was germ-free, even if I did really want to quit tennis lessons, so what? I was a minor, living under *her* roof. If, in fact, I said that I wanted to quit, why didn't she just tell me I couldn't? When I asked why, why didn't she just respond with her go-to answer for everything else: Because I'm your mother and I said so. Why didn't she just force me to play tennis, withholding allowance, food, clothing and whatever else was necessary to make me bend to her will, knowing that in the long run she'd be doing me a favor? I could have already won Wimbledon and retired by now. And I'd be too busy designing the Prince special edition Cindy Guidry tennis racquet to worry about anything other than what fabulous new Mother's Day gift I could come up with to top last year's gift *this year*.

Personally, I found the whole thing rather suspect. And the

more I thought about it, the more I began to think that my mother knew from the get-go that she didn't have a leg to stand on. So why had she brought eggs into the mix? She doesn't even like eggs. She told me just the other day that she found the thought of eating a chicken embryo repulsive. And the only other time I could ever remember my mother even talking about eggs was a few years back when she was lobbying for me to freeze some of my own.

So why was she making such a big fuss about them now, and in a totally different context? What was her motive? Did she suspect that I was on to her, that from halfway across America I'd somehow managed to stumble upon her old receipt for the one-way ticket 'to ADD that she'd bought me way back when? And if so, was she just trying to beat me to the punch? Was she adopting the offense-is-the-best-defense approach in the hope of short-circuiting my already overtaxed brain with yet another thing to think about so that I could never quite figure out how to pin the blame on her? It wouldn't surprise me. She's knows how I am.

As evidence, I offer up a trip to Home Depot circa 2000. I was in need of gardening shears; my mother came along for the ride to peruse the latest array of toxic pesticides. As we were checking out, the casher slipped my shears into a plastic bag. "Oh, don't worry about the bag," I said with a smile. "I'll just take them." He stared back blankly; I tossed in an explanatory, "Save the planet."

Well, the planet obviously meant nothing to him, because at that point, he took the shears out of the bag, handed them to me and proceeded to toss the unused plastic bag directly into a trash can. I stood frozen, an ice sculpture; completely paralyzed by his disregard for Mother Earth, until my own mother took me by the arm and said, "Keep it moving."

I kept it moving, but I was outraged. How could he do that? How could my own mother stand for that?

"Stand for what?" she asked, puzzled.

"*What?*" I replied. "That jerk just took a never-been-used plastic bag and . . . oh, wait, I forgot, you're the woman who feeds her dogs on paper plates so she doesn't have to wash anything."

Puzzle solved, she snapped back, quick as a whip. "Oh, no you don't," she said. "You're not going to make me feel bad about that. Paper is recyclable. And plus, I'm conserving water."

Damn her. I knew in my gut that serving dogs on paper plates was wrong, I just couldn't quite articulate *why* without adequate time to prepare.

"Well, what about the fact that he handed me the shears pointy end first?" I asked. "Are you cool with that, too?"

"No, I'm not *cool with that,* but what do you expect? The guy was an imbecile. He was picking his nose and staring into space as we were approaching the register. Do yourself a favor. Just forget it ever happened. Let's go get a hamburger."

"*A hamburger?* I can't eat a hamburger now! Then we'll just have more packaging to throw away. I can't stop thinking about that Indian crying on the side of the road, as is."

My mother looked around. "What Indian?"

"The one from the commercial in the '70s."

"*Indian!*" she cried out, trying hard to appear outraged. "We call them Native Americans now." Then she burst out laughing.

"Well they were Indians thirty years ago! And it's not funny, Mom. That plastic bag really upsets me."

"Well, don't blame me if some dolphin gets tangled up in it because *I love animals.* I give more money to animal charities than you ever will."

"Did I say anything about dolphins?"

"Oh, boo hoo hoo," she replied, after allowing me a three-second grieving period. "It's the sad story of the plastic bag." Then she smiled, adding, "Look on the bright side, now you've got something to waste the next six months of your life getting worked up about."

Clearly, the woman knows how I'm wired.

Could it be that she was only now learning how to use it to her benefit? And was stuff like that genetic? Was that why I was still flailing around, unable to access my own power? Would I, too, have to wait until the age of sixty? Was my mother purposely drawing attention to my unhatched eggs and instructing me to "figure it out," expressly because she didn't want me to figure it out, and knew that I would never do anything she told me to do? I couldn't tell what she had up her sleeve, but whatever it was, it wasn't working. What's more, it didn't matter. She was right. I had a problem. If only I could figure out how to fix it. . . .

Why was it that the minute I started teaching Pilates, I instantly became obsessed with opening a snoball stand? Why did I want to go back to school to become a lawyer one day and bake pies for a living the next? Why had I still not finished that stupid scarf? How could I have woken up this morning believing myself to be a well-rounded person with varied interests and now feel like an utter failure? And wasn't it ironic that I, who had never produced results or a final product of any kind, had just partnered with a friend to start our own film *production* company! Was I setting myself up for failure, or trying to force myself to *finally* produce something?

The *whys* eluded me, but I could suddenly see the faintest glimmer of light at the end of the tunnel. Knowing that Pauline, like me, didn't believe that guests should help with the dishes, I sprang from the dining room table, pulled everyone into a big group hug and dashed out the door just as fast as I could. Sure, they looked at me funny, but I couldn't be bothered to explain.

I drove home desperate to hatch an egg, even if the only thing inside it was a scarf. I figured it was a start, and just the momentum I needed. Finishing that scarf was the only thing that mattered to me anymore. I was so excited!

Then, a few blocks from my apartment, I saw something shiny on the side of the road.

buddhist

The sun was shining, I was driving down the open road, the wind was blowing through my hair and I was in a foul mood. Alice was sitting next to me, but we'd had an argument earlier in the day. I'd described something as Buddhist, she said it was technically Hindu, and frankly, I don't like being corrected by anyone who uses the word *irregardless*. On top of that we were at the tail end of a cross-country trip and as far as I could tell the only vegetables available in Middle America—where I thought some vegetables were actually grown—are either canned, frozen or fried. I wanted something fresh, I wanted something green, and iceburg lettuce wasn't it.

We'd been up half the night calling every restaurant listed in the Amarillo phone book, quizzing them on their vegetable offer-ings. Half of them hung up without responding, obviously believing our question to be so outlandish that it couldn't possibly be anything other than a prank. A number of people told us they had French fries, at which point we had to rephrase the question to include the word *green*. After being told by some jackhole that they might have shamrock shakes at McDonald's—in June, no less—Alice and I headed to a Chinese dump where we proceeded to eat MSG-saturated "vegetables" that looked more like anemic squid. I woke up with a pounding headache and elephantine feet and they were still with me seven hours later. But mostly I was in a foul mood because my big adventure out on the open road had produced very little adventure thus far.

Suddenly, Alice grabbed the dashboard. "What was that?" she asked, terrified.

"My tire just blew out," I replied.

"How fast are you going?"

I glanced at the speedometer. "Ninety-ish."

"Do you know what to do?"

"Of course I know what to do. I practically willed this to happen. Why do you think I've been driving with both hands on the wheel?"

I took my foot off the accelerator and coasted to the side of the road. Only a few shreds of rubber remained on my rim. *Beautiful.* I called AAA and flopped down on the side of the highway, where I proceeded to call everyone on my speed dial to excitedly share the good news.

A little while later a tow truck appeared, the words TOMBSTONE TOWING emblazoned on the side of it. I turned to Alice and said, "Welcome to Tombstone."

The driver emerged. He was about the size of Alice and me combined, covered in tattoos and wearing a T-shirt that bore a picture of a demented clown and the words: I LIKE YOU SO I'LL KILL YOU LAST. He looked like he'd just driven in from Sturgis. Alice's face went white, but I couldn't have been happier. "Five bucks says he kills you first," I snickered.

There was a gas station within sight, but our man Mac said we'd be better off traveling a few miles off the highway to some nameless establishment in the middle of nowhere—a place where both the locals shopped and his best friend worked. "Sounds good to me," I said with a smile as Alice made a squeal that reminded me of a sound I'd only ever heard once before, while walking down a dirt road in Greece. The sound had come from a pig, and it had coincided with the image of what looked like a handmade knife being plunged into his meaty pink neck and about seventy gallons of bright red blood gushing down the hillside.

While Mac hoisted my car onto the tow truck, Alice and I bickered just out of earshot. She didn't want to go a few miles *anywhere* with Mac and insisted that his T-shirt was proof positive that we'd never make it to our destination. By wearing the T-shirt, she reasoned that he was giving us fair warning—a warning she suggested we heed. I told her to take a hike.

"You can heed whatever you want but I'm going. This is the first interesting thing that's happened in two weeks and everybody knows that serial killers are stealthy, they have ways of doing things—they plan, they plot, they follow patterns, they only kill redheads or people who wear the same size rings. They're not random; they don't just kill anyone whose tire blows out. The T-shirt is obviously a joke. He's not spooky, you're paranoid."

I walked over to the tow truck and hopped in. Alice reluctantly followed. I smooshed in next to Mac and said, "Nice T-shirt." In response, he turned to me and said, "You like Whitesnake?" I'd never heard a Whitesnake song in my life, and it didn't really sound like my cup of tea, but this was an adventure and Mac was our host. So I nodded, "Sure." Mac popped in a tape, a song that seemed to be about oral sex started blasting out of the speakers, Alice planted her hand on the passenger door handle and we were off.

Moments later, Alice leaned into me and whispered, "Look. He's got a Curious George keychain just like you." She indicated her head toward a set of keys on the dashboard. They were *my keys*. My Los Angeles Public Library keychain card was clearly visible, as was the evil eye Alice herself had given me. "What do you know?" I whispered back, adding, "Listen, when we get home can you actually *show me* that Princeton diploma of yours."

After a little while, I screamed, "Seen any good movies lately?"

No one answered. Finally, Mac turned the stereo down and said, "You talking to me?"

"Uh-huh. I already know everything she's seen and done."

We talked about movies for a while, during which we learned that both *Seabiscuit* and *Forrest Gump* were on Mac's top ten list, a discovery that emboldened Alice to the point of inquiring, "So, did you cry?" *Did you cry?* I turned to Alice, impressed, then to Mac, expectant. "Like a baby," he replied.

Mac enjoyed animation, too. Like me, he preferred *Monsters, Inc.* to *Shrek,* but his all-time favorite was *Aladdin.* He was, however, terribly disappointed in *Aladdin* 2. I asked if he had any kids, but he didn't. What Mac did have was a Staffordshire terrier named Peanut, and a brother who lived in Phoenix. His brother had been trying to lure him there for some time, but Mac wasn't interested. "Why would I move to Phoenix when I have a broiler in my own kitchen?" Mac asked rhetorically. I agreed wholeheartedly, chiming in that his brother was obviously a lunatic.

As we drove along we passed a nudie bar. Oddly enough, in a town with a population of about thirty-seven, the parking lot was overflowing. I told Mac that I found it interesting that no matter where you went, no matter how small or religious the town, there was always room for a strip joint.

"It's fucked up is what it is," replied Mac.

"You know," I said, "where I live they sometimes have to offer free food just to lure guys in."

Mac thought about that for a few seconds then concluded, "That's fucked up, too."

Alice and I soon learned that Mac used to manage a strip joint in Washington. That is until he realized that everyone who worked at strips joints, management included, had mental problems. So he packed up and moved to Tombstone. I told Mac I was surprised to hear that because in the movies and stuff, the strippers are all actually very together and only doing it to make enough money for medical school. Mac assured me that was not the case. "I've known hundreds of strippers and only two ever made anything of themselves. One became a real estate agent and one was in Playboy."

While we were talking, Mac's cell phone rang. As soon as he answered, I seized the opportunity to turn to Alice and say I told you so.

"He's super nice," I whispered.

"You know the sequel to Aladdin wasn't a theatrical release," she whispered back.

"I know. It was direct-to-video. That's why I asked if he had kids," I whispered.

"I wish *Aladdin* 2 had been better," whispered Alice, "since Mac actually went to a video store and rented it."

"Maybe it wasn't total crap, maybe it just wasn't as good as the first one. Have you been listening to his conversation? I think Peanut has hip dysplasia," I whispered.

Alice hadn't heard. "Really?" she whispered back.

I nodded. "Yeah, they might have to put her to sleep," I whispered. "Or maybe it's a him. I'm not sure."

Sorrow swept over Alice's face. "Oh my God, I don't even know what a Staffordshire terrier looks like," she whispered back.

"They're pretty cute," I whispered. "I think they're black and white. Or maybe that's a Boston terrier."

"We passed a Chili's a few minutes ago," whispered Alice. "Maybe we should go there for lunch. I think they have salad."

"I think their salad is mostly bacon bits and croutons. I'll probably just get French fries. At least I don't expect them to be anything other than fried potatoes," I whispered back.

We arrived at the tire store before Mac was off the phone. By the time he hung up, his eyes were filled with tears. He walked us into the store and hooked us up, then he said he had to go. I couldn't be sure if he really had somewhere else to be or if he just didn't want to cry in front of us, and I didn't know exactly what to say to someone who was hurting but I didn't really know.

Alice, of course, was completely undeterred. She gave Mac a big hug and said with feeling, "I hope Peanut's OK. My mom passed away a while back so I know what you're going through." Mac stared back speechless, as did I. Then we headed outside where we took pictures and kissed our new biker friend good-bye.

Tire fixed, Alice and I made our way to Chili's. I had French fries; she had the "salad." It was mostly orange and brown. "I guess you can't judge a book by its cover," said Alice, as she flicked a crouton across the table. "Mac was awesome."

I fingered the crouton. I examined my previously frozen French fries. "If the cover says Chili's you can," I replied. Then I squirted some ketchup on my plate, picked up a fry and pointed it at Alice, adding, "But with people you definitely can't."

I wanted Alice to ask me how I knew for sure, but she was too busy picking through bacon and cheese. So I said it again. "With people you *definitely* can't." She looked at me like I was a freak and stabbed some iceberg lettuce. That's it. Nothing more.

And it drove me crazy because every single morning of our trip she'd ruined my breakfast by plopping down and saying, "I had the weirdest dream last night . . ." And did I care? No. And did I want to hear about it? No. But I did. And here I was trying to share one stupid dream with her and she doesn't even have the decency to offer me a lead-in.

So I said, "*Irregardless,* with people you definitely can't." And you better believe that got her attention.

"What's your problem?" snarled Alice, throwing her fork down.

"With people you . . . oh, fuck it. I had the weirdest dream . . ."

"Last night?"

"No, not last night. A while back."

"Whatever," she replied.

"No, not whatever," I screeched. "I've heard about hundreds, maybe thousands of your dreams over the years and now I'm going to tell you mine *regardless* of when I had it. And check this out: Mine actually has a point, a moral even."

"What? Don't judge a book by its cover?"

"That's right," I replied. "So I had this dream, it was a sex dream and . . ."

"You need to get laid."

"And it was *totally hot,* maybe even better than any real sex I've had, and *definitely* better than any real sex you've had."

"You're not Buddhist, you're Satanic," replied Alice.

"Oh really, I thought I was Hindu. So anyway, then I woke up and realized . . . *Holy shit, that was Kevin Spacey!*"

"*Kevin Spacey? That's* who you dream about?"

"That's my point. Here I was having the best sex of my life with someone who, cover-wise, totally doesn't do it for me. And yet, he did it for me. I mean, he *really* did it for me."

"He's gay," said Alice, as if he told her himself, which I *know* he didn't. And that bugged me too, except that it only strengthened my point, so I let it slide.

"Great, even better," I replied. "All the more reason why we'd never have sex in real life."

"Well, you can thank the Chinese. MSG obviously knows no bounds."

"The Chinese had nothing to do with it! I told you I didn't have the dream last night!"

"Oh, right. I forgot," said Alice, but in this totally dismissive way that sent me over the edge.

"How the hell would you know where Kevin Spacey lands on the Kinsey scale anyway?" I snapped. "Did you ask him? Have you ever even met him? Because in print he's repeatedly said that he's *not* gay."

"Whatever."

"And what do you care? I'm the one who slept with him."

"Yeah, *in a dream*."

"That's right. And I'm telling you, Kevin Spacey knows his way around a woman's body."

"So, what?" asked Alice. "You're going to start sleeping with guys you're not attracted to and see what you uncover?"

"No, that's your little game. But it did made me think that I was probably really shortchanging myself by being so cover-specific."

"*Cover-specific?* And all this time I thought you were superficial."

"No, you didn't. If all I needed was a great cover, I wouldn't be sitting here with you right now because I'd be at home having real sex with my very handsome husband."

Alice let out with a condescending sigh. "Normal people grow to love the cover of the books they love."

"Actually, they say women do that, but that men grow to love the book with the cover they're attracted to."

"Really?"

"Yeah, that's why sometimes when the cover gets a little worn, they toss it aside and go look for a new cover to love. All I'm saying is that maybe I could be happy with an average cover but I'll never know because it would have to come to me in my sleep and make me see fireworks before I'd give it a chance."

"Like in a dream, or through your window?"

"No, my little Princetonian," I replied. "That's a *rapist*."

"OK. So what's the moral?"

"Don't judge a book by its cover!"

"But you just said you're still going to!"

"I'm not *still* going to do anything because I never did it in the first place. *Judging* and *choosing* are two different things. I don't judge."

"Of course not," she snickered. "You're Buddhist."

"Right. I was just trying to illustrate how totally wrong you were to judge Mac."

"And *that's* not a judgment?"

"No, that's an observation."

what's your hook?

I guess it was bound to happen. In an industry where everyone's looking for some new way to suck in an audience, and in a town where people are working every angle they can to get into a preschool that's going to cost them $30K in tuition, $10K in donations and God knows what in birthday parties, I should have seen it coming.

Say what you will about weddings and bridal showers, the single woman's worst enemy is the baby shower. Go to a baby shower and you open yourself up to a double-barreled attack. I, of course, happened to be *cohosting* a baby shower the morning after I solved the riddle of My Last Boyfriend.

I was nearing forty when he entered my life. I hadn't been in a decent relationship in years, and I was beginning to wonder if the problem wasn't just me. But he arrived on the scene with all the gallantry of a knight, and I was duly taken. Maybe it would work, maybe not, all I knew was that I wasn't going to let my own issues get in the way.

The first couple of months were extremely promising. He was smart, fun, thoughtful, caring, sexy, and up for anything. My Last Boyfriend was a great guy, until he wasn't—until he became distant, then stopped calling, or taking my calls, much less taking me out.

Now, I know there are people who would say, "He's just wasn't that into you. Get a clue." I know because I had a girlfriend who said just that. In fact, our friendship pretty much ended over what she considered my "pathetic need for resolution."

I, on the other hand, saw nothing pathetic about it. In fact, I saw no reason why I *shouldn't* hold a grown man—who had readily entered into a relationship with me—accountable for his unexplained actions. Maybe that wasn't the "cool" thing to do, but *just going away,* as I imagine he hoped I would do, would have only made things easier on him. And just for the record, I don't need resolution in every instance. I've been blown off by guys in the past and let them go on their merry way, without a peep from me. But this was different. It wasn't simply that he wasn't that into me; he was that into me until *something* happened that had absolutely nothing to do with me. I was 100 percent sure of it. And it really upset me that he was now pulling a 180-degree turn and expecting me to just take the hint when I knew full well that there was a major piece to this puzzle that he had and wasn't showing me.

So I went to his house—an action that was, in my girlfriend's words, "the kind of pathetic move only a *girl* (said with scorn) would pull." But guess what? I *am* a girl, and I have absolutely no interest in pretending otherwise. The telephone wasn't getting me anywhere. And having spent many a weekend at his place I sure knew where he lived. So I drove over. I thought it was a pretty ballsy move myself, although, trust me, I didn't feel very ballsy at the time. I was shaking like a leaf as I approached his front door, and it took every ounce of courage I had to actually knock on that door, not knowing what might await me on the other side. But what got me through it was the knowledge that not demanding that he treat me with the decency and respect I deserved, would have made me feel pathetic. I know, because I've been there. I also knew that for every hurt I buried, I was only hardening my own heart that much more. And there's nothing cool about that.

Luckily for me, he was alone—surprised, but alone. So I went in—not swinging and screaming like a banshee, but perfectly calm and composed. I asked him about the missing piece to the puzzle. And after an hour or so of pussyfooting around, he finally forked it over. It turned out that he'd impregnated another woman while we were together.

Just kidding.

He'd actually impregnated another woman a few months *before* we'd met, before he'd asked me out, before he'd started seeing me three times a week, before he'd slept with me, and before he'd introduced me to his family.

Wow.

I left his house shortly after the big reveal, having never raised my voice. I was shaking a whole lot more than I had when I first approached the front door, but I didn't feel pathetic. I felt proud— proud of the fact that I had valued my feelings over my ego, and proud of the fact that I had stood up for myself. I walked away feeling more like a woman than a girl. And I saved myself weeks of self-torture and wondering why in the process.

Apparently, he knew about the baby all along; he just didn't think I needed to know, because . . . *what?* Because sometimes babies just stay in the womb forever and ever and never have to be acknowledged? Because it's easier to pretend that you're not a father until the date of birth? Because he was planning to discard me before then anyway?

I can't go down that path because it makes me so fucking angry for so many reasons, some of which have nothing at all to do with me. And I know he wasn't actively trying to hurt me, I know my pain and confusion were simply a by-product of the bigger mess he'd made for himself, but I can't go down that path either. Because then I start rationalizing his behavior and I can't tell if I'm being empathetic and compassionate, or if I'm just being a doormat. So I try to simplify things, and I try to remember that I, just like every other human being, am not only bound to The Golden Rule, but also deserving of benefiting from it. And all he had to do was be honest. All he had to do was tell me what I was getting myself into. But he didn't. Instead, he withheld that information, taking away my ability to make an informed decision as to whether or not I wanted to get my emotions tangled up in his mess. Even I can't rationalize that.

So that was My Last Boyfriend, and the next morning I cohosted a baby shower. The timing wasn't great, but the baby was due the following week and it wasn't going to just hang tight until I was emotionally prepared. I figured I'd see some old girlfriends and forget about men for a while. Or not. Character isn't gender-specific. And in a way, I think that by confronting My Last Boyfriend, and bringing the specifics of that relationship into focus, I'd saved myself from writing it all off to the already overused and far more general MEN SUCK. All men don't suck. I knew that. I know that. My next boyfriend would be better.

At least the shower wasn't at my place. Heavens no, these women wouldn't know what to do in a one-bedroom apartment. They'd probably think it was a dollhouse. Half of them have guesthouses bigger than my place. Instead, the shower was being held in Rose's backyard, which made the pool area at the Four Seasons look like some broken down public park in Compton.

I was slicing onion tarts when Marjorie entered the kitchen. "Are you seeing anyone?" she asked.

Mercifully, Marjorie, like most of the women in attendance, knew very little about my present life, and nothing about My Last Boyfriend.

"No," I replied, "but you know what they say: *Every pot has a lid.*"

Marjorie laughed. "Honey, you're not going to find your lid in Los Angeles. This place is the pits."

Not the encouragement I was looking for, but I carried on. "You found your lid here," I replied.

"Luck," she said. "And I found him a long time ago."

I handed Marjorie the onion tarts with a smile and sent her outside.

People love to blame Los Angeles for everything. God knows I do. It's such an easy scapegoat; maybe that's part of its appeal. But sometimes I think that in staying here all this time, I've painted myself into a corner. I mean, I would suspect that there are more single forty-year-old men in Los Angeles than say, *Omaha*. Isn't the rest of America still clinging to some semblance of normalcy? Now that I'm forty, as weird as it is, Los Angeles may be my best option.

Marjorie returned as I was preparing the poached salmon with dill sauce. She leaned on the kitchen island, and continued talking without missing a beat. "You may find *someone*," she said, "but you've got to worry about any guy who's forty and single."

Like I need a woman who's been married fifteen years to tell me that? I'm not an authority on anything, but I think I've got a bit more expertise in this area than she does.

I just smiled. "I'm forty and single."

"Yeah, but you're not a man. It's different."

And I think it's different, I think *I'm* different, but doesn't *everybody*, and how do you really know? Before I could ask Marjorie how *she* thought it was different, Linda rushed in. She looked really distraught.

"What's wrong?" I asked.

"Marjorie told me you're not seeing anyone," she replied.

I turned to Marjorie, flabbergasted. She put her hand up like a crossing guard. "I'm just trying to help."

"*I don't need help!*" I shot back, momentarily forgetting my place as hostess.

Linda was sympathetic. "You know," she said, taking my hand, "there are a lot of divorced men out there who would be *lucky* to have you."

It was all I could do not to douse her in dill sauce. Did she really think I was sitting around crying in my soup every night, thinking that a man was some unattainable goal? I don't care if some guy gets lucky, I want a man that *I'm going to feel lucky to have*. And in the meantime, I've still got a life. It may be a bit unconventional, but it's mine and I like it.

But this was supposed to be a friendly get-together, and I *was* cohosting the event, so I just smiled at Linda and said, "*Really? How many?*"

Linda then got all fired up, proclaiming that the divorce rate in California was 67 percent, as if that were the greatest news ever! Marjorie debated the statistic.

"But how can they know for sure?" I asked. "I mean, if they're counting celebrities who get divorced all the time, and not counting illegal aliens who never get divorced?"

"It doesn't matter what the number is," replied Linda. "Trust me, *there's plenty*."

"That's wonderful, Linda. Now if you'll excuse me . . ."

With that, I walked to the bathroom, which was about the size of my entire apartment, locked the door and proceeded to stuff a bar of soap into my mouth, biting down as hard as I could. What did it even matter how many divorced men there are in Los Angeles? Most divorced men my age are looking to hook up with twenty-year-old girls. And really, who can blame them? They've already had one failed marriage, they're probably looking for something a little less complicated, and pretty young things arrive here by the truckload every day. I don't think I'm all that complicated, and I look pretty good for my age, but I'm certainly not going to put up with the shit I would have when I was twenty, and I'm *certainly* not going to put up with anyone's ex-wife's shit.

I returned to the kitchen to find that Marjorie and Linda had not moved. I pushed them out of the way and starting throwing together a cheese plate.

Marjorie picked up a strawberry, pointed it at me, and said, "Well, *whatever you do*, don't go out with a forty-year-old man who's never been married. They're the worst." Then she plopped the strawberry into her mouth.

Linda nodded. "It's true, either they've got some childhood bullshit they can't get past, or they're just not interested in being married."

I wanted to tell Linda that she was forgetting a small but significant group, the group that *might* be interested in marrying me had they not sealed their fates via unprotected sex with another woman, who, quite possibly, was looking to get knocked up because really, birth control isn't all that hard to master. I met a woman at a party just the other night. She was a thirty-five-year-old single mother with a newborn baby. I asked about the father and was told that he was an asshole—he was an asshole because he didn't want to marry this woman, who he'd been seeing for two months, when she accidentally got pregnant. So I guess in that way, we're still in the 1950s, except now men are less likely to fall into the baby trap and women are lugging newborns around to parties in search of stepfathers. But I wasn't about to get into that at the shower because every time I suggest that *women*, who comprise more than 50 percent of America's population, might be partly responsible for the current state of affairs, I get attacked.

And even though my real concern is the children, I somehow end up defending men, too.

Since I was in no mood to defend men, I simply banished Linda and Marjorie from the kitchen.

Michelle came in a few minutes later with her son on her hip. I was arranging cupcakes on a tray. "Isn't he the cutest baby *ever?*" she cried. I looked over. Michelle had that Stepford smile plastered across her face. She was gearing up for something, that much was obvious. And whatever it was, I wasn't up for it. I started spiking sprinkles into the cupcakes.

"What happened to that guy you were seeing?" asked Michelle.

That was the problem. Michelle knew about My Last Boyfriend.

"Nothing *happened* to him," I replied. "He's still alive. I'm just not seeing him anymore."

"He seemed perfectly fine to me," she said haughtily.

"I'd be happy to give you his number."

"Nothing ever works out for you," she continued. "Didn't you ever wonder why?"

"Don't start, Michelle. Today's not the day."

"I'm just being honest. I thought you liked that."

Instead of stabbing her with an icing spreader, like I wanted to, I said, "Michelle, how long have you and Steve been together?"

"Three years," she replied.

"That's right." I said. "So how about this? How about you come and talk to me after you've been together seven years? I've been in relationships a lot longer than you have and just because they didn't end with a ring and a baby doesn't mean that *nothing ever works out for me*. Maybe I don't want the same things as you. Did you ever think of that?"

And then, suddenly, I was the bad guy. Michelle got all teary-eyed, claiming that she just wanted me to be happy, and insisting that I can't *really* be happy unless I have a man *and a child*. Then she ended her rant by telling me that it really hurts *her* to see me so single.

"Look," I said. "I didn't hold out for forty years just so I could drop the bar low enough for the first *perfectly fine* man who walks by to trip over it and fall into my arms."

"I know," she said, "But you're so picky. We all have to make compromises. Nothing's perfect. You think *my life* is perfect?"

"No," I replied, "I don't think your life is anywhere near perfect, which is just one of the reasons why I don't want you telling me how to live mine. And if I'm picky and I'm OK with it, then I suggest you get OK with it too, because I'm never going to be anything other than picky and I have no desire to end up with anyone who isn't."

"Fine," she said. "I'll shut up."

Then, instead of shutting up, she proceeded to complain about her life, thus illustrating what it's like to be *really* happy.

When all the food was out, I walked into the backyard and took a deep breath. Rose's garden was truly magnificent. And as I was gazing upon what must have been a good $250K in lush foliage, I started thinking that maybe I'd done everything wrong all along. Forget about My Last Boyfriend—there was no way I could have predicted that. But maybe I *was* too picky. Maybe I should just forget about chemistry and serendipity and true love. Maybe I needed to get over that. Maybe I needed to get out more. Maybe it was time to be practical.

I glanced over at Rose. She had never worked a day in her life, and here she was living in a five-star hotel. She seemed happy.

Maybe I could be happy with expensive stuff, too. Maybe I should just find some rich man, *any rich man* and . . .

The next thing I knew, Marjorie was in my face with some woman named Maryanne, who I'd never seen before in my life. "I told Maryanne all about your predicament," said Marjorie. "If *anyone* can help you, *she can.*"

Before I could respond, Maryanne gave me a quick once-over and said, "What's your hook?"

What's your hook? Did she just say that?

"There's only a few good men out there," she added. "And the competition's tough. *What's your hook?* I can't sell you if you don't have a hook."

I must have looked like the world's biggest dope, as I stared back at Maryanne, slack-jawed, dumbfounded. It was bound to happen at some point. It made perfect sense. I just couldn't believe it was happening *now* and *to me*. A gnat flew into my gaping maw. And as I spun around and started spitting into the flower bed, I heard Maryanne say to Marjorie, "She's not giving me anything to work with. I need someone who's going to help make the sale. I'm good, but I can't do it alone. I'm going to get a mimosa. You want anything?"

She sounded like an agent. I sounded like a bad, meandering script—hookless, pointless, destined to be tossed out after the first ten pages. I yanked Marjorie behind a Jacaranda tree. "*How dare you!*" I whispered, barely holding it together. "You have no idea . . ."

And then I stopped, composed myself, walked into the house, past the guest of honor, and out to my car. I slammed the door, punched the steering wheel, and cried like a baby as I drove back to my humble one-bedroom sanctuary.

But as I sit here and write about this a year later, I find myself wondering all over again. Where does kindness end and stupidity begin? Should I have ditched My Last Boyfriend as soon as I saw that he was troubled? Maybe, but that's not who I am. Was there something I could have done to make him feel more comfortable, to make it easier for him to open up without me having to hunt him down? Why did it have to come to that?

And then I start to wonder if I'm crazy. I start to wonder if his version of our relationship wasn't the accurate version; if our relationship was never anything that warranted that level of disclosure; and if I'm not the one guilty of rewriting history. Then I go back through all his old e-mails that I've saved—just like I've saved every other personal e-mail or letter that's ever meant anything to me—and I am relieved to find that, while I may not be perfect, I'm not crazy either.

the cat whisperer

The production company was up and running. I was getting scripts in, meeting with writers, working hard and having a grand old time. I was my own boss and that I could live with. But what I couldn't live with was Frankie trying to bolt out of the front door every time I left for work. He's extremely charismatic, he was kidnapped once, he's not allowed to roam the streets anymore, and I didn't even want him outside when I was home to supervise him because he hadn't had any shots in a couple of years. I needed to take him to the vet, but we sure couldn't go back to his old vet. They'd have had me thrown straight into the pokey.

Sure, Frankie looks all regal and Siamese-y, and he is when he wants to be, but he's a Dumpster cat underneath. And his old vet didn't want anything to do with him. Frankie burned that bridge on our last visit when he raked his claws across her face. Although, in his defense, she had just rammed an ice-cold thermometer up his bum.

Regardless, she pinned the blame squarely on Frankie, claiming that he had "behavioral issues" and threatening *me* with legal action, at which point I rammed Frankie into his cat carrier and we hightailed it out of there, never to return. The whole thing was preposterous. Of course he's got behavioral issues. *He's a cat!* He's got a mind of his own. That's everything that's wrong with him and everything that's right with him all rolled into one. We were both happy to be done with her. But Frankie did need shots, and a checkup probably wasn't a bad idea either, since, friskiness not-withstanding, he was about seventy-seven years old in people years.

Conveniently enough, it wasn't long before I met with a writer who told me about a vet in my neighborhood who was reputed to have some kind of cat magic. So out came the cat carrier and off we went.

Unlike that old vet's office, which looked like some mad scientist's laboratory, The Cat Whisperer's pad had a vibe similar to that of a yoga studio—water trickled from fountains, mystical music wafted through the air. Frankie dug it. He also dug the man himself, who was sort of like the Nutty Professor, but with an accent.

On our initial visit, I watched, awestruck, as The Cat Whisperer gave Frankie a thorough cavity check, leaving no orifice unpene-trated. Frankie offered little more than a contented purr in return. And when The Cat Whisperer proceeded to scrape plaque off his fangs with something that looked like the pop-top of a beer can, Frankie only gazed at him dreamily. It seemed there was nothing The Cat Whisperer could do that wasn't pleasing to Frankie. And I'm not too proud to say it stung.

I was the one who'd been scooping poop for fifteen years, not this character! And not once had I gotten the look of love from that little monster, who suddenly leaned over and bit *me*. What was that all about? Was he trying to impress his new friend? Was that my signal to split so they could be alone? Whatever his motive, it wasn't very nice, and he was messing with the wrong person. I knew all his secrets. So I turned to The Cat Whisperer and said, "You wanna hear something funny? Frankie's afraid of *aluminum foil.*" After a brief chuckle, I added, "Isn't that a hoot?"

Frankie looked at me, his slanty little eyes afire. *How dare you, woman*.

The Cat Whisperer was completely unmoved. "I'm sure he's got his reasons."

"I don't know what they could possibly be," I replied. "But I'll tell you something else, he bakes his brains in front of the heater for hours on end. I think he communicates with his mother ship through heat waves."

Frankie's eyes widened. *How did you know, woman?*

"I'm pretty sure they're cooking up some evil world domination plans."

"It's possible," replied The Cat Whisperer, while stroking Frankie. "They're a lot like people."

Yeah, extremely lazy people who only get off their ass to either eat or destroy.

"You just be careful with those instruments," I warned. "He'll scratch your eyes out. And I don't need that kind of trouble."

The Cat Whisperer showed no fear. "He wouldn't be able to if you trimmed his nails."

With that, Frankie *freaked*.

Why the big freak-out, I have no idea. I wouldn't go near his claws without a welder's mask and armored gloves, neither of which I own. Still, his lover had betrayed him; Frankie was off his high horse. But not for long. Because right after that The Cat Whisperer started massaging Frankie's temples with lavender oil and interrogating *me* about his diet. I assured The Cat Whisperer that Frankie ate only the finest, most expensive, organic cat food— pointing out his opalescent fur as proof—but apparently that wasn't good enough. He wanted me to cook for Frankie.

"You're kidding, right?"

"It doesn't have to be every day, but maybe twice a week," he replied. "Anyone can manage that. Perhaps a little chicken or fish."

Frankie looked at me. *Get with the program, woman.*

"How about steak and a movie every Friday night? Would that work?"

Frankie quickly rubbed against The Cat Whisperer. He thought he was being smooth, but it was such an obvious attempt to influence the man's response that I had to laugh.

"A movie could be nice," replied The Cat Whisperer. "But steak's probably too rich."

Ah, well, you can't win 'em all. *Get thee to Blockbuster, woman.*

Back at home, Frankie watched *The Incredible Journey* and ate salmon mousse off a TV tray, while I read a script. It was a good script, too. It was just never going to make it to the screen because the story was set in Egypt about a zillion years ago, and nobody's going to finance a movie about ancient Egypt unless Angelina Jolie and Brad Pitt decide they want to remake *Cleopatra*. But as I leafed through the script, I was reminded that the Egyptians *worshiped* cats. Nothing was too good for the little beasts. They even shaved their eyebrows off when a cat died! I started to get the picture.

With a quick call to The Cat Whisperer's office, I confirmed my hunch. He was indeed Egyptian. How could I have missed something so obvious? All the signs were there: His ability to reduce Frankie to jelly—obviously a magical power bestowed on him by the mystical order of dead cats in repayment for the goodwill of his ancestors, his complete lack of fear at my suggestion that we may be headed toward a new world order—knowing that he'd be taken care of by his feline friends, his total regard for Frankie's well-being, his complete disregard for mine, *his weird name.*

The Cat Whisperer called a few days later with Frankie's test results. Supposedly, his kidneys were not up to snuff. The Cat Whisperer needed to see him again *immediately*. "Is this a trick?" I asked. He insisted it was a medical necessity if I wanted to ensure Frankie's happiness. "Define happiness," I replied. "Because if it costs $500 and involves spending more time than I already spend *catering to a cat,* I probably don't want any part of it." The Cat Whisperer answered me, but I wasn't entirely clear on what he was saying, what with that crazy Egyptian accent and all. In the end, it was more the desperation in his voice that compelled me to return.

On the second visit, Frankie was examined again—why, I don't know—then The Cat Whisperer pulled out some contraption that looked like a miniature plastic jackhammer and proceeded to adjust Frankie's spine. I told him that I could probably use an adjustment myself, but he pretended not to hear me. Instead, I was issued a magic serum that had been concocted out of Frankie's own blood, as well as a bag of fluids—it just looked like water to me—and twenty needles. My role in the love triangle was to inject Frankie with the "fluids" twice a week.

After that, we returned to The Cat Whisperer on a monthly basis. I had a cat, he had a boyfriend, and apparently, it was my duty to finance a $200 date every thirty days. So that's how it went.

Until our most recent visit to The Cat Whisperer.

It all began innocently enough. Frankie got a full-body massage with some doohickey I'd recently seen at Brookstone, stretching out his body to about five feet in length so that not a muscle would be missed. Then, just as I expected The Cat Whisperer to whip out two cucumber slices and place them over Frankie's eyes, he pulled a fast one on me, instead, whipping out a tray of needles and issuing a quick, "I think Frankie would benefit from acupuncture."

My nodding head jerked upright. *Acupuncture?* But before I could resist, Frankie had fifteen needles jutting out of his body, and The Cat Whisperer was setting a kitchen timer for ten minutes. I looked at my little pincushion. One needle was poking directly out of his head, providing an exclamation point atop his now-frowning face.

"Don't frown, Frankie. Or you'll have to get Botox, too," I whispered sweetly.

You've pushed me too far, woman.

Again? Well, two can play that game, I thought, as I stared deep into his powder-blue eyes and thought even harder.

In case you haven't noticed, cat, I'm not the one with the needles.

You could have stopped him.

Hardly! And it'll probably cost me an extra seventy-five bucks.

Your bills mean nothing to me, woman. I sit on them.

Good, because it's coming out of your lunch money, cat.

You were supposed to protect me.

You begged me to come here!

Not anymore, woman.

Your wish is my command.

"Why are you looking at him like that?" interjected The Cat Whisperer.

I jumped.

"I'm not looking at him like anything," I replied.

The Cat Whisperer eyed me suspiciously.

"I swear. I was just looking because . . .because he's so cute."

Liar.

God have mercy, they were tag-teaming me.

We'll see how cute you look atop your catafalque, woman.

I turned my eyes back on Frankie.

Catawhat???

"Stop doing that!" ordered The Cat Whisperer.

I immediately snapped to attention; Frankie lifted his left paw and batted at his exclamation point.

You're dead meat, bitch. And I'm pissing all over your comforter tonight, too.

"Oh, for crying out loud," I said, "can you just take the damn needles out?"

Then I looked back at Frankie. *Potty mouth.*

The Cat Whisperer was aghast. "You're making a big mistake."

"That's OK," I replied. "I think it's a bigger mistake to leave them in."

As The Cat Whisperer slowly plucked the needles out of Frankie's flesh, I took a seat. Here I was, a forty-year-old woman *with a cat.* It wasn't good. I had no idea these things lived so long. And it would be one thing if Frankie were actually nice to me, but . . .

"Have you been feeding Frankie canned tuna?" quizzed The Cat Whisperer.

Shit. I was back on the stand. I knew I was supposed to be serving him seared Ahi, but confessed that I had, on occasion, given him canned tuna.

"Cat tuna or people tuna?" he asked, accusingly.

Of course, my little Egyptian god was right back on The Cat Whisperer's side, and glaring at me as if I'd committed the cardinal sin of actually serving him something unworthy of his Dumpster palette.

"Well," I replied, "it's not the Italian stuff packed in olive oil that I eat, and I don't bake it into a fish-shaped casserole for His Highness, but it's good enough. Chicken of the Sea, I think."

"It's too high in protein!" exclaimed The Cat Whisperer. "I don't want you to give him people tuna *ever, ever again.*"

Needless to say, at that point, I fully expected Frankie to spring from the metal table and latch himself onto The Cat Whisperer's head. But instead, he just hopped down and stepped into his royal cat carrier. *Take me home, Jeeves.* Not the behavior I expected, but like I said, he's a cat. So I just wrote another $200 check and chauffeured Frankie back home, where I proceeded to look up *catafalque* in the dictionary.

rob marciano is hot!

Frankie and I were in repose when Alice called to notify me that there was a hurricane headed for New Orleans. I, of course, knew nothing about it since I don't have cable television or a radio antenna. Why bother? All the news is bad, and there aren't enough hours in the day for the countless hobbies I'd like to pursue. I'll probably be floating around in outer space a week after the world ends, wondering what happened. But that's OK. I've made peace with it.

"Oh, don't worry about it," I said blithely. "Nothing ever happens. Everyone wastes their time boarding up windows and then at the last minute the thing does a jig and hits Florida. It's a much bigger target. Did I ever tell you about the time I took my dad's pirogue and rowed down the street to Karen's house after a hurric . . ."

"I think you should check it out," interrupted Alice. "Come over."

"If you insist," I replied. "But nothing ever happens."

I stroked my feline companion for a few minutes then headed over to Alice's, where I sat on the couch and quickly learned that a Category 5 (!) hurricane was heading for New Orleans. I immediately dialed my father's cell phone—my mother didn't have one—to get the scoop. Sure, they're still in marital limbo, but they're together every time I call.

I'm sorry. All circuits are busy now. Please try your call later.

Later? Were they kidding? There's no later for me. There's only now and never. I dialed and dialed and dialed. I dialed on my cell phone, on Alice's home phone, and I had Alice dialing on her cell, too. *Finally,* we got through.

"Hey, Tidbit," answered my dad. "I'm going to hand you off to the Queen."

"Hi," chimed my mother, as if she were strolling through the park. "How's Los Angeles?"

How's Los Angeles? "Los Angeles is fine. What the hell's going on over there?"

"Oh, it's a mess. We're trying to evacuate, but it's not easy. We've been sitting in traffic for hours."

Evacuate? I'd lived in New Orleans for nearly twenty-five years and never once had we, or anyone else I knew, evacuated. It just wasn't done. Every once in a while you'd hear someone reminisce about Camille or Betsy, but for the most part, hurricanes were like the boy who cried wolf. And people had stopped listening to his cry long ago.

Knowing that my parents must be in my father's two-seat truck, I asked, "Where are those animals of yours?"

"Oh, they're right here," replied my mother.

And then it was the usual routine. She shoved the phone in Remi's ear, I tried to come up with something interesting to say, Remi began barking like there was no tomorrow, my mother responded by screaming at him (but in *my* ear), and eventually she returned to the phone, threatening to give him to the SPCA because "that dog just doesn't know how to act right." Of course, Foxy probably wouldn't "act right" if he had a cell phone embedded in his ear either, but she likes him better so my theory has never been tested.

My parents were heading to Jackson, Mississippi. I told them to call me when they arrived.

They never called, and by the time I got through to them the hurricane had already hit New Orleans and worked its way to Jackson. My parents were in the only motel they could find that allowed dogs. My mother said it was filthy.

I should probably take this moment to mention that my mother is the cleanest woman in America. I can honestly say that the only place in New Orleans that I never once saw a single cockroach was in my own home. Maybe it was the boric acid–filled moat that surrounded the place, I don't know. But those foot-long flying cockroaches could have easily soared over it, so I can only assume that word must have gotten out that my mother was not to be messed with. Cockroaches simply weren't allowed in her house.

And in truth, they'd have only been disappointed if they had made it in. There wasn't a crumb to be found. The place was spotless and every food item was hermetically sealed. We didn't even have a garbage can. Garbage went outside the instant it sprang into existence. And if opening the door was forbidden because there were too many mosquitoes outside or The Fog Man was cruising the streets atomizing every living thing with his noxious bug juice, the garbage went immediately into a plastic bag, which was then tucked into a deep freezer, and removed promptly at sunrise the following morning, when it was once again safe to open the door.

The procedure was a bit labor-intensive for my taste, but it wasn't nearly as gruesome a task as wiping a dog's ass with Huggies. This is a more recent phenomenon, but again, as far as I know, exclusive to my mother. She complains that her dogs are too much work, but I mean, come on, how could they not be too much work? Every ten-minute walk is followed up with a twenty-minute rectal cleansing, and she walks them at least fifteen times a day to prevent any "accidents." If that isn't a full-time job, I don't know what is.

But here were my parents, all holed up in a motel that, according to my mother, smelled like a kennel. To make matters worse, they hadn't had electricity in two days. She couldn't wait to get home and take her dogs to be groomed.

"I don't think you're going home anytime soon, Mom."

"And why not?" she asked.

"Haven't you been watching the news?"

"Of course I haven't been watching the news. I told you there's no electricity. What do you expect me to watch it on, the palm of my hand?"

"The levee broke."

"Oh, I heard somebody say something about that, but I didn't know if it was true. Anyway, the Industrial Canal is nowhere near my place."

"No," I said, "but the 17th Street Canal is."

"I'm sure it's fine," she replied. "My place never floods. I'll talk to you later. I gotta go walk these dogs."

Things went from bad to worse. I hadn't moved from Alice's couch in days, and it would be another week before I did. I watched more television than I had in the last twenty-five years combined. Tomas called at one point to remind me that I had a cat, and from what he could tell through the window, Frankie appeared to be eating the stuffing out of a pillow. Alice brought Tomas my house keys, and he took over from there, while I continued to soak up the horrors in Alice's living room.

———

New Orleans was never a perfect place. No place is. But it was a special place. I'd been away for a long time, but whenever I told anyone where I was from, they would always respond with delight and interest. They either loved New Orleans or dreamed of going there. I have always taken great pride in the fact that I'm from New Orleans. I have always thought that being from New Orleans somehow made me special, too.

The music, the food, the architecture, the history—they all combined to make New Orleans a wonderful world all its own. But the best thing about New Orleans was the people. Despite the sweltering heat, the racial issues, the shitty economy and every other injustice, the people, for the most part, were able to smile at each other, laugh at themselves, live side by side, and keep on keeping on. *Laissez les bons temps rouler,* as they say. Let the good times roll. The people of New Orleans had a certain joie de vivre that simply could not be crushed.

So to see these people who have for so long made the best of their situation, now be reduced to this, crushed *me*. My world was darkening like never before. I didn't have the strength to walk to the stereo, and I wasn't entirely sure Dave Matthews could get me through this one anyway. But as I was climbing the walls of my imagination in search of a fantasy within which to retreat, Rob Marciano came to my rescue.

I was first alerted to his existence before the hurricane ever made landfall. I'd been up for about thirty-six hours at that point, and was beginning to nod out, when Marcus, Alice's full-time neighbor and part-time garden gnome, suddenly materialized before me, holding a bottle of red and three wine glasses in one hand, some smoked salmon and assorted cheeses and crackers in the other. He was wearing absolutely nothing but a hip-length kimono. "Quick!" screamed Marcus. "Switch to CNN. I think I've just found the man you've been looking for." Alice quickly did as instructed, and there was Rob. I think he was ducking a flying stop sign when I first laid eyes on him.

"Holy heat wave!" I screamed back. "Rob Marciano's hot!"

Where it came from is a mystery best left unsolved, but at that point, Marcus produced a cheese knife; and in a bizarre cabaret that I can only describe as Benihana meets kabuki theater, he hacked off a hunk of brie, smeared it across a water cracker, and slid the whole gooey mess into my kisser in *one seamless motion.* The performance climaxed in a chirpy, "*Merlot?*" before I had time to absorb its full hallucinatory brilliance.

Words escaped me. It was probably about 4:00 A.M., but time had lost all meaning. I nodded my head, Marcus filled my glass, and I returned to Rob. He really was the best weatherman ever—manly, but in a boyish way, the kind of guy who could bare his soul as effortlessly as he might pitch a tent, then show you who was the boss once inside that tent. He was my savior.

And so the days passed—a visual onslaught of death and destruction interspersed with periodic visits from the ever-faithful Rob who, despite the torrential rain and gale-force winds, kept watch over me via Alice's fabulous one-of-a-kind two-way television.

When I finally got in touch with my parents, they were still in Jackson. They now had electricity and knew that all hell had broken loose, and yet they hadn't done squat in terms of making an escape plan.

"Look, I don't know what you're doing Mom, but you've got to get out of there."

My mother let out a deep, annoyed breath. "You know," she replied, "you're really starting to aggravate me with these phone calls."

What???

"Where do you expect us to go?" she asked.

It was a valid question. My older brother Stephen lived in the New Orleans area, so he wasn't going to be any help, but Blair, the roaming minstrel that he is, was living in Wichita. I suggested that my parents go stay at his place.

"As if," laughed my mother. "You know how Blair likes his privacy."

There was no way to respond to that. Sure, I could call Blair and try to force him to unlock the doors to his secret lair, but who knew when I'd be able to get in touch with my parents again.

"Well, you can't stay in Jackson and you certainly can't go home. New Orleans is turning into the Wild West. The government isn't doing jack to help the situation and suddenly it's a big free-for-all. Why follow the rules? I can't even tell the difference between right and wrong anymore. I'm warning you, Mom. This is no time to fool around."

"Maybe," she said. "But it's not so easy with these dogs. What do you expect me to do? Take them out back and shoot 'em!?!"

The dogs, the dogs, the dogs. Always the dogs. The woman has pictures of the dogs in her wallet, but not a single picture of me. And she doesn't even need pictures of the dogs because they're with her *constantly*, at the end of a leash that sprouts from her hand like a sixth finger.

"Send the dogs to me!" I blurted out, not knowing where the hell I'd put them, only knowing that my parents would die in Jackson if I didn't take the damn things off their hands. And then *I'd* have to go there. "Just make sure they know I'm not going to be wiping their asses before they get here," I added.

"I don't think so," said my mother. "The big, bad wolf wouldn't like that too much."

The big, bad wolf is my mother's designation for Frankie, whose only real crime is that he's not a dog, meaning he doesn't roll over, jump through a hula hoop, and wet himself trying to please her.

"I'll deal with Frankie," I replied. "Just send me the dogs."

Having seen my mother in action during the garage sale, I was familiar with the whole denial routine. But it was maddening nonetheless. And now I had two obnoxious dogs on the way. It was a lot to process, and Rob Marciano was nowhere to be found. It was just Anderson Cooper, Anderson Cooper, Anderson Cooper. So I decided to check my e-mail, which I hadn't done in days.

My inbox contained nearly fifty e-mails from close friends, old friends, new friends, work friends, and a few people I didn't even know were my friends—checking in to make sure I was OK, asking after my family, offering money, their homes, anything and everything they had to give.

I was in the midst of shooting off responses, when I received a text message from my dear friend Paul. It read: JUST SAW YOUR PARENTS LOOTING ON TELEVISION. THOUGHT YOU'D WANT TO KNOW.

I'd cried more than I thought physically possible while watching the details of Katrina unfold, and although Rob had afforded me random moments of escapism throughout, it was only now, for the first time in over a week, that I laughed—I laughed loud and hard, without hesitation or restraint, never thinking about what might be stuck in my teeth, or worrying about what anyone else might think. I laughed the way I learned to laugh years ago and in another world, from so deep inside that all the collected pain and sorrow momentarily dissipates, replaced by the reminder that life, although often unfair, is still better than the alternative. I laughed the New Orleans way.

Alice was at my side in a heartbeat.

"Are you all right? What happened?"

I showed her the text message, and, seeing that it was safe to crack a smile, she too began to laugh. A few minutes later, Paul called. We quickly conspired against him.

I'm not sure what his opening line was, but Alice suddenly adopted a solemn demeanor and said very slowly, "I need you to tell me *exactly* what you said to Cindy." I shoved my head next to Alice's, listening in as Paul confessed his sin and tried to convince her that he would have never said anything to upset me, that it was just a joke, a desperate, misguided attempt to bring levity to the situation. Alice, in turn, assured him that it hadn't worked, that it had only driven me to the bathroom, where I'd been locked away crying ever since. Paul continued to plead with her to *please* tell me how sorry he was and that it was all a big mistake, but Alice dismissed his appeal, closing the case with a curt "I can't talk to you now. I've got to go try to undo the damage you've done."

Alice and I extracted as much laughter as we could from the moment. Then we called Domino's.

A Domino's thin-crust pizza never tasted so good. I hadn't eaten in days, but Alice and I now ate an entire pizza each. And as we did, we continued to watch the news.

I'd already seen every recognizable sight, every place I knew and expected to always be just as I'd left it, turned into something at once familiar and yet, completely foreign. It was as if I'd been watching a disaster movie and these were just sets and locations. There was so much of me that still refused to accept that it was real.

At this point, a lot of the people from the Convention Center had been bused into the suburbs, near Lakeside Shopping Center, and walking distance from my childhood home. It was slightly less awful that what we'd seen previously, but it was by no means good, and for some reason stranger to me than all the rest. Hundreds, maybe thousands, of people were camped out on a patch of grass I'd traveled past every single day of my life.

Powerless, I sought asylum in guilt.

I felt guilty for being emotionally consumed by this tragedy when I knew other tragedies were occurring around the globe every single day. And I felt guilty for blinding myself to the news of those other tragedies simply because it hurts too much to know, because I couldn't bear to be another well-informed, self-righteous blowhard who rants about every injustice on earth while *doing* absolutely nothing. I mean, if that's the end result of awareness, why subject myself to the horrors?

But there I was, taking it all in, and feeling guilty for everything, including the pizza I was wolfing down while my fellow New Orleanians, wrangled together like cattle, were going hungry. And they were going hungry in the middle of a town filled with empty homes and grocery stores where literally tons of food was rotting by the minute in the middle of #$@! America. I wondered how that could happen. I wondered what being an American really meant. I grabbed one of the five boxes of Kleenex strewn about Alice's living room and balled up on the couch, feeling as useless as all the guilt and impotent outrage in the world. But good ol' Alice, she just let me cry.

After I'd emptied my tear ducts, I sat back up and pulled myself together. When the coast was clear, Alice rewound her TiVo. "Check this out," she said.

This was a very curious incident. One-way buses out of hell were being loaded with passengers, but only women and children were being allowed on.

So this funky-looking woman was boarding the bus, a baby cradled in her arms, when a security guard stepped in, blocking her path. The woman stopped, then, out of the blue, the security guard grabbed her hair and yanked it right off.

It was wig! It was a man! It was a borrowed baby! And the expression on the guy's face was priceless. *Uh-oh! You got me.*

Then it got even weirder. The guy started laughing. I was floored. I mean there are plenty of drag queens in New Orleans, so the getup was proof of nothing but a penchant for women's clothing, but he had to have been 100 percent desperate to get out of the city at that point. Who wouldn't have been and why borrow a baby otherwise? Yet here he was laughing as he was being tossed off the bus. And I guess it could have been the laughter of a madman, but it didn't sound like that. It sounded like genuine laughter—a laughter that was soon accompanied by more of the same from a number of onlookers.

My God, I thought, New Orleans isn't dead yet. There are still a few freaks out there keeping the spirit alive.

Alice and I watched the incident play out again and again. And as we did, I found myself thinking about the Ignatius Reilly statue on Canal Street, in front of what used to be the old D. H. Holmes building. If he thought he was living amidst a confederacy of dunces before, I can only imagine what he would have made of this. Oh, how I wished Ignatius had been sitting on the couch between Alice and me. I would have loved nothing more than to hear his commentary on the whole hideous mess. God knows the man would have been outraged—he was outraged by everything else—but I doubt he would have felt even the slightest twinge of guilt about eating pizza.

After a few hours had passed, Alice and I figured it was time to let Paul off the hook. I called him, and he instantly launched into apology mode. In service of the ruse, I contained my laughter as best I could. When that was no longer an option, I unleashed it on Paul, who replied quite simply, "I hate you."

My mother eventually came to her senses. She called to inform me that the dogs would be heading to Los Angeles at the end of the week. She and my father were in Memphis now, at some diner. And she was acting as if she were on some weird vacation.

"Everyone's sooo nice," she said, sweetly. "We get discounts everywhere we go."

"That's great, Mom."

"Yeah, it is. Except I'm trying to act like a refugee, and this buffoon I'm with keeps making jokes. I told him if he keeps acting jolly, they're going to start charging us full price."

"I think as long as you've got a Louisiana license you'll be fine."

"I guess so," she replied. "You just be nice to my dogs."

"I will."

"And I'm sending some Huggies along too, in case you're feeling adventurous."

I hung up the phone without ever telling my mother that I'd scoped things out on Google Earth. My dad's place was fine, but my mother's first floor had flooded and was by now undoubtedly morphing into a verdant marsh of mold and bacteria. Nothing could be done about that at this point, and it was way more than a lot of people had to go back to, so I figured I'd just let her enjoy her discounted vacation.

I returned home to Frankie that evening. Tomas came over a little while later. I offered him a glass of wine, sat down and patted the couch beside me. Tomas looked at me, looked at the couch, and looked suspicious. "What do you want from me?" he asked. I smiled back. "You know how you've been talking about getting a dog?"

Tomas didn't have any idea what he was in for, but he's a big softie underneath and my hometown had just been destroyed, so he agreed to keep the dogs at his place. "But I'm not doing it for you," he pointed out. "I'm doing it for Frankie."

"I know," I replied.

Of course, we both knew that he was doing it for me, but after so much ugly reality, what was the harm in engaging in a little make-believe?

"What about your parents?" asked Tomas. "What are they going to do?"

"Well," I said. "Once those dogs are here, my mom won't be able to stay away for long. I'm not sure about my dad though. He'll probably want to go to his fishing camp or something. But nothing's going to happen for a week or so. They're on vacation now, which is good, because I've got *a lot* of cleaning to do before my mother arrives."

under my roof

My younger brother is the most fascinating creature on earth, and my mother's favorite child. I'm not sure which begot which, but you can tell she thought he was special from the get-go just by his name. Only 1 in every 12,500 American males is named Blair; 5 of the 25 girls in my high school Spanish class were named Cindy.

I'm pretty sure Blair is also the smartest member of my family, although, given what a rare bird he is, no one has come up with a way to measure his kind of intelligence yet. And there's probably no point in even trying. Some things are just unknowable.

Like my mother, Blair is ultra clean. Everything in his house is white, you're not allowed to wear shoes inside, and he makes you scrub your feet with a wire brush and Borax before entering. Of course, this doesn't happen often, because he never invites anyone over and you can't just pop in for a surprise visit because he relocates every three months and doesn't tell you where he is until he's loading up a moving van and heading to his next secret location.

Yet my mother calls *me* a gypsy.

The last time my father was granted an audience with my younger brother, Mr. Clean washed his truck upon arrival. My father called me from his cell phone as it was happening. When he told me he was at Blair's house, I just about fell off my chair.

"*Really?*" I replied, "You mean he actually exists? I thought you guys were just making him up."

"I'm looking at him right now," said my dad. "He's Windexing my windows as we speak."

"Wow. Do you have a camera?"

"Yeah, but it's in my truck and I'm not allowed over there because my shoes are dirty. I think that might be why he's washing it. He doesn't want it messing up his driveway."

"That's all right," I said. "He probably doesn't photograph anyway, but listen, does he do interiors?"

"I don't know yet," replied my father, with a chuckle.

Then we moved on to deer.

My father was giving me a blow-by-blow of his latest hunting trip, when suddenly he leapt in with a "Whoop! Look's like I'm next."

I heard Blair cackling in the background. He had turned the hose on my poor father, who, unfortunately, doesn't move too fast.

Blair used to be an aircraft mechanic, but now he sells penis enhancement products on the Internet because "Why work sixty hours a week and leave the house to do it when I can make more money in four hours sitting at my own computer?" Say what you will about the effectiveness of penis enhancement products, it's hard to argue with a statement like that. And I know he's not lying about his income, because he's got the Midas touch. He always has. Why else would my dad have taken an eight-year-old to the racetrack every weekend? I'm convinced my mother slept with a leprechaun back in '67 because I swear you could lock Blair in a padded cell, and six months later, when you unlocked it, he'd be doing a jig and hugging a pot o' gold. Which is pretty much what happens anyway, except that it only takes three months. He may poop golden coins for all I know. It would certainly be a lot more sanitary than the alternative, and God knows Blair is no friend of germs.

Also, this one time when we were all home for Christmas, I snooped in his Dopp kit and found a bar of *Irish Spring* soap.

But perhaps my greatest proof that Blair has the luck of the Irish on his side, is the fact that he is repeatedly able to buy homes, then have a hurricane strike his neighborhood and destroy everything in sight *except* his own house, which he then turns around and sells for more than he paid for it. It happened with Ivan, and it happened again with Katrina—on a house he had closed on just two days before! I told him it was wrong to capitalize on a disaster; he told me that's how capitalism works. And I don't know about Ivan, but Katrina sounds suspiciously Irish to me.

I only learned about Blair's power to change the course of hurricanes when my mother came out to stay with me after Katrina. Apparently, he tells her a lot more stuff than he tells anyone else in our family because they have some weird love connection. Of course, it doesn't translate into room and board, despite the fact that my mother is probably the only person on earth capable of upholding Blair's sanitation standards. So instead of taking shelter in Blair's three-bedroom house in Wichita, she came to stay with me in my one-bedroom apartment. I was a little concerned about my mother and me living under the same roof for the first time in twenty years, but the thought of her and Blair scrubbing everything to death was more than I could handle. I'm sure he had a top secret mission or two he had to jet off to—he's been all over the world—and I knew what trap I was setting when I had my mother ship me those dogs of hers anyway.

––––––

"So," I asked, "where is Blair's magic rainbow taking him next?"

"Oh, I don't know," replied my mother, but I know she did.

"He sure is one interesting character," I said, hoping to loosen her lips.

"He's very smart you know, just a little unconventional."

A *little* unconventional? The guy seems to exist on a diet of raisins and broccoli, he's memorized every show that's ever been broadcast on The Learning Channel *and* he can pull money out of thin air! Maybe I'm a square, but that sounds *a lot* unconventional to me.

"I guess you could call him eccentric," added my mother.

"Uh-huh, because he's got some dough. If you're poor and eccentric, they just call you crazy."

"I don't know about that," she replied.

"I do."

My mother, sensing what I was after, instantly changed the subject. "I want to go see my dogs," she announced. "I know that little Foxy must be missing me something awful."

What I wanted was to hold her prisoner, make her squirm, and force her to give up the goods on Blair. But I didn't have much to work with. I had thought that maybe as she was unpacking I'd be able to make my move, slipping in a casual question while she was distracted, and feeling victorious after extracting some small nugget of information about the all-powerful Oz. Unfortunately, my mother had nothing to unpack. She'd left home two weeks earlier with an overnight bag, thinking she'd be back the next day. But no one was supposed to return to New Orleans for another month, and even then, her home wouldn't be anyplace she could actually live. My father had called before she'd arrived to say that he'd snuck back in and worked his way to my mother's house, and was ditching everything on the bottom floor and knocking out the drywall, before heading off to some rural Louisiana town I'd never heard of where he knew somebody who knew somebody who had a hunting camp.

In addition to that, there was no way even I could pretend that Foxy *and* Remi weren't missing my mother something awful. Those damn dogs had been howling like werewolves since the moment her scent had wafted over to the other side and through the window of Chez Tomas, where they were to remain for the duration. That was the setup. I do have a cat, after all.

But really, the racket was nothing new, because in addition to being funny to look at, my mother's dogs have the charming feature of barking at anything that moves—be it another dog, a passing jogger, or a blade of grass swaying in the breeze. And you can't really tell which animal is the instigator because in a bizarre act of canine solidarity, they've somehow managed to figure out a way to perfectly synchronize their barks. But while it pains me to do so, if forced to point the finger of blame, I'd point it at Remi. Sure, he's got some faults, but he's no follower. That dog is his own master, he's been flying his freak flag since the day he was born, and I love him for it. Foxy's his bitch, and Remi humps him twice a day just to make sure he doesn't forget it. Foxy wouldn't make a peep without Remi's OK.

Tomas had all but abandoned writing the previous week to undertake the self-appointed task of training my mother's dogs. I told him not to bother, that it was a lost cause, but miraculously, in just a few days' time, Tomas had them completely silenced and doing the goose step. He also had this strange idea that Foxy and Remi were members of the French Resistance.

Tomas reported to me daily on the progress of his charges, and whenever he did, he did so in a French accent, and with a red beret atop his head. Occasionally, he would get on all fours to reenact a scene, and in every scene, Foxy addressed Remi as "Boss." Then, when Tomas was done with his performance, I'd look down at him and say, "That's wonderful. Don't pee on my leg."

Despite the theatrics, Tomas truly had achieved the unachievable. And my mother's arrival instantaneously reversed his efforts, like a 5,000-piece jigsaw puzzle tossed into the air. Tomas was not a happy man.

I took my mother next door, where Tomas greeted her with a smile. But then again, he is a trained actor—a trained actor who leapt at the opportunity to run, not walk, over to The Grove and take in a double feature. My mother and her dogs soon launched into a lovefest, and when Tomas returned, she wandered back to my apartment.

Knowing that I do not watch television, the first thing my mother did was pick up the remote and poke at the buttons.

"What's wrong with this gadget?" she asked.

"I don't know," I replied. "I've never used it. It probably doesn't have batteries. Not that it matters, seeing as I don't have cable and free TV went out around the same time as shoulder pads."

"You don't have cable!" she exclaimed, as if this were all a big surprise.

"No, Mom, I don't have cable, but I've got an idea. Why don't you read a book?"

I handed her *Naked*. "Check this out. It's funny."

My mother eyed the book. "Oh," she responded with delight. "I love this guy. I used to listen to him on NPR. Maybe we can get him to come clean this place up."

I rolled my eyes and pointed out my *Strangers with Candy* box set. "You can watch this if you get bored with reading. It's his sister. But you will have to walk to the DVD player to turn it on."

"Which sister?" she asked, as if trying to impress me with her intimate knowledge of the Sedaris clan.

"Amy."

While I was out buying batteries, my mother called to ask me if I had any sunblock. She wanted to take a walk. Day 1, and trouble was already brewing. I did have sunblock, and I knew exactly where it was, I just didn't want her anywhere near that particular cabinet, because it housed a few things that contained no UV protection whatsoever. But being the good daughter I am, I gave her the coordinates, knowing full well that I was setting myself up in the process.

I reentered my apartment just as Amy's character, Jerri Blank, was asking someone to pee on her, and my mother was bouncing up and down on the couch, laughing hysterically. My eyes instantly zoomed in on the bottle of Juicy Lube beside her; and at precisely the same moment, my mother's laughter ceased. She picked up the Juicy Lube and said, "What, may I ask, is this, and why, may I ask, does it come in flavors?"

My first instinct was to start crying and promise that I'd never do it again, but then I remembered that I was a forty-year-old woman. If only I still lived at home, I could blame it on my brothers. But I knew that wasn't going to fly now. So I gathered all my courage and said, "I thought you were going for a walk."

"I asked you a question."

Uh-huh. And not only did she ask me a question, she stared me down in an attempt to pull her kooky Jedi mind trick on me. But I kept my cool and carried on. "It's exactly what it looks like. I bought it for you."

"Very funny," she said.

"What's wrong? Are you mad because it doesn't taste like black jelly beans? I swear I looked all over for something in licorice. Watermelon was the best I could do."

But she was already done with me, and back to Amy.

I sat on the couch beside my mother. "Can I ask you a question?"

"I don't know," she replied.

"How come it's funny that Amy Sedaris wants someone to pee on her, but it's not funny that I have sex potions?"

"Oh, that's easy," she said. "Because Amy's not my daughter."

"OK, sure, but I am forty years old," I replied.

"OK, sure, but you're still my daughter."

And for maybe the first time ever, I realized that she hadn't been actively refusing to treat me like an adult all these years; she simply couldn't stop seeing me as her child. She didn't want to keep me locked away; she just wanted to keep me safe and innocent. All at once, I was filled with a sense of warmth and well-being. I'd forgotten what it was like to feel that someone in the world was watching out for me.

"Plus," she continued, as I gazed at her, half-hoping, half-fearing, that this tender moment was about to give birth to some profound declaration of a mother's love, so pure and sweet. "Amy doesn't want anyone to pee on her—that's Jerri's thing."

Silly me.

"I don't know, Ma. I think it takes a special woman just to play Jerri."

"Oh, who cares?" she replied, springing off the couch. "You're going to do whatever the hell you want anyway."

By day 3, the living situation was completely intolerable. The dogs could be heard throwing themselves at Tomas's front door round-the-clock, my mother was consumed with guilt, Tomas hated me, and Frankie was just about to scratch through the window screens and finalize his escape. It was time to hit the streets.

"Where are you and the big, bad wolf gonna go?" asked my mother.

"I don't know. I haven't quite figured that out yet."

"Why don't you just stay here with me and let him camp out with Tomas," she suggested.

"No, that won't work. Frankie gets very depressed when he's separated from me."

"I'm so sure," laughed my mother. "He acts like he'd rather not know you half the time."

"That's all right. I don't need the constant reassurance of a dog. We're sticking together."

She shook her head. "I don't know what you're going to do when that cat dies."

"I already told you what I'm going to do. I'm having him skinned and made into one of those tiger rugs with the head still attached."

"Oooh, you're so tough," she replied.

"No, I'm not. I just think he'd make a good bath mat. He's soft."

"You don't fool me for a second, young lady. The last time that cat was out of commission, you got so worked up I thought I was going to have to have you committed."

"He was on his deathbed!" I cried.

"Get real. He had a tooth pulled."

"Yeah, well, it was a big one."

The next morning, Frankie and I headed off to Stephanie's house, and the dogs moved into my apartment with my mother. It wasn't ideal—leaving my mother unsupervised *and* within spitting distance of Tomas—but it seemed like the best solution.

And so it was for the next six weeks. I spent as much time as I could with my mother, and I had the cable turned on to keep her company when I couldn't, although she claimed she only needed it for her dogs, because they *love* Animal Planet. I tried to visit Tomas once or twice as well, but all I ever got was the cold shoulder; he had befriended the neighborhood stripper to punish me. And all the while, as I was making myself crazy trying to please everyone, my mother was consorting with Tomas behind my back.

I learned of this about a month in. I was approaching my apartment, when Tomas cut me off at the pass. "Diana's really sweet," he said, in a saccharine voice. "And she *really* wants to get you married."

"*Diana?*" I replied. "You mean my mother?"

"She may be your mother, but she's also her own person."

"Whatever," I replied, knowing that it was his least favorite word in the English language.

"I hate when you say *whatever*," snapped Tomas. "It's an ugly word, and it really doesn't reflect well on you."

"Whatever."

Tomas was really chapping my hide. He hadn't given me the time of day in weeks, and now here he was drawing some weird line between me and my mother, or my mother and I, or my mother and me . . . whatever. The point is I didn't like it. And not only was he trying to make me jealous by positioning himself as her best buddy, he was painting *me* as her persecutor.

"Look Tomas, what my mother *really* wants is to go home. She's bored out of her skull. Her routine's all messed up. She's used to having a job and going out dancing five nights a week."

"That may be, but she asked me to help her find you a husband. She's got some crazy idea that you're a kind person who would make a great wife . . . *and mother!*"

"I'm sure you set her straight on that one,"

"No, I just played along. She was *crying* after all."

"Well, thank God you're a trained actor," I replied.

"I'm just trying to clean up your mess."

"Oh really? Well if you knew as much about human psychology as you think you do, you'd know that she was *crying* because she has no idea what awaits her back home. I know I've only known her forty years longer than you have, but trust me, she doesn't normally weep over the fact that I'm single."

"Whatever you need to tell yourself," said Tomas. "And by the way, Foxy's got a rash."

I'll probably never know what really transpired between those two, but Foxy did have a rash. So I made an appointment with The Cat Whisperer. He does dogs, too.

I hadn't seen The Cat Whisperer since he'd outlawed canned tuna on Planet Frankie, but my mother was well aware of his existence, as I'd called her with a full report after the acupuncture incident—a report that she responded to by informing me that I had the I.Q. of a fried egg, and advising me to find a new vet. But now that Foxy—a squirrelly little specimen found alongside some Louisiana highway—had a rash, my mother couldn't get in to see The Cat Whisperer fast enough. So off we went.

Remi even came along for the ride.

Curiously enough, my mother seemed to have the exact same effect on The Cat Whisperer that he'd had on Frankie way back when. Everything my mother said was charming and interesting. It certainly helped that she was a refugee, but even before that was revealed, there was no denying that she'd cast a spell on The Cat Whisperer.

Where did I go wrong? The Cat Whisperer's examination room was clearly some kind of mystical energy field, like a mini-Sedona. Whether it was due to all the crystals scattered about or not, I couldn't be sure; all I knew was that magic was criss-crossing every which way, yet somehow it had managed to miss me in both directions.

But boy did my mother score. The Cat Whisperer even offered to give Remi a free exam. Of course, when he leaned over and attempted to lift the curly chap, his back practically snapped in two.

"A diet might not be a bad idea," suggested The Cat Whisperer, as he strained to heave Remi onto the examination table.

"I barely feed him, as it is," replied my mother. "I guess it's because he eats rocks. I try to stop him, but he's pretty quick for a fatso."

"Shake him," I said to The Cat Whisperer. "He sounds like a rainstick."

"I thought you liked Remi!" scolded my mother.

"I do like him! I like him more than you do! I thought it was funny."

But there was no room for my humor on their bicycle built for two.

"I'm going to wait in the car," I said.

And there I sat, perplexed once again. How come they could talk shit about Remi, but I couldn't make one little joke? How come I got sent to the poorhouse and my mother got a free dog exam? How come I got scolded for not cooking for Frankie and my mother got no reprimand whatsoever for freely admitting that she allows Remi to eat rocks? And the dog isn't even fat! He's just stocky and feels like he's carved out of stone, because in addition to rocks, she lets him eat boulders.

It was all Foxy's fault—him and his stupid attention-seeking rash. We should have just squirted some Neosporin on him and called it a day.

I glanced in the rearview mirror and saw my mother exiting. The Cat Whisperer was hot on her heels with a bag of Skittles. Unbelievable.

"I love that vet!" exclaimed my mother, as she opened the car door with one hand and waved good-bye to The Cat Whisperer with the other. "And his wife is from New Orleans! Can you beat that?"

Having already learned my lesson, I didn't even try.

My mother settled into the passenger seat, waved her Skittles in front of my face, and said. "Door prize! Want one?"

But while our trip to The Cat Whisperer did provide a temporary distraction, the truth was that my mother was getting more and more homesick by the day. She was trying to put up a good front, but I could tell she wasn't happy. Time had passed; reality had set in. She was no longer able to convince herself that she was on vacation. She already knew that she didn't have a job to go back to. The time had come for her to go home and see what kind of a life she had to go back to.

My mother arranged to stay with her sister—whose house had made it through Katrina unscathed—while she sorted things out. But with so much uncertainty, Foxy and Remi wouldn't be able to return until later. They were going back to shack up with Tomas. He just didn't know it yet.

The night before my mother's departure, we had a dinner party at Alice's house. It was just my mother and me, Alice, and Marcus, who had been given strict orders to dress like a normal person. Tomas had been invited as well, but by this time, his fate had been revealed, and he opted to bow out of dinner. I imagine he was back at home either mentally preparing for the return of Diana's dynamic duo, or getting a lap dance from his stripper friend, but I didn't press him for details.

Now first off, let me just say that I have never seen my mother take a single drink in her entire life. She claims it's because she gets excruciating migraines, and occasionally goes so far as to spend days on end lounging about in a cool, dark room to support her claim. But I myself have long suspected that Blair actually demanded that she take a vow of sobriety before bestowing the title of confidante upon her.

Wait, that's not true. I did see my mother have a drink once—a Whiskey Sour—at my cousin Helen's wedding. She must have thought it was safe to sneak one in since Blair was not in attendance.

Nor was he in attendance now, at Alice's house, where my mother proceeded to drink *an entire glass of white wine.* When I saw that she was approaching tipsy—and I had already passed it—I decided to make my move. I was running out of time, after all.

I got a quick lay of the land. Alice was making goo-goo eyes at her dog through the French doors; Marcus and my mother were talking about face creams. I clinked a spoon against my wine glass.

"Mother!" I called from out from across the table, "Did you or did you not have sex with a leprechaun in 1967?"

My mother looked at me briefly, very briefly, then she turned to Marcus and said, "I knew I shouldn't have been wearing that girdle when I was pregnant with her."

"I think girdles are fabulous!" gushed Marcus.

"It can't be any worse than smoking cigarettes and drinking martinis," Alice chimed in.

These two were no help whatsoever.

"Oh, I never did that," swore my mother.

"My mom sure did," replied Alice, as she topped off her wine.

"Enough!" I blurted out. "You people are distracting the defendant. Not to mention condoning one of her many crimes."

"*Defendant?*" giggled my mother.

"Just answer the question, lady."

"Don't be ridiculous," she said, brushing me off.

"Then how do you explain Blair's endless streak of good fortune, huh? How do you explain his ability to turn water into wine?"

"Who's Blair?" asked Marcus, intrigued.

Alice leaned into Marcus. "That's her little brother."

"Oh, for heaven's sake," replied my mother. "He's just a hard worker."

A hard worker? Since when does sitting around in your underwear four hours a day qualify as hard work?

"What's that supposed to mean?" I belted out, trying to sound offended.

"Nothing," she giggled. "It just means he has a stronger work ethic than some other people."

"Oh, I wonder *which* other people you could be referring to? Alice, give the defendant more wine. We'll get some answers out of her before the night is over."

Alice did as instructed.

"Blair wasn't born in 1967 anyway," added my mother. "He was born in 1968."

"True, but last I checked Homo sapiens still had a gestation period of nine months, and he was born in *August*. So what are you saying? Does it just take less time to fully bake a half-leprechaun?"

"I don't think I'm saying anything, but you've got quite an imagination."

"Well, I guess that's better than nothing," I replied, temporarily pacified by the notion that perhaps I hadn't gotten completely gypped. Although in terms of a cross-examination, I hadn't come away with much.

While plotting my next move, I leaned back and watched Marcus cozy up next to my mother again, like they were best girlfriends.

"You better watch out, Marcus," I warned. "You get too close to Diana and Tomas may challenge you to a duel."

Marcus didn't seem too concerned. He was all about the '70s now, and practically sitting on my mother's lap.

"I bet you were going to key parties and doing blow off shag carpets, weren't you?" asked Marcus, desperate for a little splash in the gutter.

Alice spit a stream of wine across the table and started choking on her own laughter. I, on the other hand, was appalled.

"Marcus!" I screeched. "That's *my mother* you're talking to!"

My mother handed Alice a glass of water.

"If you can ask her about leprechauns, why can't I ask her about the '70s! I was too young. I missed all the good stuff."

"Tough shit. Ask your own mother."

My mother looked at me. And then she laughed at me. "I wasn't born yesterday, you know. It takes more than that to shock me."

Marcus put his arm around my mother and glared at me. *See.*

"And stop cursing," added my mother.

"Check please," I called out to Alice, as I secretly prayed that Marcus wouldn't say anything that actually *would* shock my mother. Because I knew he could if he wanted to.

"So?" repeated Marcus with urgency. "Were you doing blow off shag carpets?"

"Lord no," replied my mother, giggling again. "I didn't have time for that. I was too busy raising children. I was a cookie-baking, costume-making, storytelling mother."

True, but . . .

"Oh, right," I interjected. "Like you'd have had your nose anywhere near some dirty old shag carpet if you didn't have a batch of cupcakes in the oven."

"There are lots of things you don't know about me," replied my mother, sounding surprisingly mysterious, although I knew even if she did have a secret or two they definitely weren't drug-related.

"I know you smoked Eve cigarettes once because I found them in your nightstand when I was about twelve."

"Is that so," she said. "And tell me, was that before or after you and Karen stole her mother's car and went cruising off to the lakefront?"

"Don't try to skirt the issue, young lady."

"*Young lady?*"

"Don't deny it! You'll only make things worse on yourself if you lie to me."

Giggle. Giggle. Giggle. "I'm not denying anything," said my mother. "I don't even know what you're talking about, but I *did* have a life before you came along. Back when I was a stewardess . . ."

Marcus sprang up like a jack-in-the-box. "*You were a stewardess!!!*"

"That's right," she replied, proudly.

"I've always wanted to be a stewardess!" shrieked Marcus. "Tell me what it was like!"

"Oh, not now," she said, offering me a mischievous glance. "I don't want to say anything that might shock Polly Purebred over there."

"Traitor!" I called out. "Go ahead. Tell him everything. And why don't you give him a map to Blair's house and a secret decoder ring while you're at it."

My mother just giggled on. "Blair said he's happy to give that information out on a 'need-to-know' basis."

"Ah-ha! So you have in been in communication with the little weasel!"

"You better be nice," cautioned my mother. "He could send an earthquake your way."

"Do you think you could make me a stewardess costume?" interjected Marcus. "I'll pay you."

"No, goofy," I piped in. "She's leaving tomorrow and she's got plenty of her own stuff to do. Alice, cut that man off."

"Alice, I think you better cut her off, too," added my mother. "In fact, maybe we should call it a night."

"Good idea," I concurred. "I don't think this is the best environment for someone your age."

Then Marcus showed my mother his tattoos and Alice walked us to the front door, bidding my mother farewell with a salute.

It wasn't easy saying good-bye, but the time had come for us to both fly solo once again. As my mother was packing up her things—and some of mine—I asked, "So, how'd you like living under my roof?"

"It was interesting," she replied. "But I think I prefer living under my own roof." Then after a pause, she added. "I just hope I still have one."

"Well, if you don't, you can always come back."

"Oh, no, that's OK. I'll figure something out."

"Don't worry about the dogs," I said. "Tomas is a freak, but he's nice to four-legged creatures. One time he even hand-washed Remi's rear after an unfortunate incident involving the consumption of cactus."

"I'll miss those little guys," she replied, gazing over at them. "But I know they'll be in good hands. You just take care of yourself."

I nodded. "Mom, can I ask you a question?"

"I guess so."

"Do you wish I had a husband and kids?"

A bittersweet smile swept across her face. "Whatever makes you happy."

And then, she was gone.

it's only natural

In need of a little R&R, I made the mistake of joining some friends for a weekend in San Diego. They're married. They've got three kids. They were meeting up with a bunch of other families.

I was lounging around in my bikini, minding my own business, with munchkins zooming all around, when this guy Greg turned to me and said, *"You don't have kids?"* But the way he said it, you'd have thought I was some freak of nature who still managed to live and breathe despite the absence of a liver, three feet of intestine, and a heart. "Nope," I replied, as I sucked on my Piña Colada. "Then why on earth would you subject yourself to *this?*" he asked.

It annoyed me. *First he implies that there's something wrong with me for not having kids, then he implies that there's something wrong with me for not avoiding kids?* I wanted to ask him why he spent his *entire family vacation* talking on his cell phone, but instead I simply said, *"Why?* Because being around you people reminds me that *not having kids* ain't so bad." Then he looked at me with disgust and said, "Really? Most women want to have children. *It's only natural.*"

What I wanted was to cram a bottle of suntan lotion down his throat.

My biological clock went off when I was thirty. At the time, I was living in San Francisco with The Elf. The Elf was not short, as one might expect an elf to be, it was instead his pointy ears and passion for the outdoors that inspired the moniker. I loved The Elf. So when the alarm went off, I suggested he plant the seed. But The Elf, instead of giving it a shot then and there, simply hit the snooze button and told me he had to kayak around Baja for a month.

Fine.

While The Elf was communing with whales, I began looking at two-bedroom apartments and buying *very small clothes*. I couldn't wait to have our baby. There was not a speck of space in my brain for thoughts of anything else. I started ingesting prenatal vitamins and reading up on all the latest child-rearing techniques. When The Elf returned, I showed him a brochure on the great Lamaze class I'd found, and suggested we make a list of baby names. He suggested we go to the movies instead.

We went to see *Junior,* which was a comedy starring Arnold Schwarzenegger. The Elf thought it was hilarious; I found it downright disturbing. It could have been a dream sequence, I don't remember, but somewhere in the middle of the movie, Arnold, through some trick of science, gave birth to Junior—a creature approximately the size of a large eggplant who, through some trick of camera, had Arnold's face superimposed on his body. I leaned in close to The Elf's pointy ear. "That baby gives me the willies," I whispered. The Elf, in turn, laughed uproariously. I guess he thought his trick of turning me off to babies had worked.

In reality, it did nothing of the sort. Junior was grotesque, but *our baby* would be an elfin beauty.

With each passing day, I wanted a baby more and more. When I couldn't bear it any longer, I mentioned to The Elf that we should really start trying. "It doesn't always happen the first time," I said. The Elf hit the snooze button again. This time he had to go climb some mountain in Argentina. The trip, like all his trips, would take a month. We'd talk about it when he returned. "We're not going to have much money for the little elf," I said. "Not if you spend all your money on climbing harnesses and crampons." The Elf took this in, and then he headed off to REI.

Around this time, it began to dawn on me that I might be the only one interested in procreation. So I called my mother and told her to hold off on the baby shower.

By the time The Elf returned from Argentina, I'd gained fifteen pounds. To make matters worse, he acted as if he didn't even notice. "Aren't you going to ask me why I'm fat?" I demanded. He stared back nervously. "You're not pregnant, are you?" "No," I screeched. "*I'm depressed!* Everybody gets to have a baby except me. Even stupid Arnold Schwarzenegger!" The Elf sighed in relief; I burst into tears.

And then, I went completely mad.

For the next several months, I wore empire-waist dresses and walked around with my stomach jutting out and one hand on my back. I'd go into the bathroom and make vomiting noises. I'd plop down on the couch with a peanut butter and pickle sandwich in my hand. I'd talk about how much my feet hurt. I even swore off alcohol! But all my delusional efforts were in vain. They did nothing to sway The Elf, who'd been sitting on the couch, staring at some nature video that had been playing on a loop since he'd returned from Argentina.

As the alarm continued to sound, I turned to The Elf and snarled, "There's your cue. Go hit the snooze again." The Elf, however, did not respond. How could he? He was in a trance, his eyes glued to the television screen, as he watched a flower bloom in slo-mo for the umpteenth time.

I felt as if I'd been conned. How could someone love nature *that much* and yet refuse to respond to its call in his own home? And sure, I could have conned him right back, except that that seemed like an awfully big responsibility to inflict on someone just to get my way. I couldn't be sure that he would take on the responsibility either, and I wanted my child to have a loving father. I guess I could have left, too. Gone off and found someone baby-ready. But I didn't want to leave The Elf. I loved him.

So together we sat, The Elf and I, neither of us budging, until, just like every other clock, the alarm on mine finally turned off on its own. Then I gathered up the very small clothes and whatnot, packed them into a large box, and marked it FUTURE BABY. It's still around here somewhere.

What once felt like a biological imperative has since been reduced to a choice. Sure, I'd still *like* to have a baby, but I don't *need* to have a baby. And what I need even less is some fifty-year-old man, with a cell phone welded to his ear and a silicone-injected wife on his arm, telling me that *I'm* unnatural. Especially when *I'm* the only lifeguard on duty to make sure his in vitro–fertilized triplets don't drown.

future ex-husband

Once again, I was experiencing problems with my computer and had to call tech support. Some guy in India answered. After sharing my secret password with him, we shifted over to the topic of marriage. I told him that I thought they were really on to something and that I personally have often contemplated moving to India or really anyplace where they have spicy food and arranged marriages. I told him I felt confident that if you went into it with the right attitude and really *tried,* you could love just about anyone. God knows I've shacked up with complete jerks, and I found a way to love them.

Back in the old days, when I was simply trying to fill the same role in a never-ending story, it was all so easy. I'd find someone who looked the part, and after a quick audition, we'd move in together for a few years. Simple as pie. But ever since I got myself straightened out in therapy, that just won't do. Now that I'm actually conscious of what's happening in the relationship, now that I actually desire a healthy relationship, I can't get out of Act I. I'm just lost in a maze of dysfunction and red flags. Sure, the steamroller approach has its flaws, and the relationship may prove to be only temporary, it may even prove to be a disaster, but at least you get to have a relationship, which even when flawed has its benefits. For Christ's sake, married men *live* longer than single men.

I said it before, and I'll say it again: I like black and white. I know how to be a partner and I know how to be single, but this in-between shit is for the birds. Either you're in or you're out. Dating? Courtship? Who needs it? It's a completely flawed concept. It's no wonder the steamroller technique was invented. *Let's storm through this fickle fog of ambiguity as swiftly as possible to see if there really is a warm placid sea of devotion on the other side!* Because in the time it takes me to properly assess someone else, I've got my own self-doubts popping up left and right. It makes my head spin. It makes my stomach do flips. That's why I sometimes think it would be better if I were just assigned someone. We'd be stuck with each other and there would be nothing more to think about. My brain could shut down and we'd just get on with it.

And that was exactly how I was feeling when Suzanne called and announced that she'd found my future ex-husband. She'd met him at a party at a friend's house. He was smart and charming, and really, she was so certain about it all, that on her way out the door she'd interrupted his conversation with another woman to demand that he fork over his phone number. I told her that seemed like an awfully aggressive move, and her husband went so far as to label it obnoxious, but Suzanne didn't care. She was on a mission. After all, she did phone me on January 1 to proclaim that her New Year's resolution was to find me a man.

"Is he a Viking?" I asked.

"He's kind of a Viking, I guess, but with better manners," she replied.

And yes, it's true, I'm over Vikings, but I still like to ask just to weed out the hobbits. How tall is he? What color is his hair? Fat? Skinny? What color are his eyes? Was he smart? Was he witty? Was he self-effacing? I like self-effacing. What was he wearing? Nice smile? What does he do for a living? Where's he from? How was his vocabulary? How old is he? The more questions I asked, the more eerily similar he sounded to someone else I knew. "Suzanne," I said, "I think my future ex-husband is my former ex-boyfriend."

This was a guy I had gone out with thirteen years earlier. I was working as an assistant at the time and he had come in for a meeting with my boss. I saw him, I loved him, then I went into the bathroom and looked in the mirror. *What on earth was I wearing?* I looked like crap. How could my boss have scheduled a meeting with a cute guy and not warned me? I wanted to flush her phone sheet down the toilet and spit in her coffee.

After he was gone and I'd calmed down, I went into my boss's office and demanded that she concoct some reason for him to come back in the following week, giving me adequate time to prepare.

At the time, I was making about fifty cents a week, but that didn't stop me from buying a $300 sundress, visiting a tanning booth, and having my hair blown out professionally for the big day. He returned; I flirted shamelessly. We soon discovered that we lived only ten blocks apart, and the following Sunday he came over to help me stain a table. And it was there, in my dining room, that I learned he had a girlfriend. But that didn't stop me from being his "friend," which basically amounted to talking on the phone and hanging out together until he finally saw that he wasn't getting rid of me and broke up with his girlfriend.

After that, he was *all mine.*

I think the first time we broke up was at the Ivy. We were having dinner, and during our conversation he mentioned something about a girl he'd gone on a date with . . . recently. *Excuse me?* After all the time, effort and credit card debt I'd put into snaring him, he had the audacity to date other people? I blew a gasket. I screamed, I cried, I tossed a bowl of sugar packets into the air. Then, just to show him, I paid the bill.

I spent the next month eating Ramen noodles and working on a letter that clearly outlined all the reasons why this had been stupidest mistake of his life, while making it equally clear that were he to crawl back to me, I would most likely embrace him and we would live the rest of our lives happily ever after.

I mailed the letter, and then I wondered. Has he received it yet? Has he read it yet? Did he see the truth and wisdom in it, or has it just been disregarded as twelve pages of insanity? Time passed. Was he still seeing that stupid girl? Had *she* read my letter? Had they giggled over it in bed together? More time passed. Had I put the right amount of postage on the letter? Should I send another one? Would I ever be able to write another masterpiece like that again? I wondered and wondered, and then, a year later, as I was still wondering, he called. He'd *finally* come to his senses. Luckily for him, I'm no quitter when it comes to love. After letting him sweat it out for a few weeks, I took him back.

And in love we were. I went to meet his family. We hit it off like a house on fire. Everything was moving ahead swimmingly. Then work took him to New York.

A week or two later, I went to visit him. We'd just come back from dinner and I, wanting to have Crest-y clean breath for my man, was looking for toothpaste. Instead, I found a Costco-sized box of condoms, which wouldn't have been a problem, except for the fact that I was in a monogamous relationship *with him,* and we were not using condoms. I blew a gasket. I screamed, I cried, I threw the box of condoms into the air.

But according to him, it was all my fault. According to him, I'd once said that if my husband had an affair, I'd rather not know about it. He was just trying to be safe.

I corrected him. What I had said was that if my husband had,

not an affair, but a single random indiscretion, that I would probably prefer to just never find out about it. In fact, I think I made
it pretty clear that if my husband found himself in love with
another woman, and was having a full-blown affair with her, that
I would actually like to be *the very first person* to know about it.
Then I pointed out that a box of five thousand condoms was clear
evidence of both premeditation and intended repetition. Then I
pointed out that he was not, and never would be, my husband.
And that was the end of that.

"Bollocks," said Suzanne. "And you never spoke to him again?"

"Nope. Never saw him, never spoke to him, nothing. It's kind
of amazing, actually. You'd think I'd have run into him at some
point."

"Well, at least I was on the right track. I picked someone who'd
already been preapproved for sex, and that's not easy with you."

Suzanne was crestfallen. Here she thought she'd satisfied her
New Year's resolution with ten months to spare, only to find out
that I'd been there, done that. Twice. But Suzanne's no quitter
either, and before she would release the bone, she did some fact
checking to make 100 percent certain that these two men were
one and the same. They were, although, according to him, he'd
changed a lot since then. And what do you know? I was "the one
that got away." Flattered, I decided to give it a whirl. Maybe I'd
see him and fall in love with him all over again. We already had
two years of dating under our belts. I didn't know if we'd get credit
for all of it, but some of it had to be transferable. If everything
seemed kosher, we'd just get married and be done with it.

I met him for lunch and a stroll down memory lane, during
which he reminded me that I *had* actually seen him once more
after that night in New York. I'd gone to his house a month later,

unannounced. I was in tears and demanded that he tell me why he came back into my life just so he could pull the same shit all over again. He was caught completely off guard and responded with a nervous smile, at which point I ordered him to "wipe that smirk off your face." I, of course, remembered nothing of this, and it made me cringe to think I would say something like that, but given that I'd heard my mother say those very words a thousand times, I had no choice but to accept his statement as truth.

Apparently, he didn't do as instructed either, because after that I supposedly socked him one. I asked him what happened next; he told me that he blacked out. All he remembered was that he woke up on the ground and I was gone. I found it highly unlikely that I'd hit him hard enough for him to see stars, but he insisted it was true, claiming it had something to do with the angle I was coming from, and the iron gate next to his skull.

We laughed. It wasn't exactly love, but the thought of having to start all over with someone new and go through that dating fog again was more than I could bear. So I told him he had three months to decide whether he wanted to marry me or not.

We never made it that long, but this time what tore us apart had nothing to do with condoms or anything else; it was just us. For me at least, it was all the things that, thirteen years earlier, when I desperately needed him to love me and only me, I had either overlooked or disregarded. He had changed some; that was true. But I had changed, too. And now that I no longer needed the validation that only his love could once provide, I realized that, well . . .

It all became crystal clear to me the day we were to see *Prairie Home Companion* live at the Hollywood Bowl. I'd heard about it and suggested we go. He'd agreed wholeheartedly and gotten two tickets. By the time the date rolled around, the writing was on the wall.

I left him a message saying that I wasn't feeling well, and suggested that perhaps he might want to find someone else to join him. I received a response via e-mail that simply read: I hate Garrison Keillor. I wrote him back, telling him that, if that was the case, he should have never agreed to it in the first place. He then clarified his previous statement, informing me that he'd only just realized that he hated Garrison Keillor, and the reason he hated Garrison Keillor had to do with the fact that he was a white man living in a world filled with crocuses, rutabagas, porch swings and root cellars, which somehow added up to him being an L.L. Bean–wearing Aryan.

Now, I could love a man who hates something I love. I could probably even love a man who agrees to things he doesn't want to do simply to please me, and then turns around and resents me for it. But I could never *marry* a man who can't back up his statements with a decent argument.

For starters, how do you *just realize* that you hate something? Hate is a pretty strong emotion. It usually rears its ugly head without much need for thought. I only had to listen to Tom Leykis once to know that I hated him, so how can someone who listens to NPR regularly *just realize* that he hates Garrison Keillor? Oh my, I *just realized* that I hate cats. I better get rid of this one I've had for fifteen years.

Secondly, *crocuses + rutabagas + porch swings + root cellars = Aryan?* It's so nonsensical that it's hard to even know where to begin, except to say that there's something very wrong with that math. I like crocuses and porch swings. I've never had a rutabaga, but I've liked every root vegetable I've ever tried. I've never seen a root cellar, but I've been to The Container Store and I do like things to be stored away properly. I've even got a pair of slippers from L.L. Bean. Does that make me an Aryan? Or do you have to be from Lake Wobegon? Because I'm not, I'm from the South. And in the South, our Aryans, they're called Klansmen, and they don't usually sit around on porch swings gazing at crocuses and talking about what they've got in their root cellars. They're usually at the shooting range, staring at bulls-eyes and talking about something else entirely.

I felt it was my duty as a fellow NPR listener to inform him that Garrison Keillor, in addition to being an Aryan, was also a liberal Democrat. I asked him if being a white liberal from Minnesota makes you an Aryan, then what does being a white liberal from California make you? And then I begged him to *please* go back to law school and get his degree, like he'd been threatening to do, promising that I would, too. That way, even though we weren't going to get married, and we'd never get to go through a messy divorce, I'd still be able to fight him in court.

Of course, all that said, it's not like he'd gone out and bought a ring.

Not long after that, I went to my favorite Indian restaurant. Darshem came over and greeted me with a smile. After giving him my order, I said, "Darshem, how's that arranged marriage business working out for ya?"

"My wife is a lovely woman," he replied. "We have been married for thirty wonderful years."

"And do you think something like that could work for someone like me?" I asked.

Darshem just about tripped over his dhoti.

"*You? Never!*" he cried. "The trick only works if you are young and stupid."

hell

I was cruising the Internet just as happy as a clam when I came across a story about this woman in England. Only she wasn't really a woman, *she was a skeleton!* They found her sitting on the couch in her **one-bedroom apartment** in front of a television that was still on and next to a heater that was still heating. She'd died at the age of **forty**, but she'd been hanging out decomposing for three solid years! Apparently, no one noticed that she was missing because she was **single.** There was evidence that she'd owned a **cat** but I'm thinking it probably escaped once the mail piled up so high and the cat got so skinny that it was able to launch itself out the mail chute. I can't remember how or why they found her; I just know they needed dental records to identify her. They said that she had **never been married** and had **no children.** Her only living relative was a sister, who I imagine must have felt like a complete heel upon hearing the news, unless of course she's cut from the same cloth as my dear brothers who probably wouldn't notice I was dead until I failed to show up at their funerals.

I sat there, dumbfounded. I couldn't believe there was a place in the world where you could totally blow off your rent *and* utility bills for three solid years and get away with it. *Holy doley,* I thought, I'm moving to England. I looked to the heavens and thanked God for sending me this sign.

Then, as I was I packing, it struck me that *on paper* I myself seemed like a prime candidate for the same gruesome fate. But in real life, I'm not.

For starters, my landlord is Johnny-on-the-spot. I wouldn't make it three days without him and half the Russian mafia busting in here to evict me. And even if I did, Tomas is constantly sniffing around my window to see what's for dinner. He'd catch wind of my stink long before I ever got to the skeletal stage. I do have a couch but I don't watch television. I do have a heater but the gas company is almost as obnoxious as my landlord. I do have a cat but I don't have a mail chute. And besides that, in real life, I don't feel like the poor, over-the-hill, spinster cat-lady that I'm supposed to be. I'm pretty sure I don't look like her because I've got the high school hooligans a block away whistling at me every time I walk out the door. And I know I don't act like her because all the children I come into contact with seem to think I'm just an oversized version of them.

Still, I couldn't shake the similarities, and I couldn't help but wonder: *How the hell can I possibly have more in common with some skeleton chick in England than any of the live women I actually socialize with here in Los Angeles?* I mean, all my Hollywood girl-friends are rich, married homeowners. And they don't have time to mess around with cats because they have actual offspring.

Sure, there's Alice and she's single. It's just that she does own a home, she has been married, she is hot on the hunt for husband #2, she has threatened to adopt and, really, who can blame her? She's from Connecticut. They'd probably revoke her clam-baking license if she weren't doing everything in her power to rectify the situation. We may be in the same boat for now, but if there's a life preserver, she's taking it.

The thing is, what really irritates me, is that none of this crap would have even entered my brain if not for the Internet, the stupid fucking endlessly seductive Internet. I swear to God, it's the devil's own TBS. *Cyberspace* is just a code word for hell. I'm convinced that Lucifer's sitting down there in his red leotard poking on a keyboard with his pitchfork uploading porn and whatever spooky tales he can conjure up while clinking glasses with a flying monkey and toasting his own cleverness for figuring out a way to screw up the world once and for all. *I'm telling you, I wasn't even looking for that story. It just popped up.*

Be that as it may, it was the last straw. Sure, the Internet had provided me with hours of amusement while vastly improving my detective skills, but it was undermining my confidence now, and trust me, living in Los Angeles, you need every shred of confidence you can muster. This place breeds insecurity. They may even put it in the water supply. And there's only one proven defense, a strong sense of self. Without that, you're screwed.

So with God as my copilot, I made a solemn vow to never go on the WWW ever again—not even to Google someone—and in one swift move, I slammed my laptop shut. That's when I saw it—the forbidden fruit—staring back at me, the modern-day Eve. There it was, an icon of a juicy little apple missing a bite, and a clear sign that the devil was branching out beyond mere content. *Chilling?* You better believe it, but at least it explained that recall on spontaneously combusting batteries.

Damn it. I cursed myself for having given in to temptation. I wanted to order a righteous new Dell computer then and there, but that would have involved going online. I wanted to do a little research, see if anyone else had discovered the link between Apple and evil before me, but that too would have involved going online. I wanted to do all kinds of things, but pretty much everything I could think of doing involved going online. And then I remembered, oh yeah, there's a great big world outside my front door. I can leave this apartment and interact with actual human beings. So I walked over to Alice's to get the ball rolling.

———

Alice was sitting at her computer scoping out the goods on Match.com when I arrived.

"Perfect timing," she said.

"For what?" I asked. "The Apocalypse?"

"Check this out," she replied, turning her computer screen to face me.

"No, thanks."

"Just look at it."

"I can't. I've got a little soul cleansing to do before judgment day."

"Will you just shut up and look at it."

It was the profile of a Hollywood executive. It was strange too, because I read somewhere that most of the men on Internet dating sites are under 5 foot 9, and this guy's like 6 foot 2.

"It's a shitty picture," declared Alice.

"Speak not with the devil's tongue," I replied.

"*What?*"

"It got your attention, didn't it?"

"*What the fuck are you talking about?*"

"The shitty picture. It got your attention, didn't it?"

"Hardly. Jessica sent it to me as a joke."

"Ah, so *that's* how Internet dating works!"

"Sometimes."

"You're gonna burn in hell."

"Sit down," instructed Alice. "I want to read you his profile. Or will that make your ears burst into flames?"

"I don't know yet. Just shut up and read it."

And so began Matt's merry myth. Really, it was one absurd fabrication after the other. I didn't want to react; I didn't even want to listen, but it was impossible not to. That's how evil works.

"What a crock of shit," I blurted out halfway in. "I mean, I have no idea if he really plays the harpsichord naked, but that is one distorted version of the truth."

"How do you know?"

"Because I went on a date with him —a 'date & switch,' actually. One of those things where he had his assistant schedule work drinks then totally tried to turn it into a date, rubbing his hand up my leg and everything."

"Isn't that more like a switch-a-date?"

"Whatever it is, trust me, he's not that interesting in person."

"I can't believe you went out with him," replied a bewildered Alice. "He's not good-looking enough for you."

"I just told you he tricked me, woman."

"It's weird though, aside from the physical, he sort of seems like your perfect match. He's into puppetry and tennis, he loves heirloom tomatoes and lima bean purée, he cooks, he's a master hula hooper, he sews and snowboards, and sometimes he juggles to unwind."

"That's not a perfect match, that's identity theft."

"*Good God! Did you know he owns a second home in Micronesia?*"

"All right, so it's not identity theft. He's gay, he needs a beard, and he's trying to lure me back in."

"Maybe you should let him."

"No, thanks, but I'm curious, does he mention anywhere in his profile that he's bipolar?"

Alice gave it a quick scan. "Nope. I guess he ran out of space."

"Yeah, right. Or maybe he had to go feed his pet giraffe. That's the problem with Internet dating. Everyone conveniently leaves out the fact that they're socially handicapped, emotionally retarded, a mass murderer, a bed-wetter, *a liar.*"

"I think that's because they're trying to sell themselves."

"Ooops, my bad. I thought you were on Match.com, not _eBay_."

"They're not that different."

"No, they're not. Except that false advertising in the consumer world is, uh, wait, you come from a family of lawyers, _illegal_. Honestly, I don't know why you waste your time with that crap."

"It's not a total waste of time. It's funny. And at least you get to narrow it down."

Narrow it down. This is what they always say and it makes me crazy. Narrow it down to _what?_ Like and dislikes? I mean, come on, people are more than the sum of their parts, not to mention the fact that I already have someone who likes and dislikes all the same stuff as me: _Me_. And as luck would have it, I'm available to me 24/7. So what do I care if someone else loves Spalding Gray and Indian food? I'm looking for a man who might actually add something _new_ to my life. And what it is, I couldn't tell you. It's a mystery. It's supposed to be a mystery. Similarities don't cause people to grow as human beings; differences do. I don't want someone who's going to allow me to be the same fucked-up version of myself that I already am; I want someone who's going to stand up and tell me what I need to hear, when I need to hear it. I want someone who's going to help me become a better person; I want to help someone become a better person. I certainly don't want a carbon copy of myself. A little friction is what makes a relationship interesting. Otherwise, ribbed condoms wouldn't exist. Not to mention the fact that my longest relationship was with someone I had virtually nothing in common with. But even though we didn't both have a passion for falconry, there was some _je ne sais quoi_ that created its own little magic and overrode all else.

Honestly, I couldn't write my perfect man's profile to save my life. I know because I tried.

I was sitting in Celeste's backyard; she was kneeling in the driveway, a tub of Sidewalk Chalk beside her. The whole thing was her idea.

"What color do you want?" she asked.

"Blue's good."

"Great," said Celeste, as she pulled out a hunk of blue chalk and wrote the word *Viking* on the driveway. Even though I have told her repeatedly that I've decided to branch out, and even though I haven't been with a Viking in ages.

But she never listens.

For instance, every time anyone asks about me, at a party or something, Celeste always laughs and says, "Oh, she's probably cleaning her apartment." Even though I have told her repeatedly that I don't want her saying that, and even though I have explained to her that I find it offensive, given that both she and whomever she's chatting with can afford a housekeeper, and I can't. But that's Celeste. She only hears what she wants to hear, and everything's *great!* All you get to do is go along with it.

"OK," she said, "so he has to be a Viking. What else?"

"Well, I've been thinking a widower might be the way to go."

"Great. That way we know he can commit but you don't have to deal with an ex-wife. What else? Kids?"

"Yeah, he can have kids."

"I just meant does he have to *want* them? You could still have your own, you know."

That's another thing about Celeste. She wants everyone to have a baby. She *loves* babies. If I had one, she'd probably steal it. Then she'd drop it off on my doorstep on its second birthday.

"If I have a baby the old-fashioned way, fine, but I'm not really looking to jab needles into myself and all that. You can give him a couple of kids. Or we could adopt. Or not. Just put *Kids?* and we'll figure out what it means later. It's not a deal breaker either way."

"Great. What does he do?"

"Besides rape and pillage? Hmmm. Well, I'm not getting any younger, so maybe a doctor. And L.A. is probably some kind of cancer capital, so how about an oncologist?"

"Great. What about hobbies and stuff like that?"

"Yes."

"I need a little more than that."

"*Whatever makes him happy?* It would be nice if he played tennis, and even nicer if he were a little better than me so I could improve my game. But I don't want someone who's going to pout if I win. I hate that. What's-his-name did that and it drove me crazy. I used to always have to let him win at everything—tennis, Scrabble, you name it."

"I'm just going to put *plays tennis, good sport.* How's that?"

"That's fine."

"Great. And he needs to love food since you're always cooking."

"No, he doesn't have to love food. He just needs to eat food, appreciate a hot meal, and be able to put up with me talking about food all the time."

"Great."

"But he does have to have good table manners. A Viking is nice in the bedroom, but I prefer a gentleman everywhere else."

"Great. How do you feel about football?"

"I have no feelings about football."

"Do you care if he watches it every Sunday like Jack?"

"No. He can do whatever he wants. I won't be delivering him nachos while he's screaming at the television, but I'm happy to make him something before I leave."

"Great. What about location? Eastside? Westside? Beachfront?"

"Is this a real person or some guy who's going to appear when you wave your magic wand?"

"Same thing."

"All right. If he has a pool, then up somewhere in the hills would be nice. Otherwise, closer to the beach."

"Great. Can you think of anything else?"

"Other than the fact that this is ridiculous? Let me see, OK, if he could live here only six months out of the year, that would be perfect. That way, I'd still have plenty of me time."

"Great. Where's his other home?"

"Wow. You really cover all the bases, don't you?"

"It's going to be half yours."

"If you say so. How 'bout Corsica?"

"Great," said Celeste, as she followed her blue chalk bread crumbs back into the driveway. "Corsica it is."

"*And how exactly is this supposed to work?*" I asked.

"Time management!" exclaimed Celeste.

Celeste is all about time management; the woman could travel the country doing seminars. According to her, *anything's possible* as long as you manage your time properly. And she may be the only woman I know who truly has figured out how to have it all. She's married with children. She earns twice as much as her husband. The entire family eats dinner together every night and goes on entertaining and educational outings every weekend. She sews her kids' Halloween costumes. If she could only learn how to cook and didn't have so many allergies, she'd be a perfect candidate for cloning. It's a little suspect that everything's always *great,* but there's no denying that she can whip through a list of twenty errands in a day. Or that I've had clothes I need to take to the dry cleaner in the backseat of my car for over a month.

According to Celeste, the more specific I can be about my mate, the easier the search will be, and the less time I'll waste on undesirables. But how finding that guy is supposed to be easy, I have no idea. And who's to say I'd even want him if I found him? Who's to say he'd want me? Wouldn't I just be better off leaving myself open to the possibility that I could fall in love with a man who doesn't fit some goofy prefabricated mold? Not to mention that, aside from the insincere specifics tossed in for Celeste's benefit, my mold seemed as easy-to-fit as a newspaper horoscope, and I know I'm pickier than that. So why bother trying to narrow it down?

And as far as the Internet goes, what people are narrowing it down to, first and foremost, is who they think looks good. Anyone who tells you otherwise is full of shit. If you don't believe me, register without a picture and see how many people want to get to know you better based on your great personality. *Zero.* (Unless of course they're looking to do something extra freaky and can't afford to be choosy.) People act like they're cutting through the bullshit with Internet dating but the profiles I've seen are nothing but bullshit. And why shouldn't they be? Anyone who's honest and earnest gets laughed at. In that way, it's eerily similar to both a John Denver album *and* real life.

"Shit," said Alice. "I'm sorry. I would have never laughed at your ex-boyfriend if I'd known you still had feelings for him."

"He's not my ex-anything," I replied. "And this isn't even him. This is some quasi-sardonic, wildly idealized version of what he could be if he were on medication and worked sixty hours less a week. And even if it were true, I don't want to know all that stuff right off the bat. What's Internet dating supposed to be, some kind of microwave oven for relationships? I like *real* baked potatoes. So what if they take longer—they taste better. And isn't part of the beauty of getting to know someone in the discovery, anyway?"

"Sure, but you've got to meet the person first and really, when's the last time you met anyone interesting in the real world?"

"OK, fine. It's been a while. But that's only because everyone's inside messing around on the Internet."

"So maybe that's the place to be."

"*What are you, a lemming?* And not for nothing, but if it's the place to be, then why are you still single?"

"Because it's all bullshit, OK? And it's a huge time suck too, but at least it makes you realize you're not alone. It makes you realize the things you want aren't that crazy. Take Matt, for example. Every time I see the guy, he acts like he's got it all figured out. But now I read this, and I see that he's desperate to connect with someone just like we are."

"*Of course he is, he lives in Los Angeles!* This is the lonely-hearts capital of the universe. But saying that's what you want on the Internet doesn't mean you're actually capable of it in real life. Matt wasn't even capable of asking me on a *real* date. It's easy to be a superhero when you're sitting in front of your computer. It's easy to be a sex goddess. It's easy to be vulnerable. It's easy to be whatever the hell you want to be. It's *too easy*. And anyway, you have to have a *soul* . . ."

"Yeah, yeah, I know, before you can have a soul*mate*. So what, you think he's just full of shit?"

"I don't know. Not necessarily. The desire for human connection is natural and universal, but I think if everyone were as open as they claim to be on the Internet, Match.com wouldn't exist. There'd be no need for it."

"But there is a need for it because everyone's become really isolated."

"Sure, because of the Internet!"

"It's not just the Internet," said Alice.

"No. You're right. But it certainly doesn't help. And now we're supposed to think online dating is the greatest thing ever when in truth it's nothing but a booby prize—a booby prize whose very existence was necessitated, *at least in part,* by the goddamn Internet."

"Can we just call it a consolation prize?"

"Call it whatever you want. I'm not buying into it. I'm going to find myself a man the old-fashioned way."

"Good luck, sister."

"I know. I'll need it. But I'll tell you something else, presenting yourself as a deep soulful guy is a great way to get a lot of stupid girls to drop their undies. I don't know if you remember this, but way back in the '90s, a man would actually have to spend a little time with you in order to figure out what he needed to say and do to get you in bed. All you're doing here is handing him a dossier upfront."

"Sure, but it works both ways."

"But women are born with everything they need to get a man in bed instantly! If it's just about sex, then why waste your time filling out a form? Just walk outside and rub against the first guy who appeals to you. It's not that difficult. Or, I don't know, maybe it is now. I don't know what's what anymore. That's the problem. But I'm telling you, the answer's out there somewhere, and I may not actually *find* it, but I'll stumble upon it eventually."

"Great. Let me know when you do, because I don't even know what the question is."

"I'm just not wired to be the aggressor. And I don't want to be a cave*man.* But sometimes I think that's what it's come to. There are so many aggressive women out there, and half the men are so confused, not knowing if they're predator or prey, that sometimes I think I'll have to club a guy and drag him back to my cave before he gets the picture. And that's after first clubbing ten women out of the way just to get to him! How did that happen? All this "sexual freedom" has made meaningful relationships more elusive than ever. Sex. Sex. Sex. It's everywhere and nowhere. And the Internet, that's the worst. Sex is so in your face in every possible perverted permutation that people are becoming completely desensitized to everything and forgetting how to just fucking care for another human being, how to just let another human being care for them. When did watching a video of two drugged women vomiting into each other's mouths, or some guy eating shit straight from the source, become entertainment? Because it is now, people send that stuff and worse around and laugh their heads off, and if you don't think a steady diet of that has any effect on the human psyche, you're wrong. We're all going to hell in a handbasket. Just last week . . .

"*Crap.* I forgot what I was going to say. You see, I was just about to tie it altogether and then *Poof!* it was gone. What was I talking about?"

"You got me," shrugged Alice, completely uninterested in the death of humanity. Except that I know she isn't really. Just when boys are involved.

"What's that quote?" I asked. "The higher a monkey climbs, the more you see of his behind?"

"That's funny."

"I guess. If you like monkey ass. You know Tomas was telling me about some online virtual reality game the other day, only he didn't call it a game, he called it a community. And . . ."

"Tomas is The Grim Reaper. Don't listen to anything he says."

"He's only like that because he's super sensitive and he doesn't have anywhere to put his emotions, or he's afraid to because he's super sensitive. Hence the black cloak and scythe. It's just a defense mechanism. His heart is in the right place and he's extremely articulate and erudite. You just have to stop the flow of booze before his eyes cloud over and he turns evil. Anyway, he was much more positive about this 'community' than I was. It seems that because we no longer have a genuine community, we now have a virtual substitute. You can go online, buy a house, have friends, start a company, go to a nightclub, the whole deal. To me it's just exacerbating the problem, but Tomas thinks it has value because it gives people a *sense* of community. It's called Second Life, but I said it should be called Fucked Up Imitation of a Real Life."

"I know some people who are on it. They love it."

"*Really?* How many hours a day do they love it? Because most people I know who *aren't* on it, people who are trying to live first lives, don't have enough time to do all the things they want to do. Time is a precious commodity; we only have a limited amount of it. How can anyone have time for a second life unless their first life, their *real* life, is empty? And then wouldn't it make more sense to concentrate on that one? I seriously doubt anyone will ever think to themselves on their deathbed, *Damn. I wish I'd spent more time dicking around on the Internet. My virtual life wasn't nearly rich enough. If only I'd gotten to know those avatars better!*"

"It's just a game," said Alice.

"Fine. Just remember what your pal Steve said the other night: If you're looking for a relationship, don't go out with any guy you find on the Internet because they're just looking to get laid."

"OK."

"I hate the Internet. You know it was invented by Satan, right?"

"You'll be online tomorrow."

"No I won't. I made a vow."

"Whatever. I'm familiar with your 'vows,' and I thought Al Gore said he invented the Internet, anyway?"

"I don't care what he said. Unless he's got a forked tail and cloven hooves, he's full of shit."

"How do you know? Did you *Ask Jeeves?*"

"No, smart ass. I figured it out on my own. And if I were Al Gore I wouldn't be bragging about inventing the Internet. He should stick to global warming. All I'm saying is that you, my friend, are playing with fire."

Then, a miracle occurred. Alice actually turned away from her computer screen and looked at me. In the eyes and everything.

"And all I was saying was that *on paper* Matt sounds like someone you'd really hit it off with."

"Oh great, *on paper!*"

"Yeah, *on paper,* the computer screen . . . whatever."

"Well, it's funny that you say that because I've just discovered that *on paper*, I look like a poor, over-the hill, spinster cat-lady freak."

"That's absurd."

"Not really. That's one way to paint it."

"I guess, but that makes you sound like a loser. Nobody would ever put that kind of stuff on their profile."

"I rest my case. I'll see you later. I've got to start managing my time better if I'm going to find that man of mine. But you know what? That's not a shitty picture of Matt. That's what he looks like. You just think it's a shitty picture because so much is missing. A person's presence, the way they walk into a room, move, talk, laugh, all of it, those are the things that paint the real picture of who someone is. It can work either way, but in Matt's case, it's too bad. He wasn't the guy for me, but he's much more appealing than that picture would lead you to believe."

"Did you come here just to piss in my punch bowl?"

"Oh, no. Thanks for reminding me. I have a question for you."

"I can't wait."

"Do you think anyone would notice if I died?"

"*What?*"

"I mean I know my brothers wouldn't, but do you think anyone else would?"

"Dude, we'd have to rent out the Shrine Auditorium for your stupid memorial service."

"I'm not fishing for compliments here; I'm asking you a serious question."

"And I'm being serious. All I have to do is throw up an announcement on MySpace."

"Very funny."

"Seriously. I've already got like four hundred friends."

"Those aren't *real* friends, Alice."

"*Really?*"

"Sad but true."

"You don't think I could call all four hundred of them in my darkest hour?"

"I don't even think you have their phone numbers."

"All right, I guess I'll just call you. So why are you freaking out about dying, anyway?"

"I'm not freaking out about dying. This is something else. This is fear of people getting my story all screwed up after I'm gone. So can you just do me one favor, I mean, if I do die?"

"Yeah, sure."

"Can you write me a really good profile?"

"*Profile?*"

"Profile, obituary, whatever you want to call it. Pack it with lies. Give me a hook. Use Matt's thing. I don't care. But whatever you do, don't let people think I was a poor, over-the-hill spinster cat-lady, because I'm not!"

"I know you're not."

"I have a lot in common with my live friends."

"I know you do!"

"And no shitty pictures!"

"Fine."

"Because once that stuff gets posted on the Internet, there's no retrieving it."

"Are we done?"

"Actually, there's one more thing. If I still don't have a boyfriend when I die, can you find me a good-looking necrophiliac? Just get him to come to the funeral and pose as my boyfriend. He can have his way with me after that. I won't have a soul anymore so it won't matter."

"How convenient," replied Alice. "Any idea where I might find this necrophiliac?"

"Oh, I think the answer's pretty obvious."

the last single woman
in america

I was at the beach the other day when someone asked me how old I was. I squinted my eyes. I mulled it over. "What year is it?" I finally asked. Of course, once that was established, I was able to compute my age with lightning speed.

Part of the problem is that I live in a place where there are no real seasons to denote the passage of time. It's just one big endless summer. Everyone cruises along in their convertibles thinking they've got nothing but time. Then one day a cold breeze blows in; a clammy hand taps them on the shoulder. Could it be . . . *winter?* No, babe, that's Death, and your big beach party's over. *Shit, how did that happen? Where did all those years go? I've been tricked. The leaves never even turned orange!*

Another part of the problem is that I lie about my age constantly, although, in my defense, I always lie up. When I was thirty-eight, I started telling people I was forty just so it wouldn't freak me out when it really happened. Now that I'm forty, I routinely tack on half a decade or so in an effort to elicit compliments. *Oh my god, you're forty-five! You look great!* To me, it makes a lot more sense than pretending to be thirty-five and having people talk about how I'm starting to look a little worn.

Oh, and people do talk. You can bank on it. Like Alice's dad once told me, "Never put yourself down. Someone else is already doing it for you."

And when you come from a place where people get married at

the age of eighteen, you better believe that the fact that you're forty and *still single* is something they talk about. I'm pretty sure half my extended family thinks I'm a lesbian. And frankly, I'm happy to let them think it. It's a lot better than trying to explain *why* I'm still single.

What I'm not happy about, however, are suggestions of girl-on-girl love coming from the mouth of a "man" who is just as old and just as single as I am, but who is living under the convenient delusion that it's cool to be a single man *no matter how old you are,* but if you're a single *woman* at the age of forty, there's got to be something wrong with you. Because you know what? Single can be cool regardless of age or sex, but single is never cool if the reason you're single is because you're too emotionally retarded to engage in a decent relationship with an equal. I don't care how much testosterone you've got coursing through your veins.

As evidence, I offer up a recent movie premiere. I, as usual, bowed out, unable to stomach any more glad-handing. The more I can ignore that aspect of the movie business, the easier it is for me to be a part of it. But Alice, she keeps on truckin'. Then she feels compelled to report back to me on all the bullshit I was trying to avoid in the first place.

At the premiere, Alice ran into this producer—a guy whose advances I've been rebuffing for the last fourteen years. Why? Well, for starters, I crave *human* interaction, and this guy is most definitely *not* human. He's an alien. And he's not even a sexy alien; he's just rich, which does nothing at all to light my fire. I'll never do what it takes to prove it, but I feel confident that were I to strip him down, I'd find both a battery receptacle and a smooth, plastic groin area, much like that of a Ken doll.

So there's that, and then there's the fact that he's emotionally retarded. But I mean really, if I'm going to engage with someone who's emotionally retarded—and I probably will because we *are* in the midst of an arrested development epidemic—then I'm going to make damn sure that he's both sexy *and* human. It's not going to be this weirdo. Not ever. I think I made that pretty clear fourteen years ago. Yet, whenever our paths cross, he makes me reject him all over again. He's like a boomerang. It makes me crazy. He's like some horrible accounting error, like a bill that you paid but never got credited to your account. And no matter how many times you call to deal with it, it never gets fixed and they just keep sending the bill over and over and over again.

Anyway, Alice went to the premiere and ran into the alien, who asked after me by way of a *kittenish* inquiry as to the whereabouts of her "other half." Honestly! Just because I would *rather* sleep with a woman than sleep with him, doesn't mean I *am* sleeping with women. And certainly not Alice.

But queerly enough, he's not alone in his assumptions. In fact, I've got the wedding invitations to prove it. Two names. One address. They're usually mailed to Alice's house.

Now, I know some people can't bear to go to a wedding without a date, but I ain't one of them. In forty years I haven't learned much, but out of necessity, I have learned how to handle a few basic power tools without losing a finger, and I have learned how to enter a room without someone holding my hand. And even if I hadn't, isn't the rule that if you're not invited *plus guest,* you're not supposed to bring a guest? And even if I didn't know the rules, wouldn't it be better to simply tell me not to bring a guest than to insult two people who mean enough to you to invite to your *wedding* by sending them a joint invitation?

When the third one came in the mail, Alice hit the roof. "Fuck 'em," she said, zinging the calligraphied invite into the shrubbery. "I'm not going."

The question is, which is worse? Inviting two straight women to your wedding as a lesbian couple, or seating the only one who

RSVPs at the Singles Table with a bunch of frat boys half her age?

So there I was sitting with seven guys ranging in age from twenty-three to twenty-eight, listening to one of them espouse his theory that the only girls worth dating are fives and sixes, and getting revenge the only way I could—by drinking for two. Apparently, any girl who's hotter than a six has mental issues and is more trouble than she's worth. But often, even sixes are too screwed up; you're better off with a five. He didn't get into why fours and below are unacceptable; I guess that was supposed to be self-evident.

It took everything I had not to tell him he was a three. And that was *before* he started talking.

The whole thing made me think of a poll I'd recently seen in some women's magazine. They had a bunch of women rate their physical appearance and something like 63 percent described themselves as above average, which seemed a little fishy to me, given the nature of the word *average*. The thing is, most women don't take compliments very well, and a lot of them proactively cut themselves down. So if all these women secretly think they're hot stuff, then why are they running around pointing out their flaws? Especially since, as far as I can tell, you set your own value. Other people just run with what you give them.

A girlfriend of mine was recently bemoaning the fact that she'd gained weight and felt uncomfortable being naked with a man. I told her to get over it. Nobody cares if you're ten pounds over-weight, as long as you're fun. In fact, I had a lot more suitors when I was twenty pounds heavier. Being thin is no guarantee of any-thing. Looking good isn't either. A male friend of mine recently quoted a guy who, upon breaking up with a supermodel—a woman most women would love to look like—said, "No matter how hot she is, you get tired of fucking her." So there you go. Maybe 13 percent of those polled women are really average. And if so, maybe they're better off. According to the jackass at my Singles Table, that's what guys want anyway.

I, on the other hand, wanted another glass of wine. I was on my way to the bar when the DJ called out for all the single women to come up to the dance floor for the bouquet toss. Naturally, I played deaf. But it got considerably harder to ignore what was happening when the hyperaggressive bride took me by the arm and dragged me onstage for all to see.

And there I stood, alone. Feeling not like a ten or an eight or a six or a four or a two or even human; feeling more like a two-headed cow, like some strange curiosity paraded out for others to gawk at. Wondering all the while why I didn't simply take Alice's lead and boycott the entire affair.

One hundred eyes bore holes through me; fifty pitiful smiles were cast my way. I hissed at the bride as she moved into position, "Just give me the goddamn bouquet and go to Tahiti already."

"You're not the only single girl," she chimed back, smiling brightly.

Just when I didn't think it could get any worse, another "single" joined me on the dance floor. She was, I don't know, three or four. Unlike me, she was thrilled to be in the spotlight. And unlike me, she had Down's syndrome.

While the bride dicked around with her princess costume, *commanding* her husband to fan the train out around her, I tried to wrangle my fellow single. All I wanted was for her to stand still so she could catch the stupid bouquet, but man was she slippery. To make matters worse, her mother was staring at me from the sidelines as if I were trying to abduct her precious child. Fine, I thought. If the bouquet comes my way, I'll just let it bounce right off me. She'll pick it up eventually.

Then I went back to watching the bride publicly humiliate her husband. The poor guy was on his knees, crawling around, desperately trying to please his master, who, from what I could tell, wanted to achieve some sort of Christmas tree skirt effect with her dress. But the thing was never going to form a perfect circle. That's not how it was cut. So every time the groom tugged at it the slightest bit in one direction, it gave somewhere else, ruffling his little lovebird's feathers all the more.

The whole thing was captured on video by some character who looked like he actually *did* abduct children in his free time. I thought the tape would make a nice piece of evidence during the divorce—irrefutable proof of abuse that it was—and made a mental note to tell the groom as much before leaving. And as I continued to watch, I started to wonder if maybe I wasn't just too nice to men. Maybe that was my problem. My friend Suzanne once told me that all men secretly think they're assholes, so it's important to treat them like assholes from time to time. According to her, it makes them feel understood. And well, she's married and I'm not, so maybe she's right.

But in front of God and everyone? At your own wedding? I don't think so. These two were definitely taking the whole S&M thing too far.

Once the bride was satisfied with the placement of her train, and looked to me like she was standing in a pool of Marshmallow Fluff, her castrato was dismissed. He quickly got off his knees and scurried out of the way. The bouquet was soon airborne. *And closing in on my face at a rapid rate!* I frantically reviewed my floral avoidance plan and found that it provided no instructions whatsoever should the thing be on a collision course with anything above my neck. And all this time I thought I'd make a great lawyer! How deluded was I? Where was my other half when I needed her most? Was her absence proof that she was also my smarter half? My own lack of a contingency plan certainly did nothing to challenge that notion. I couldn't bear the thought that Alice was smarter than me, but there was no time to convince myself otherwise. So I threw my hands up, figuring I'd just spike the bouquet into the arms of the competition. But no sooner were my mitts in the air than those wily flowers hung a left, nosediving into the butterfingers of my little rival, and leaving me looking like the kind of desperate asshole who'd actually try to snatch a bouquet away from a three-year-old with Down's syndrome!

Then, as if that wasn't embarrassing enough, she looked down at the flowers, looked up at me, and started crying. I couldn't believe it. *She dropped them!*

I momentarily considered reaching down and handing them back to her, but thought better of it when I saw her mother sprinting toward us. I headed back to the relative comfort of my Singles Table instead. And as I did, I wondered: *Smarter than me? Smarter than I?* Which was it? And would Alice be able to answer that question *with conviction?*

Returning to my post at the Phi Beta Butthead Table, I grabbed the fullest wineglass I could find and lifted it to my fraternity brothers. "Well, boys, it's been a long time coming, and tonight we can finally make it official: I am indeed *the last single woman in America*. Somebody get me a napkin and a notary public! This shit's going down in history."

"Screw that!" blurted out the guy who liked fives. "I'll marry your ass."

I couldn't help but laugh.

"That was awesome the way you nailed that kid with the bouquet!" he added.

Nailed that kid with the bouquet? "I hate to disappoint you, my friend, but I was framed."

"Really?"

"Really."

He shrugged. "That's all right, I'll marry you anyway."

"Thanks babe, *but I'm no five.*"

"You don't seem *that* screwed up."

"No more than anyone else, I don't think."

"Then why are you still single?" asked some ginger-headed guy.

And there it was, that burning question.

I looked at Ginger. I looked around the room. Why *was* I still single? What did these women have that I didn't? I mean, besides the obvious husbands and children.

I looked back at Ginger. "I have no idea," I replied.

"It was your choice," said the guy who liked fives.

"I suppose."

"If you could do it all again, would you make different choices?" asked another guy.

"Nothing major, that's for sure."

"Like I said, you're single by choice," repeated the guy who liked fives.

He was starting to bug me all over again. "Life isn't that simple."

"It's pretty simple," he countered.

"Not as simple as your theories."

"I'll second that," blurted out Ginger, saving the day.

"I stand by my theories," replied the guy who liked fives.

I wanted to ask him if he'd stand by them in a corner somewhere far, far away, but opted for the less antagonistic, "Can we just change the subject?"

Ginger was on it. He looked to me and said, "My girlfriend wants to get married, but I don't know if I'm ready."

With that, his friends all groaned, and in under a minute, it was just the two of us.

"Way to clear a table," I remarked.

"That was the goal. You want some more wine?"

I eyed Ginger. "Sure."

"So what do you think?"

"About what? You and your girlfriend?"

He nodded.

"I think I'm the last person on earth you should be going to for relationship advice, that's what I think."

"So I'll consider the source. Let's hear it."

"OK. Marriage. I think it's not enough to commit to a person. People change. You'll change. She'll change. I think for a marriage to really work, two people have to be committed not just to each other, but to the concept of marriage. People used to *have to* commit to that concept for a lot of reasons that no longer apply. But because we don't *need* each other in the same way anymore, I think the idea of committing to the concept has gotten lost. But I think we still need each other, and I think that for a marriage to work, you still have to commit to that concept as if you did, in fact, *need* that other person. Because shit happens, and at some point your relationship is going to be tested, and at that point, if you're not committed to something other than your mate—who you could want to throttle—if there's not something bigger than that other person keeping you there, the whole thing's doomed. So what do *you* think? Does the concept of marriage appeal to you?"

"Yeah, definitely. I'm gonna get married *one day,* there's no doubt in my mind about that, and I love my girlfriend, it's just that I'm only twenty-seven, and that's a big leap I'm not sure I'm ready to take. So I don't know. But I know I don't want to *not* get married just so I can sit around and wank off with these wankers for another ten years."

"Well, that's a start. And maybe you'll never *know* when to take the leap. Maybe you'll just have to guess. I have no idea. Maybe you're not supposed to think about this stuff so much. But I'm going to tell you something. It's not going to sound like much fun, but I assure you it's better than the alternative. Until you're ready to take the leap, whenever you're about to have sex, put on a condom. Then, when that's securely in place, put on another condom. Then, before the big moment, pull out. You got that? Wear *two* condoms *and* pull out. If I've only learned one thing of value in my entire life, that's it. And I can't even use it. I can only share it. How's that for a kick in the pants?"

Ginger stared back at me, slack-jawed. I lifted his chin back into place.

"You care to elaborate on that?" he asked.

"No. But trust me, darling, that's sage advice. Do that and you'll be saving yourself and everyone else involved a lot of heartache."

"I trust you."

"And don't waste too much time on the Internet, either," I added.

"I figured that much out on my own."

"Good."

"How old are you, anyway?" asked Ginger. "Thirty-five?"

I indicated upward with my thumb.

"Thirty-six?"

"Fifty-seven," I proclaimed proudly.

Ginger laughed. "Wow. You look *good*."

"*Good?*"

"*Great!*"

"Thanks, I do what I can."

"I like you," he said. "You're funny."

"Well, there you have it. Maybe that's why I'm still single. I read an article the other day clearly stating that men do *not* like funny women."

"Is that true?"

"I don't know," I replied. "You tell me."

Then Ginger looked straight into my eyes and said, "I already told you. I like you."

Holy shit! Was Ginger hitting on me? I looked at him. He looked at me. A shiver went up my spine. *A clammy hand tapped my bare shoulder.* Oh God, say it isn't so! I didn't dare turn my head, but my eyes zeroed in on the hand. If that was Death, he was way chunkier than I'd ever imagined.

"Excuse me," came a voice not unlike Peter Lorre's. "Were you in *Wes Craven's New Nightmare?*"

Was this really happening? I *was* in *Wes Craven's New Nightmare,* but not long enough for anyone to actually recognize me. It was mostly just a cleavage shot. *Who was this pervert?* I looked up. It was the videographer, getting a fresh shot of my cleavage with his own beady little pig eyes.

"Yeah," I replied, scooting out of his line of vision. "For about three seconds."

He smiled back. "I saw you on TV last night."

It creeped me out to no end. "Great. I guess that means I'll be getting a residual check soon."

"Can I get your autograph?"

"You can't possibly be serious."

And yet, he was. "You can just sign that napkin," he said.

"Oh no," I replied, grabbing my purse. "That's for an official document. We'll find something else. I just have to run to the bathroom first."

And off I ran to the bathroom. I just didn't stop there. I kept going, down the hall and through the exit. I felt bad about ditching Ginger, but such is life. He had a girlfriend, anyway.

Too intoxicated to get behind the wheel of my car, too sober to think I wasn't, and unable to bear the thought of an obituary announcing the death of The Last Single Woman in America, I chose to abandon my convertible and call Yellow Cab.

Sitting on the curb, awaiting my chauffeur, I tried to add it all up. But it's so hard when everything is knotted together, when you can't even pull the threads apart, when everything feels so connected. And it's not just Hollywood; it's bigger than that. I know, because online dating sites are springing up all over the place.

Wake up, read the paper, you've got to be tough just to do that and not be crushed under the weight of it all. Head out, drive past a thousand advertisements telling you how much happier you could be if you only had this thing. Arrive at work where everyone else has driven past those same advertisements, where everyone is trying to keep up with the Joneses, get ahead, have it all. You've got to be tough. You've got to be ready to get fucked over, ready to fight. You've got to keep your eyes on the prize, remember who's number one. You can't get caught up in anyone else's problems because they will only drag you down. And then we drive home and scream at everyone who isn't driving fast enough, slow enough, well enough; we go to the movies and cry in the dark, where it's still safe to be human.

A friend was telling me the other day how amazed he was when traveling through Cambodia because the people in these villages had so much less than we have here and yet they seemed so much happier. And I thought, yeah, because they're all they've got, they can't afford to put up walls, they need each other just to survive, they don't have time to think about all the things they don't have, or if they do, those things are so out of reach that they don't ever matter. Retail therapy isn't an option so they seek comfort the only way they can, through human connection. But does life have to be that hard in order for the things that matter to be sought and appreciated? And how do you remain open to human connection when you have to shut down just to survive? Sometimes I think a happy marriage is nothing less than a small miracle. We have so much and yet . . .

"Hey, heartbreaker," purred Ginger. "What ya doin'?"

I looked up and smiled. "Just trying to figure out what it all means, as usual."

"And the answer is?"

I shook my head. "The world is spooky enough. You don't need to be poking around in my brain."

"I'll take your word for it," replied Ginger. "You know, your boyfriend is still waiting. He really, really thinks you're coming back. He said he wants to marry you."

"He'll get over it."

"Yeah, you're probably right. I imagine he's had quite a bit of experience with that. You need a ride?"

"Nah, my spaceship should be touching down any minute to take me home."

"Spaceship? *Cool.* What's it like on your planet? Is everyone single?"

"Either that or I'm not. I'm not sure yet. I've never been."

Ginger smiled. "There are other single woman in America, you know."

"I know. Men, too."

"Things have gotten kinda fucked up, huh?"

"I don't know. I think they probably always were. They're just fucked up in a different way now."

Ginger nodded. "Well, it was really nice meeting you. Thanks for the advice."

"You're welcome. You want some more?"

"That's a tough call," said Ginger. "I'm still reeling from the last bit."

"I'll take that as a yes. Here it is: You can say *one day* and *some-*

day for a long time, but time can play tricks on you, and the longer you put things off, the easier it gets to keep putting them off, and the bigger and scarier they can become."

He squinted his eyes at me. "You mean, like my taxes?'

I smiled. I liked Ginger. If only he were ten years older and free of attachments. "Yeah," I replied, "like your taxes, but good things, too. We've made *codependent* a dirty word, but really it's not. It's nice to have someone to depend on, and to have someone depend on you. That kind of responsibility is good; it helps keep you from becoming a big, self-centered baby. There are a lot worse things than being alone, but I think there's something better than being alone, too."

"Sharing your life with someone?"

I nodded. "Don't do anything stupid, but if you've got a good girl and you think you can make it work, don't walk away from it just because you imagine some other grass might be greener. Grass is green, whether you're rolling around on it alone or with someone you love."

Ginger disappeared into the parking lot; I looked across the lawn and up at the trees. The grass was green; the leaves were, too. But I knew if I went to the Farmer's Market all the vegetables would be orange. Fall had come. And I was still single.

love

Other people might fall for it, but I'm rarely affected by onscreen romance. It's not that I'm heartless, it's just that I know that what *may* have begun as some earnest screenwriter's blood, sweat and tears, has almost certainly been futzed with by a team of development executives who have since perverted the very heart of that script, hiring as many rewriters as necessary to properly screw it up and slap a happy ending on it. It's true. I've seen it happen with my own eyeballs. I've probably done it. I'll probably do it again. God knows I can't keep an opinion to myself. That's why, when I write, I lock the whole world out and never show the final product to anyone I haven't known for ten years and whose mouth isn't sealed shut with duct tape. I'm not interested in hearing from the peanut gallery. This is *my* story.

But it's not just that. I watch a movie and half the time all I can think about are the countless butt-numbing hours everyone involved had to sit around waiting for the scene to even happen while someone important was misbehaving. The rest of the time I'm thinking about all the behind-the-screen crew members who were quietly sneaking off to the Craft Services table, and wondering if their on-set snacks were better than mine. It's hard to get sucked into the big romance when you know that not only did the people on that film probably get better snacks than you, the "lovers" in that film are getting paid boatloads of money to "love" each other. There's nothing real about it. Unless the "lovers" actually are lovers, which is to say, screwing around offscreen, but even then, sex isn't love, so who the hell knows?

Music, on the other hand, sucks me in.

Music is my whirlpool. And unlike movies, it doesn't require that you drive to a theater, sit on a couch, or even look at it. You can dance to it, naked, in your own kitchen, with your eyes closed. It's just there, enveloping you in all its heart-wrenching beauty, coming at you straight from the source. That's where the real drama is.

As evidence, I offer up my two latest musical obsessions:

Exhibit A: Ray LaMontagne's *Trouble*

Exhibit B: Richard Ashcroft's *Alone with Everybody*

If you don't have them, get them. Or just hang around in my driveway with Tomas. Both CDs are in heavy rotation over here, blasting through the windows. I mean why do it when you can overdo it? And not only do I listen to the stuff ad nauseam, I pore over the lyrics as if I were cramming for the LSAT.

I'd walk one mile on broken glass just to fall down at your feet? *Yes, please.*

At first I wondered if depth of feeling was a trait peculiar to musicians, then I remembered that I'm not a musician, and, oh, yeah, CDs aren't recorded and pressed exclusively for me either; zillions of other people around the world are feeling the pain, hope, sadness and joy; being moved, or at least moved to buy the CDs, just like me. And I don't even know how anyone could possibly read music. To me it just looks like the scribblings of a madman.

So I ask you, if everyone's feeling the same things and looking for the same thing, then why is love so hard to find? I know we've put some obstacles in the way, but isn't love supposed to conquer all?

Plagued by these very questions, I headed over to Alice's house, making a pit stop at my local gas station. The attendant is an East Indian man named Fred. I would have preferred something a little more exotic, but there you have it. Nevertheless, he's super nice and I love to hear him speak—that Indian cadence just makes me smile—so we usually chat while I'm filling 'er up.

But not this time.

Arriving at the gas station, I spotted Fred in the cigarette hut. I waved to him, and the next thing I knew, he was standing beside me, letter in hand. A wordless moment passed. Then he handed me the letter and returned to his post.

Only it wasn't just any letter; it was a *love* letter—a love poem, to be exact. Three full pages of handwritten rhyming couplets, offered to me as if it were nothing, as if it were a coupon for $2 off my next car wash. But reading it, I was struck by the thought that it was, quite possibly, the purest love letter I'd ever received—not in content so much as in the gift itself. I could call Fred's act courageous, but I think doing so would cheapen the spirit in which the letter was given. It seemed to be given simply for the joy of giving, without fearing, or even knowing, that it could be received as anything other than a gesture of fondness and admiration. His letter exposed my own fears and shortcomings in its eye-squinting radiance. It humbled me. And while I couldn't return Fred's feelings, I was filled with gratitude, for he had reminded me, right here, in the heart of Bullshit Central, that expressing one's feelings should never engender shame, that only a fool would ever laugh at sincerity and kindness.

Mercifully, Fred was busy with another customer when I looked back toward his hut. I don't even think he noticed when I blasted out of there, panic-stricken, nearly taking his nozzle with me.

What the hell was going on? Who was this quixotic Indian man stepping out of the shadows of a gas station? Why did he think I was a gift from Almighty? Did I really have a voice as sweet as honey? Where did he get the *samosas* to fork over a letter like that? Was he supposed to be my man, or was he just a sign, sent to me to reveal that some men actually *are* pure of heart? And if he was supposed to be my man, how the hell was I going to get out of it?

I arrived at Alice's house, desperate for guidance, only to learn that my problems were going to have to take a backseat to a much more immediate crisis of her own. Billy, an ex-boyfriend, had beaten me to the punch, landing on her doorstep that morning—coming down, crashing hard, but still very much out of his mind. Ah well, these things happen. Perhaps to Alice more often than most, but that's only because she has not yet learned how to turn her back on the pain of others. And certainly not when the pain in question is someone she once loved. Yanking me into her house, Alice quickly informed me that Billy was heading off to rehab in two days. Although, judging by the looks of him, he'd obviously felt compelled to polish off everything in his possession before then. It was not a pretty sight. And he didn't smell too good, either.

After being told by Billy for the *fifteenth time* that everything happening was top secret and no one was supposed to know that he was going to rehab, I started to lose patience.

"All right already, so stop telling me," I said. "I would have forgotten by now."

The guy could barely speak, and yet he was repeatedly able to gain command of his motor skills just long enough to announce that I'd proposed to him a year ago. It was a little uncomfortable, given that this alleged proposal occurred when he and Alice were together. It would have been *really* uncomfortable, if not for the fact that it was complete hogwash.

At first I thought he was just trying to make trouble. Because he was so insistent, I surrendered to the idea that he actually believed what he was saying, and ultimately acknowledged the possibility that I may have asked him to marry me *as a joke*. But I know I never asked him seriously. I didn't even want Alice going out with him. Be that as it may, he remembered a sincere proposal, and he wouldn't drop it.

"So tell me, was I down on one knee when I popped the question?" I asked.

While Billy's eyes glazed over, presumably in an attempt to review his mental image of the event, I turned to Alice, assuring her that he had the story *all wrong*. She took a drag off her cigarette and shrugged.

"He might not even believe it himself," she said. "He could have come up with it when you walked in the door. Sometimes he just makes up lies on the fly."

Suddenly, Billy was back with the living, and ready to furnish some important details. According to him, the big proposal had taken place . . . at a friend's wedding. *Uh-oh!* A wedding—the perfect setting for senseless behavior to be sure, and yet, I managed to hang in there, suggesting that perchance I'd mistaken him for my old Viking, who was also at the wedding. Although they look nothing alike, and I wouldn't marry either of them. But Billy refused to accept defeat. Over and over again, he accused me of wearing an amazing dress near a swan-filled pond. While over and over again, I attempted to explain to him that those facts did *nothing* to support his claim that I really wanted him to be my husband, but he wouldn't shut up. Instead, he laughed triumphantly, like a bear swooping down on a salmon that was never getting upstream. *Swim little fishy. Ha! Ha! Ha!*

Alice, of course, found it all wildly amusing. "If you really want him," she said, "you can have him now."

Then Billy repeated the entire idiotic tale all over again.

"You're looping," said Alice.

Apparently, he'd been doing this all day.

"He's got about five stories that he repeats over and over and over," added Alice. "Just ignore him."

"Ignore him? How can you ignore him? He's infuriating! I don't know how you think you're going to get through forty-eight hours of this."

"I'm not," replied Alice. "He's going to his parents' house tomorrow morning."

"So why would you wear an amazing dress if it wasn't a special occasion?" belted out Billy, thinking he'd finally caught me.

Thankfully, Alice stepped in at that point reminding him that is *was* a special occasion. It was a wedding. Then I reminded them both that the old Viking was there with his *new girlfriend*—not just someone he was sleeping with, but an actual girlfriend, whom I'm assuming he called more than once a week. I certainly didn't go to the trouble of making myself look like a goddess just so I could propose to someone else's ex-clown. I had much bigger fish to fry. I had a bruised ego on my hands. So what if I didn't want the Viking back; that didn't mean I didn't want him to want me back.

No one debated Billy's claim that he hadn't bathed in a week. Instead, Alice confirmed his fear that he looked like shit, at which point Billy immediately began touting the wonders of volumizing shampoo. For some reason, he was convinced that everything would be A-OK if his hair were just a little fluffier. When I suggested that it might take more than the right shampoo to cure what ailed him, he responded by bursting into big, heaving sobs and declaring—*for the eighth time*—that he'd been doing blow for the last thirty days straight.

"We know!" Alice and I replied in unison.

He claimed he hadn't slept for as long, but I'm not even sure that's physically possible. And really, what difference did it make? He was awake now, and suddenly laughing his head off, while talking about how ashamed he was to have us see him like this because we knew him when he was normal.

"*We did?*" I replied. But mostly I was just baffled by his shame. We both knew people who'd been doing blow for the last ten *years* straight, and bragged about it. We both knew people who had pretended to be alcoholics and joined AA just to make friends. In Los Angeles, going to rehab is *nothing* to be ashamed of. It's practically a badge of honor. Alice and I assured him that being a drug addict wasn't a very unique problem. Billy, in turn, insisted that the future of the planet rested on his shoulders.

"Before you save the world," said Alice, "would you mind wiping the drool off my chair?"

When Billy finally spoke, it was to proclaim that Alice was an angel. It was a huge promotion, given some of the things he'd called her when they were breaking up, but in addition to that, it came with a million dollar bonus! She just had to wait until he was out of rehab and back in the workforce to collect.

"What about me?" I asked. "Don't I get anything?"

"Cindy," he mumbled, "every time you speak, I love you more and I hate you more."

"That's cool," I replied. "But what exactly does that translate to in terms of hard, cold cash?"

And to that, Billy replied, "Can I have a glass of wine?"

For the first time all night, neither Alice nor I had a comeback. Here was someone who had been doing blow for the last month, but who'd been an alcoholic for *way* longer than that. Alice felt especially conflicted about the request because, as it turned out, this was all her doing. Billy had called her two days earlier, at which point she'd phoned his family to get the rehab ball rolling.

"But I'm not a doctor," said Alice. "I don't know what'll happen if he just goes cold turkey."

"Well, I guess we can either let him have a glass of wine or you can get all your belts out and we can prepare to restrain his convulsing body in a few hours," I replied.

"I wish he wasn't asking. Last night I found him in the kitchen at 3:00 A.M., chugging a bottle of vodka. At least I didn't have to give him permission."

Last night!?! I swear, nobody tells me anything, but before I could get into that, Billy interrupted our conversation to apologize for stealing vodka and mumble something new.

"What did he just say?" I asked.

"He's just mumbling. Don't worry about it," replied Alice.

Then I told him to shush, and he did. Just like that. I turned back to Alice.

"I guess we should let him have a little, but can't we get something out of it?"

We both turned to Billy. *What on earth could we possibly get out of him?* While we were wondering, he sniffed his armpit. It was immediately decided that he could have one glass of wine in exchange for taking a bath. Billy nodded in agreement, got up off the chair and walked straight into a wall.

"Fuck," he shouted.

"Sit down," instructed Alice. "We'll be with you in a minute."

At that point, Billy crumbled to the ground, only to lean his head against the wall, plant his eyes on me, and blurt out, "You got seriously fucked over when you got fired."

I couldn't believe my ears. He was right, and he knew it because he used to work at a law firm that handled a lot of the exiting executives, but why the hell was he bringing it up now, five years after the fact? And why did the one thing he had to say that made any sense at all have to do my misfortune?

"She's fully aware of that," replied Alice.

"No," he continued, "I mean *seriously* fucked over. Everyone else made out like bandits."

"Thank you," I replied. "I know that. And yet I'm the one who was sexually harassed for years on end. Isn't life funny?"

Billy started laughing again, and Alice cast a grave look my way. "He can't bathe himself," she said. "He'll drown."

"You're the one who slept with him."

"You're my best friends!" Billy called out from the floor.

"That was a long time ago," said Alice. "And you're the one who wanted to marry him."

I looked at Alice. She looked at me. A stare-off ensued. I couldn't deny her request, but I was pretty sure I could get something out of it. My wheels were turning.

Finally, I said, "You're taking me to dinner at Lucques if I do this."

"You can both do it," offered Billy.

"Pipe down," I called back.

"Fine," said Alice, "but you're getting something off the bar menu. I don't want you ordering that $44 steak just to be an asshole."

"You know I love that steak. I would never order it *just* to be an asshole."

Alice shook her head. "You're not getting it. Bar menu."

"Nuh-uh, no bar menu. How about Sunday Supper? It's prix fixe."

"Deal."

I told Alice I wasn't going below the neck. She told me she wasn't going below the waist. I suggested we get Marcus to do the spooky bits. Billy repeated that we were the only two people who could *ever* know. And I nodded my head, certain that he'd send out a mass e-mail cheerfully announcing his fall from grace the minute he could type.

"The top half is better than nothing," said Alice. "His mom can do the rest tomorrow."

Billy sat on the toilet (seat down) as Alice drew a bath and I mentally prepared for what was to come. It's not every day you see someone else's obliterated ex-boyfriend naked, after all.

Clothes fell to the ground; Billy placed his foot in the tub. First the water was too cold; then it was too hot. Finally, Alice told him that he was getting a bath from two hot chicks and to quit complaining.

"Don't tell him that!" I screamed. "I don't want him remembering this. Let him focus on the reward."

At that point, Billy blurted out *"Volumizing shampoo!"* having apparently forgotten about the wine entirely.

I asked Alice if she had any volumizing shampoo, but she didn't. I was flabbergasted. Every party/premiere/charity function in Hollywood is sponsored by someone. You can't leave your house without being handed a swag bag. I myself have enough shampoo and conditioner to last a lifetime just from going to parties, and even though I don't go to nearly as many parties as Alice, I'm pretty sure at least one of those shampoos is volumizing shampoo.

"This is good enough," said Alice, handing me some highlighting shampoo for blondes.

"But his hair is practically black!" I protested.

"Tough."

I began washing Billy's hair. It was incredibly slick. "He feels like a seal or an otter or something," I commented to Alice, prompting Billy to clap his hands and emit seal noises, which in turn prompted Alice to stick a rubber ducky in his flippers. Meanwhile, I continued on the path to nowhere.

"This stuff isn't even penetrating the oil," I whined. "You got any Tide?"

A spasmodic fit ensued. Billy completely wigged out at the mention of laundry detergent touching his tender locks.

"*Are you kidding?*" I asked. "You've been doing blow for a month and you're worried about *your hair?*"

"Would you rather this end?" asked Alice.

I checked out her end. She'd been washing his feet for ten minutes. They were spotless. She was just afraid to start moving up his legs. There wasn't a chance in hell that we were switching ends.

"You guys are beautiful," said Billy.

"Did you give him Ecstasy?" I asked.

Alice gave me the finger.

Then, the phone rang. Happily abandoning my role as shampoo girl, I fled the bathroom and grabbed it, only to be "greeted" by Billy's mother, which is to say, she promptly demanded that I inform her who I was and what I was doing there, insisting that I was never to tell anyone about what was happening, and making it clear that the apple hadn't fallen far from the tree. She wanted to talk to Billy, but I told her he was taking a bath. She wanted to talk to Alice, but I told her Alice was out getting Advil. When I returned to the bathroom, Billy was telling Alice that he really didn't want to go to rehab, and Alice was insisting that he really did.

"Everything's under control," I announced. "Billy's mom said all he needs is some warm Ovaltine. I'm going to call Betty Ford to share the good news."

Billy then proclaimed that he'd be happy with Tang, because that's what astronauts drink! Alice, in turn, informed him that he wasn't an astronaut. And Billy started crying all over again. Incredible. I wondered if that much drama lurked beneath every stoic male veneer.

Next up, Billy began singing Alice's praises, and talking about how she was the only person in the world who understood him. Forget rehab, he just wanted to stay at her house.

"Are you going to help me out here?" asked Alice.

Help? How could I? The highs, the lows; I was emotionally exhausted. Grabbing at straws, I said to Billy, "Look, rehab doesn't look like much fun right now because you're comparing it to being bathed by two girls, but I have a feeling that after spending twenty-four hours with your mother, you'll be chomping at the bit to go to rehab."

With that, Billy bolted upright and screamed, "I can't go home!" Then he fell right back down, and I just about busted my kneecap trying to catch his head before it hit the porcelain.

I turned to Alice. "Maybe you should just let him stay here until he checks in. It isn't *that much* longer."

"Will you shut up," she replied.

"Babe, I'll shut up *and go home*."

Of course, once I said that, she was my best friend.

As Alice was repositioning Billy in the bathtub, I heard her whimper. "He's getting an erection." I lowered my gaze to water level just in time to see his penis rise above the bubbles.

"It's a miracle!" I proclaimed. "All those drugs, all that booze, *and he can still get it up!* Maybe I was wrong. Maybe you shouldn't have broken up with him."

Alice handed Billy the soap and told him to finish himself off, then she reminded me that she didn't break up with him. He dumped her.

"Wow," I replied.

"Yeah, wow," said Alice.

"I'm going to rehab and you two are the only people who know!" added Billy.

Alice headed into the kitchen to get herself a glass of wine, and eventually we all made our way back into the living room. Billy was wrapped up in a puffy, white robe, looking like a guest at the short bus spa, but now that he'd earned his reward, he only wanted warm milk.

"This is tragic," said Alice.

"You're telling me," I replied. "He'll probably meet all kinds of interesting new people at rehab while we're stuck here with the same old crew. I may need drugs to deal with that reality."

"That was the best bath ever," interjected Billy. "I love you guys!"

"Glad you liked it," I replied. "Disappear for another few years then come on back. I'm sure Alice'll take you in."

And suddenly, tears were streaming down Alice's face, because the truth is, she would. Love's just like that.

I got up to heat some milk, and on the way I passed a painting on Alice's wall—a painting of a woman and a dog, alone on a playground. Obsessed with a band called Gomez, I'd dragged Alice to an artist's studio outside of London a few years earlier. The artist's name was Reggie Pedro and, in the beginning, his paintings were used for all of Gomez's CD covers. Alice fell in love with the painting and bought it on the spot. Looking at it now, a few lines from a Gomez song unexpectedly sprang to mind:

> *And when it's all been said and done*
> *It's the things that are given, not won are*
> *The things that you want*

And with those words playing in my head, it dawned on me that what at first glance appeared to be nothing more than an inconvenience was actually a gift—a well-disguised, foul-smelling gift, but a gift nonetheless. It dawned on me that by seeking shelter in Alice's home and exposing himself to her in his most vulnerable state, Billy was in effect acknowledging her incredible capacity for compassion. And it dawned on me that the opportunity to taste love, regardless of form, should never be shied away from or shunned, regardless of the giver.

Standing there, I suddenly found myself feeling so heartbreakingly fortunate for having stumbled into their beautiful mess, instead of spending yet another night in Hollywood listening to people talk about another movie falling apart, another actor holding up production, another rewrite not coming in as expected, but oh, how absolutely fabulous they are otherwise. And I don't want to sound cynical, but I don't know where honesty ends and cynicism begins either. I want to believe that all people are basically good, but it's so hard to know what anyone's ever really feeling inside, and nearly impossible when everyone's desperate to be a part of the same stupid club. The casualties are far easier to understand; they've had everything stripped away.

Returning to the living room, I found Alice and Billy gazing into each other's eyes. I wondered if she was looking for the guy she used to love, or if she still saw him sitting right in front of her. I had no idea what he was looking at, or if he could even see. But all of the sudden his face lit up, as he smiled at Alice, and said, "You look like a rainblow."

"That's nice," I added. "That's almost like a rain*bow*."

I handed Billy a mug. "It's not Ovaltine, but I melted a Hershey's Kiss in there and mixed it around."

"Dude," he replied. "You got *seriously* fucked over."

Moved by the night's events, I went home, thanked God for allowing me to share walls with an eighty-five-year-old deaf woman, cranked the stereo, and sang louder than David Bowie and Freddy Mercury *combined*. The blinds went down. My clothes came off. I danced into the kitchen and popped a few of *the most amazing Italian cookies* into my mouth, thanking God for those, too. Then, once I was all danced out, I sat down and wrote Fred a letter, thanking *him* for his letter thanking me for a gift I didn't even know I'd given him, because more than anything, his letter had thanked me for brightening his days and restoring his faith in humanity. That's what floored me—partly because I felt unworthy, partly because it was the same goddamn thing that I had been completely unable to do when faced with Dave Matthews, and partly because he made it look so simple. So while I'll admit that I fudged a bit in the section about how our love could never be because my boyfriend would scour the globe crawling through broken glass to find me were I to ever leave him, I'd like to believe that my heartfelt appreciation eclipsed that.

I dropped the letter off the following morning.

A few days later, I returned to the gas station. Fred was outside sweeping when I arrived; he looked up and smiled. It was a big, bright, genuine smile that instantly let me know that there were no hard feelings. My letter had been well received.

Putting his broom aside, Fred said, "I wondered if you weren't afraid to come back."

But his voice was different somehow—softer, less lyrical, perfectly content; it caught me off guard, not so much stripping me of my defenses, as dissolving all need for them. And left behind was nothing but this pure overwhelming emotion. There was no thought. There were no obstacles. There was only this strange dreamlike moment that held everything within its embrace. I may have stopped breathing.

"You know," he added, "I can take you as a friend. I never expected anything more." Then he placed his hand on his heart and said, "It was just something from in here that I wanted to share with you. I think you're a very special person and I want you to have a happy life."

I smiled at Fred. "I knew that," I replied. "That was the most beautiful part."

As I spoke, I heard my voice cracking. My brain was switching back ON. I suddenly felt, I don't know, like an astronaut reentering the earth's atmosphere? Out of sorts, out of place, scared, exposed. I didn't understand what was happening.

I kissed Fred on the cheek, hopped into my getaway vehicle and got away just as fast as I could. I'm still not sure why. What was there to run from? It was one of the most intimate, spiritual moments of my entire life, and it was all so beautiful—strange, but beautiful. Standing at an Exxon station in front of a five-foot-tall Indian man I knew nothing about other than the fact that he was addicted to off-track betting, I had experienced something that I'd only experienced once before, during mind-blowing sex. For just one fleeting moment, I actually saw God in another human being.

And I say *God* because I don't know what else to call it. But it's not about any one god or religion or what you do or don't believe in—it just is. And it's bigger and more powerful than any concept or construct that can be explained or understood. It can't be. It can only be experienced, at which point it can no longer be denied. And if you've never experienced it, *I know* it probably sounds as ludicrous as I think it sounds when people tell me about their interactions with ghosts. But there are these moments in life, these rare ephemeral moments, wherein you lose all sense of Me, and are suddenly aware of being completely connected, not just to one other person, but to all of humanity and the entire universe. I don't know enough about birth or death to say for sure, but I strongly suspect that the time surrounding both events would be fertile ground for such an occurrence, although I think it happened to Alice once when she was giving a homeless woman a pedicure, so you just never know. And it's not something you really talk about because it sounds so kooky and who's to say what someone else experienced. But what I do know is that when it does occur, it is an absolute blessing. And if you're like me, it's also a curse. I learned that much the last time around. Because it allows you a glimpse of what could be, which not only gives you something to aspire to, but something to judge everything else against. But maybe there's no room for judgment within it; maybe judgment only serves to obscure it. Maybe that's why it's so resistant to capture. Maybe it can only be aspired to. Maybe it's not meant to be anything other than a reminder, like the water bottle handed off to the marathon runner when hope is waning and all might otherwise seem for naught.

But alone in my car, sobbing uncontrollably, as I came crashing back down to earth still half caught in the embrace of that *thing* that I still cannot name, I knew instantly, and with absolute certainty, that despite the lack of romance in my life, despite what was happening in any one life at any point in time, love wasn't that hard to find. It's out there, always and everywhere. Even in the most unlikely places.

simon says

Simon says he's never been in love. I gaze back and wonder how it can be that this forty-year-old man could have never been in love, given that I myself have been in love oodles of times. Then he asks me what being in love feels like and I suddenly find myself groping in the dark, stumbling around as I search for an explanation that will make sense—not just to him, but to me. I've spent a great deal of my life trying to figure out what love is, but none of what I've come up with seems to truly apply to the concept of being *in love*.

I once saw a movie called *All the Real Girls*. In it there's a scene involving a boy and a girl, in which the girl is talking, flirting, and doing so with ease and abandon. Watching it moved me to tears. There was nothing particularly sad about the scene, except that I felt like I was seeing it all through a pane of glass. The innocence, the honesty and openness with which she expressed herself, was something I knew so well but at the same time felt I would never again experience. Something that I thought belonged to the young, something that I thought I was too damaged, and therefore too closed off, to ever know again, something that I could see but not touch.

Then I met Simon.

Looking at him sitting across from me, as he waits for me to string together words that might magically define the indefinable, I want to ask him how he feels *right now*, and then, no matter what he says, I want to smile my most mischievous smile and inform him that *that* is what being in love feels like. That's what the girl in the movie would do. She'd say it without thinking; it would be weightless and endearing. But I stop myself. Then I wonder if there really is some magic that exists in every moment just waiting to be unleashed, some magic that I've simply chosen to ignore again and again in order to protect my own bruised heart. I wonder if innocence is ever really lost, or if it's something that we simply tuck away once life teaches us that the price we have to pay for it is just too high.

For quite some time now, my life has been void of romantic illusions, which I guess is both ironic and tragic, given that I'm a hopeless romantic. But there I was, in all my conflicted glory, flipping burgers at a friend's barbecue, when Simon appeared, poolside. He recently asked me to pinpoint the precise moment in time when I knew I liked him. What was that moment? Was there *one moment?* He was like a magnet to me from the very first; something about him just made me happy. Otherwise, I'd have found the idea of going for a swim downright laughable. It was 10 P.M. No one else was swimming. There were two twenty-five-year-old Playmates in the pool, but they were just frolicking near the fringe. So I guess if I had to pick a single moment, it would be the moment that I rose up like a zombie and headed off to the bathroom to change into a bikini.

No, that wasn't it. It was actually the moment that I walked back *out* of the bathroom and into a throng of fully clothed people. That's when I realized that everyone and everything else had ceased to matter, that my life had suddenly been reduced to a single objective: being near Simon. So I made my way back through the crowd, entered the pool, waded past the Playmates, and got just as near to him as I could.

I was so happy in that pool with Simon, as he carried me around, protecting me from the imaginary sharks. Or maybe he was the shark. I don't remember. I just remember laughing, not a care in the world.

In the days that followed, I found myself thinking about something that happened long ago, when I was maybe seven years old. I was with my mom and we were dropping my little brother off at day care. When he realized that he was being left behind, he became hysterical. Then later, when we returned, we asked if he'd settled in OK and were informed that after no more than five minutes he'd forgotten all about us and become the life of the party. We walked outside and found him swinging happily on a jungle gym. He was having a great time. Then he saw us. In that one moment, it all came rushing back to him. He remembered what he'd lost. He burst into tears and ran into my mother's arms as fast as he could.

Having thought that innocence was lost to me, it was with great surprise that I found myself feeling so young and free and fearless with Simon. And in much the same way that a certain song can become inextricably linked to a specific time and mood, Simon is now inextricably linked to the return of innocence. I thought I was doing just fine without it, but now that it's reappeared like the Ghost of Christmas Past, I'm finding myself feeling oddly emotional. Sometimes when I see Simon, I want to burst into tears and run into his arms. The other night I did.

In fact, now that innocence has returned, I'm finding myself doing all kinds of odd things—allowing Simon to read stuff I've written, listening to his comments, believing him when he tells me I should be sending my work to publishers, *agreeing to write this essay for him about what it feels like to be in love*. And I've only known Simon for four weeks! But I feel at home with him. He's got a good heart and an easy laugh, that seems to be doing the trick, and I'm not questioning it. Now that innocence has returned, I'm finding myself truly appreciating what a magical thing it is, and I'm finding myself both willing and wanting to pay the price for it. It's not that I'm no longer afraid; it's just that I'm suddenly a lot less afraid and feeling totally, happily up to the challenge of fighting through the fear that remains. Maybe that's not true innocence, maybe that's just renewed optimism, but it feels better than that, and *the return of innocence* sounds so much more romantic.

So how do you describe being in love? It's illogical and therefore defies rational explanation. I'm pretty sure it's a temporary form of insanity brought on by a weird chemical reaction that's been cleverly designed to trick people into agreeing to spend the rest of their lives together. It's a nice idea, locking in someone who'll *have to have sex with you,* even when you're one hundred years old and incontinent, but clearly it's not the kind of thing most sane people would willingly agree to, given that it involves risking several decades in the hope that you'll receive the full return on your investment, which to be fair, includes not only geriatric sex, but a live-in funeral planner who's willing to change your diapers until you're ready for the big dirt nap. This, I'm fairly certain, is the reason being in love was invented. The fact that I have little-to-no interest in seeing anyone I've been in love with ever again gives credence to the notion that it is, indeed, a temporary condition.

Oh, and how great the temptation to redefine terms once the heart-shaped glasses come off! I mean, who wants to admit that they were in love with someone who didn't love them back, someone who dumped them, or worse, someone they now wouldn't touch with a ten-foot pole? It's far less painful and embarrassing to simply rename it delusion, dysfunction, or the all-inclusive *immaturity.*

Finding myself "doubting" whether I'd ever actually been *in love,* I tested my immaturity defense on Stephanie, who responded by saying, "Are you kidding? Would you tell a five-year-old who's reading *Dick and Jane* that it isn't *really* reading because it's not *War and Peace?* Like it or not, you've been in love."

So if Stephanie's right, I guess being in love sort of feels like you've just landed in Oz. Black and white turns to color; the mundane is suddenly infused with magic and meaning. It's a state of euphoria that, while under its spell, allows us to believe that someone has arrived to replace all the black clouds with endless sunshine and edible rainbows.

Now, in my experience, that's never actually come to pass. I've never eaten a rainbow. However, by feeling that way for even a brief time, we are filled with hope and possibility, driven to pay closer attention to the object of our desire, and, in the best case scenario, able to penetrate the superficial and find the universal—which I believe is the very pain and suffering we are so keenly aware of in ourselves—resulting in a connection that provides a reason to stay once the state of being *in love* subsides.

But maybe it's easier to think of being in love as a glance at a crystal ball, and into a future where we have everything we need, although, again, it's not true. At least, no one can do that for you. And it's ridiculous, because all these lies and tricks that were designed to get us to love only serve to make love itself seem highly suspicious.

The good news is that I actually think we already have within us everything we need to be everything we could ever be. So forget about being in love, and just think of the object of desire. Think of that person as salt. Because the right person can bring things out in us that might otherwise go undiscovered and unrealized, in the same way that salt is able to release and enhance the flavors that already exist in a roasted lamb, an heirloom tomato or just about anything else. And that being the case, it's really no surprise that salt is the number-one spice in the world.

Unfortunately, when I mentioned to Simon that I thought being in love was a temporary state too intense to be maintained indefinitely and that its main purpose was to get us to plain old love, which actually is sustainable, he said he'd have to think that over. But the way he said it led me to believe that he thought I was *totally off base*. It hardly seemed fair, him contradicting me, when by his own admission he didn't have a clue, but the most disturbing part was my sudden realization that he wasn't going to just swallow any convenient self-serving definition of love I fed him.

Of course, I still think I'm right. You can't live off fairy dust forever—walking around with your head in the clouds and doodling hearts in a notebook when there are bills to pay, things to do. It's completely impractical. Unless you're independently wealthy, you have to fall out of love. But that doesn't mean you won't fall back in. Love isn't perfectly linear; the heart does whatever the hell it damn well pleases. There's no set order in which these things must occur. Sometimes they even occur individually.

On the one hand, you've got people in love with being *in love*. These people allow themselves to be swept away, but once the euphoria wears off, they lose interest and look for someone else to fall in love with. This, I'm fairly confident, requires a lethal dose of projection and an almost complete lack of self-awareness. At least that's been my experience, and like I said, I've been in love oodles of times. For these people, falling in love is but a needle to the vein, a temporary retreat from an otherwise unpleasant existence that is inevitably followed by both a loud crashing sound and a desperate scramble for another fix. These people may never pass Go, collect $200 or progress beyond being *in love*.

On the other hand, you've got family, a group that frequently includes people with whom you have zero chemistry, people you might never willingly choose to pay attention to long enough to find a way to love. And yet, often even in the face of great personal resistance, you do mysteriously find yourself loving them. Why? Because you're stuck in close quarters with them for years on end. They're in your face. No matter how much you try to avoid them, no matter how much they try to avoid you, eventually you're all exposed for who and what you are. You see their bad behavior, but you also see the pain that produces it. You understand them. Empathy begets compassion and the next thing you know, they've got you.

Thinking about all this, I began to wonder if, in the past, Simon simply hadn't been paying attention, or had perhaps even actively resisted falling in love. Maybe something happened to make Simon fear love. I don't know what Simon's specific issues are and I gave up my junior psychiatrist license years ago when I realized how much effort all that analysis required and how infrequently I produced anything that even remotely resembled an accurate diagnosis. But he is human, and we're all broken. Maybe that's why we so often seem to stand in the way of love.

I once had a fight with someone over a package of brown gravy, although it wasn't actually a fight; it was more of an attack. I'd been seeing this guy for a few months; it was Super Bowl Sunday. I was cooking dinner for him and his friends when I ran out of chicken stock, which I needed in order to make gravy. I wanted to walk down to the store. He insisted that I use the powdered gravy mix he had in his pantry. I told him I'd prefer to make my own

gravy, and, well, that did it. The next thing I knew he was screaming in my face about how I made him feel low-rent and nothing
he did was good enough for me, which was completely absurd
because the first time I went to his house and got a glimpse of his
walk-in closet, I had a full-on anxiety attack. My own closet is the
size of a thimble and stuffed to the gills and I felt certain that
someone with a large, well-organized closet would never consider
me worthy. Yet here he was using a ninety-nine-cent pack of gravy
as a metaphor for our entire relationship. I was completely bewildered. Then as I watched his face turn bright red, it slowly dawned
on me that he had mistaken me for his mother. But how could that
be? We'd slept together. Fearing what I might discover along that
path of reasoning, I grabbed my iPod, plugged it into my ears and
walked to the store. Along the way, I realized that the brown gravy
incident, while somewhat comical in and of itself, was actually
indicative of a far greater problem: He'd stopped seeing *me*. Oh,
I think he saw me just fine in the beginning. It's easy enough to
put your baggage aside when faced with something shiny and new.
But once the initial fascination wears off, past injustices and
betrayals can move in pretty quickly and start clouding one's vision.
I thought about the things I'd heard about his mother, and about
past girlfriends; I thought about how eerily similar they all sounded;
and I realized that I too was being lumped in with them. I'd been
erased and replaced by the evil cardboard cutout that he seemed
to consider a suitable stand-in for *any woman*. So it would appear
that carry-on baggage, much like a sharp poke to the eye, causes
blindness.

Another great way to keep love at bay is by not revealing too
much of yourself. That way, no matter how much someone claims
they love you, it's easy enough to convince yourself that it isn't *real*
love. It can't be real love if they don't *really* know you, and they
can't *really* know you without your consent and participation. In

the past, this was my favored method of avoidance. It allows you to give of yourself without ever feeling that you're getting anything back. It breeds resentment, transforms the soul into an echo chamber and pretty much guarantees that you will end up feeling shortchanged, unappreciated and misunderstood. If you're like me, eventually you get bored with that routine, realize that you're the driving force in what previously felt like a universal conspiracy, spend thousands of dollars on therapy and reenter the world at some point committed to putting an end to a vicious cycle. Whereas I was unable to truly reveal myself to another in the past, I am now able to do so. Still, it produces anxiety.

Take for instance the first time Simon came to my apartment. I was approximately 63 percent OK with it, while the other 37 percent of me was 100 percent convinced that he would walk in, find that at the age of forty-one, I was still living in a one-bedroom apartment, instantly decide I was a complete loser and hightail it out of here. It freaked me out, but I had to face the music because I knew that telling him we'd have to meet somewhere other than my place, due to the fact that my place was a mansion in Bel-Air that had just been tented for termites, was tantamount to me breaking out a case of dynamite and blowing up one of the numerous bridges along love's path. Even if Simon were to fall madly in love with me, I'd simply never believe that he *really* loved me if I thought that his love for me was founded, even just in part, on my giant unseen mansion.

Apparently, I've got something going for me that makes up for my pathetic square footage because Simon's visits both continued and increased, eventually leading to a conversation about sex. Simon said that it was something he'd been thinking about a lot, and frankly, so had I. Unfortunately, he followed up the suggestion of sex with an announcement that he wasn't really ready for its *after-*

math, which I soon discovered was a codeword for *relationship.* Crestfallen, yet grateful for his honesty, I told Simon that if that was the case, I couldn't have sex with him. I hated saying it, but how could I agree to have sex with the man who represented the return of innocence when he'd just extracted hope and possibility from the equation? And why was the man who represented the return of innocence using words like *aftermath* at a time when I was actively avoiding the temptation to let my own brain drift to thoughts of outcomes and repercussions? I felt duped, not by Simon, but by the universe. Why did it send Simon *and* innocence my way simultaneously, knowing I would link them in my mind, only to reveal that they were not actually appropriate for simultaneous usage? Was it trying to teach me some weird lesson? And, if so, what the hell was it? Before I could figure it out, Simon said he was coming over.

I was feeling rather vexed when Simon arrived and announced that he was feeling rather vexed. Having expected our diametrically opposed views to result in a standoff, I was happy to discover that they'd only managed to produce mutual vexation and greatly amused by the forty-eight hours of comedic sexual negotiation that ensued.

Here's the thing about Simon: He's able to drop a bomb, then instantly defuse it. I'm not sure exactly how he does it, but I suspect helium may be involved. Weight lifts; the bomb suddenly looks like a balloon. I'm laughing. Simon's funny. He's this wonderful combination of boy and man. He's kind of neurotic in a way that both tickles and moves me. He's charming and disarming. I can't imagine anyone not liking him, and I'm pretty sure he could lure anyone into anything, just by being Simon.

Simon went to London yesterday, leaving in his wake one bottle of iron pills, two rolls of paper towels, a Violet Crumble, an interesting combination of fear and excitement, and this, my assignment to write an essay on being *in love*.

With Simon no longer around to distract me, I started thinking about a friend of mine in New York. When I met her, I loved her. And as I listened to her tell stories about her family, I soon surmised that they were all perfect people living an idyllic life. Then I met them and found that they were all out of their minds. Not only that, they had as many issues both individually and as a group as my family or any other family I'd ever known. What made her family *seem* different was that I'd heard about them through a rare filter: someone who was not judging anyone against her own expectations, but simply embracing them all for who they were and choosing to see them in the best possible light. I already knew that love, much like a Hollywood premiere, is a playground for those who are eager to see and be seen. What I decided then, was that love was not something that occurred by chance, but was instead an active decision to continually let go of expectation, to resist looking for our own validation and redemption in others, to allow events to unfold as they will and people to be who they are without opposition, to accept the unexpected, to embrace the opportunity to learn and grow when the results are not to our liking, to seek out and be awed by the beauty in what *is*.

Sure, it's a tall order, trying to be Jesus. I try all the time and I'm pretty sure no one's *ever* picked up on the fact that it is He of the thorny crown that I'm attempting to emulate. But I think it's a noble goal, and I'm not going to stop trying just because I fail far more often than I succeed. The world needs dreamers, after all.

Another thing I'll say about love is that I don't think it's something you get from another person or some outside source. I think it's something that exists inside each one of us. It's not something that is given or received, as much as it is shared. An open heart is capable of both giving and receiving love; a closed heart is capable of neither. It's just a little thing, but lately I've taken to scratching Simon's head a lot. I rub his back too, but he seems to like the head-scratching most of all. On the surface, it may look like I'm doing something *for him,* and while I would happily do it for him, that's not really what's happening. Any act of genuine kindness is as beneficial to the giver as the receiver, and since it is mutually beneficial, negates the very notion of giver and receiver. Plus, I just like touching him.

Simon was lying on the kitchen floor the other night while I was making blueberry pancakes. He asked me if I was in love with myself. I thought it was a peculiar question, but then again, Simon is a curious sort. I've quickly learned to both expect the odd and accept it as commonplace. I told him that I thought I was all right; some days I like myself more than others, but no, I wouldn't say that I was in love with myself. But in writing this essay, I realize that I am *in love* with writing. And given that writing begins with nothing but a blank sheet of paper, I'm now beginning to wonder if being in love doesn't require some degree of willing surrender. I know writing does. Only once you've surrendered can the romance begin. And writing, like a great love affair, is romantic because it allows you to romanticize. Here, in my own little kingdom, I can be completely naked and vulnerable, safe in the knowledge that no one will ever hurt me, confident that with just the stroke of a key, I am certain to live *happily ever after*.

I tried to put my writing analogy into broader, more flowery terms and told my friend Alessandro that I thought being in love felt like you'd just arrived on the most beautiful island imaginable. What's more, you're utterly embraced, endlessly welcome and soon discover that the island only exists because of your arrival. There's nowhere else you'd rather be and you couldn't be anywhere else anyway because—and this is the best part—*you and the island are one!*

He cut me off as I was peaking to tell me that being in love isn't that elaborate; being in love is simply a feeling of curiosity that takes you by surprise. I would have expected more from an Italian, and was left to wonder if gender wasn't the rock that smashes nationality's scissors, rendering all men incapable of processing more than a one-sentence definition. And if so, would Simon fancy me too complicated upon receiving my essay? As Alessandro lit a cigarette, his wife assured me it had nothing to do with gender or nationality; it was simply that her Italian husband had never actually been *in love*. But it's not true. Alessandro is still in love with Suzanne. I see it in his eyes whenever they're not fighting. But they're both in love with fighting too, so I guess that makes it OK; they wouldn't have it any other way.

I asked Suzanne what made Alessandro *the one* and she told me that he was the first person she was ever in love with at the same time he was in love with her. But then again, she also told me she didn't think they'd have ever made it down the aisle had they not lived in different countries throughout their entire courtship. She was certain she'd have sabotaged the relationship somewhere along the way. So who the hell knows?

The next day, as I was en route to meet yet another friend for dinner, it struck me that my musings on being *in love* were void of one of the condition's most common symptoms: nausea. I wondered if I could get away with just mentioning the gumdrops and lollipops, while ignoring the stomachache that accompanied them. Unsure, I arrived at the restaurant, plopped down before Gary and asked him to define being *in love*. He responded with a single word: *fear*. Gary and I spent the next two hours talking about the butterflies, the paranoia, the terror, the insecurity, the not eating, the not sleeping, the waking up in the middle of the night and making smiley face cupcakes and the dumping them in the garbage the next day when you suddenly decide that all this foolishness can only end one of two ways: bad or worse. Who was I trying to kid with that beautiful island crap? Being in love is more like being in a torture chamber.

Gary was thrilled to be celebrating his tenth anniversary the following day, but assured me that it all began with months of freaking out and wondering what it all meant. Then he smiled and abruptly proceeded to amend his definition, asserting that being *in love* is not actually fear, but the difference between being in a haunted house alone and being with someone: Walking through it alone is terrifying, but then you bump into another terrified person, you both look at each other and think, *Hey, you're here, too*. You're still terrified, but it's OK because you're not terrified alone. I liked the visual of ghosts and vampires leaping out from dark corners, but after spending two hours talking about the horrors of being in love, it seemed contradictory for Gary to now define it as some weird sort of alleviation of fear. I told him I thought all the fog at that haunted house must have confused him, but Gary wasn't interested in quibbling. He just shrugged, insisting that being in love was all about contradiction and confusion. "It's everything," he said. "It's everything all at once."

I walked to the bathroom thinking about how weird it was that I'd forgotten about all the spooky bits until so late in the game, but maybe that's just how love works. Maybe the passage of time allows us to remember the magic without reminding us that even in fairy tales witches sometimes try to cram small children into ovens.

As I returned to Gary, I began to think about a conversation I'd had with Alice, about how people like to fantasize about true love and forever and ever and all that, but how they often fall short of achieving it. I started to think about an old couple Simon and I had seen holding hands as we were walking back from dinner one night. And all the while, Gary kept talking about how his relationship was the greatest achievement in his life and how he couldn't imagine anything more satisfying. And even though I knew he'd worked hard at it over the years, because I was around for most of them, he was using words like *gift* and *honor*.

There was no way of knowing if Gary had actually been able to sustain that feeling of being in love any longer than anyone else, but I did know that he acted like he was able to, that he always spoke of his relationship in the most sacred terms, and that he never seemed to lose sight of its value, even when everyone else thought he was crazy.

But maybe you have to be a little crazy. Maybe two people have to be a little crazy at the same time. Maybe that's what it takes to transform fantasy into reality. Maybe that's how you find yourself old, gray, and walking down the street holding hands with someone whose life is so completely intertwined with yours that they feel like one and the same. And maybe then you go home, help each other out of your diapers, laugh your heads off, have hot geriatric sex, and top off the night by silently praying to God that the clown lying beside you doesn't screw up your funeral. I don't know. I haven't made it that far yet.

But driving home, I started to think that trying to define being *in love* was like trying to pick up a loose blob of mercury. I was having a really hard time getting a handle on it and wondering if it was even possible to come up with a universal definition. Ultimately, I just decided that being in love is like skunk juice. People try to describe its smell, but there's no way to accurately describe it. Then one day you're out in the world, you smell something funky, and you think, *Hey, this is it—skunk juice!*

———

What more can I say? The heart speaks its own language, a language that the mind is not always capable of understanding or properly translating. But because the mind is a smug and highly competitive organ, it can't bear to be outshined by the infinitely more complex heart and will often try to thwart it if left unsupervised. It's just something to be aware of, especially if you're kind of neurotic already.

❦

I loved writing that essay for Simon, but by the time he was back in town, I wasn't so sure I wanted to give it to him anymore. I was starting to second-guess myself. Still, I couldn't shake the feeling that the turning it over was about something bigger than Simon. This mattered and it had to be done. I knew that in my gut. So I told myself that it was just ink on paper, and I pressed SEND. Of course, once that was done I instantly decided that e-mailing Simon his essay was a massive irreversible misstep, which led to me taking yet another massive irreversible misstep . . .

"*You did what?!?*" cried Tomas, as he fell to the ground theatrically.

And yes, I could have told him that I felt the same way, but that would have been a third misstep, and allowing Tomas access to my Achilles heel was where I drew the line. I had to own this baby. So I glanced down at my Canadian neighbor and said, "I don't know why you're being so dramatic. It was just an essay."

"No it wasn't!" cackled Tomas. "You've been in love with the guy since the moment you stepped out of that pool."

"Wrong," I replied. And he was wrong, absolutely 100 percent wrong. I was in love with Simon before I ever stepped into that pool. Of course, I didn't say that. I just kept smiling at Tomas who kept laughing at me.

"You know," I said. "You don't have to be *in love* with someone to be happy they've entered your life."

"Maybe not," replied Tomas. "But you *are* in love with Simon."

"No, I'm not."

Tomas sat up, concerned. "What happened to you? Just last week you were flying around on your magic unicorn acting like life was beautiful."

"It still is."

"You *said* you were in love with him," insisted Tomas.

"Whatever."

"Noooo!" he shouted, as he leapt up off the pavement. "*Don't do this!* Don't suck the romance out of it. You were so happy. Be in love with him. Don't whatever it. Leave the darkness to me."

"I'm not being dark, bozo. I'm being realistic."

"It's the same thing, you dope!"

"No, it's not. And anyway, I thought you'd be happy that I gave him the stupid essay. I'm actually allowing myself to be *vulnerable*. Come on, acknowledge it."

"I know," replied Tomas. "It's a miracle, and it's also proof that you're in love with him so stop pretending you're not."

"*Will you just let it go?*"

Tomas threw his hands the air. "I can't believe you're doing this. You're so selfish. You were the best shot this neighborhood had at true love."

"Are you done?" I asked. "Because I still have to finish the essay."

"I thought you already sent it to him?"

"I did, but I couldn't really finish it until after I knew how I felt about handing it over."

And that right there was another massive irreversible misstep.

The next thing I knew, Tomas was congratulating me on becoming an artist, talking about how I'd thrown myself on the chopping block, telling me that there was no turning back. "You grab little pieces of what's around you, you put it together and you expose yourself for the sake of your art. That's what an artist does and that's what you did," explained Tomas.

I told him I got the connection, but assured him that giving Simon the essay wasn't a sacrifice to the gods of art.

Tomas smiled at me like he knew better. I wanted to strangle him.

"Well, then that's completely fucked," I replied, "because this is my *life* I'm messing with."

"I know," he exclaimed. "It's amazing. I wasn't sure you had it in you. I'm just sorry to hear that your relationship with Simon has come to such an abrupt end."

"What are you talking about!?!" I demanded angrily.

"Oh, you won't be hearing from him again. A *twenty-page love letter, after one month?* He's probably on his way back to London by now just to get away from you. And it's too bad because you *are* in love with him."

"It wasn't a love letter, you jerk! *It was an assignment!* You don't know anything! You haven't even read it! And what's the big deal, anyway? Who cares if it was a love letter? *Love's not a crime!*"

Tomas grinned back like a jack-o'-lantern. "Exactly."

"Fine," I said. "Then so be it. It's about time I start practicing what I preach. I'm glad I gave that essay to Simon. I'm sick of interacting with people on some stupid superficial level. I want to get beyond the surface, and if Simon isn't interested in going there, then he probably should have never mentioned love in the first place, and he *definitely* isn't the guy for me."

"I think that's all really admirable," replied the jack-o'-lantern. "And I hope you're right about Simon. I'm just happy to see you finally blossoming into the art . . ."

"Nuh-uh, don't even say the *A* word again. This is not about *A*. And just so you know, when you smile like that, you look like a pumpkin."

Then Tomas said the *A* word again and I stomped off, cursing him.

I cursed Cupid and his stupid quiver of arrows, too. I wanted to snap them in half. Why did he have to shoot me with his stupid arrow? Why did Simon ask me to write this stupid essay? Why did I take his stupid assignment to heart? I started to think about every word that had come out of Simon's mouth, every question, every comment. I started to think that he had sent a lot of mixed messages. And now that I'd given him an answer to his question, everything seemed to be changing.

Unbeknownst to Tomas, I'd already heard back from Simon. He called just after I sent the essay. He said he thought it was funny, well written. He didn't really get into it; I didn't ask for more. It was our first stilted conversation and mostly I just wanted it to end. Maybe the essay freaked him out. Maybe he *is* afraid of love. Or maybe it's just my love. Maybe he thought I was some psycho chick who was going to key his car if I didn't get the right response. But what was the right response? I hated the idea of being misunderstood, but how could I explain something that I didn't entirely understand myself? I think I just wanted to be like Fred. I wanted to be able to give the gift of love and be content with the giving. I wanted Simon to know how happy I was that our paths had crossed, and what a wonderful gift his arrival had been. I wanted that to be enough.

But I'm not Fred; I'm me. And I didn't know what was going to happen next or how I was going to deal with it. Falling in love with Simon was one thing, but acknowledging it? Advertising it? What was I thinking? Vulnerability terrifies me. It's so much easier to be admired from afar than to let someone get close and actually *see* me.

My mind was all over the place, zooming around searching for something to think about that wasn't Simon. But everything kept coming back to him.

I thought about work, about the production company. I was quickly learning that facing a boss every morning is a cakewalk compared to . . . not having a boss to pin the blame on, or hide behind, no big company to back you up, to give you legitimacy, having nothing to face every morning but yourself, knowing that it all rests on you. That's *hard*. But I was still glad I'd done it. And I was glad about the essay too. Because regardless of what happens with the company, with Simon, with anything, I'm stuck with me for the rest of my life, and that means I've got to keep trying to be the person I want to be, even if it lands me flat on my face.

I started to wonder if my life really was as random and unplanned as it seemed, or if everything wasn't linked somehow. Maybe I needed to start that company. Maybe I needed to prove to myself that I could do something on my own before I felt up to taking on a worthy opponent. Simon thinks that's a funny way to put it, but to me it makes perfect sense.

I think about tennis, about how playing with someone much better or far worse just isn't fun for anyone. No matter how cute they are, it gets boring, fast. You can't even keep the ball going unless one person is playing down to the other. But play with someone at your own level and it's not only fun, it's interesting. Two equal players with different strengths and weaknesses can keep the ball going for a long time while providing each other with challenges, opportunities to learn and grow. The right partner can make you a better individual. Maybe that was Simon; maybe not. He'd certainly gotten under my skin and found his way into my heart. And even though God knows I'm the first one to roll my eyes whenever anyone starts up with all that "Everybody comes into your life for a reason" stuff, I knew there was a reason for Simon.

My heart hurt, but I was trying not to let it break until I had to. I sat at my computer. I looked at my bulletin board. I looked at my quote. Then I pulled down another quote. I found it on a box of Celestial Seasonings tea.

As you think, you travel; and as you love, you attract. You are today where your thoughts have brought you; you will be tomorrow where your thoughts take you. You cannot escape the result of your thoughts, but you can endure and learn, can accept and be glad. You will realize the vision (not the idle wish) of your heart, be it base or beautiful, or a mixture of both, for you will always gravitate towards that which you, secretly, most love. Into your hands will be placed the exact results of your thoughts; you will receive that which you earn; no more, no less. Whatever your present environment may be, you will fall, remain or rise with your thoughts, your vision, your ideal. You will become as small as your controlling desire; as great as your dominant aspiration.

—James Allen

The weirdest thing about that quote is that I first read it in the '80s and then at some point in the '90s I suddenly found myself thinking about it again, to the point where I actually went to the grocery store and read every single tea box in sight. Not finding it, I called Celestial Seasonings and asked them to send me a list of their quotes. I read it again, and it sounded good but that was about it. Then in 2006, I found myself thinking about it yet again, and e-mailed Celestial Seasonings. I received another copy of the quote just before meeting Simon. And *finally*, after twenty years, I began to understand why that quote might have lodged itself in my subconscious.

Surprisingly, the first thing that struck me was *not* Simon-related. It was that part about your present environment. It made me think about a conversation I'd had with Tomas. He asked me why I stayed in Los Angeles if I was so at odds with my environment. And once asked, I realized that I've stayed here because I like black and white. Because living in an environment this exaggerated has made so clear what I do and don't want, and what I do and don't want to be; this place has helped shape me into the person I am today.

The second thing that struck me *was* Simon-related. It was that part about being attracted to that which you secretly most love. It was a nice surprise too, because, secretly, I think Simon is the closest thing to the male version of me that I've ever come across. I mean, he's his own freak for sure, but I see so much of myself in him. In fact, that time he asked me if I was in love with myself, the first thought that popped to mind was, *Well, I didn't think I was but I guess I am if I'm in love with you.*

God, I've gotten so lost in relationships. So maybe I needed to define myself, to figure out how to hold on to me, before I could surrender my heart again.

I thought about the rest of the quote. I wondered what my controlling desire was. The only thing I could come up with was the desire to protect myself. But apparently, I'd just thrown that out the window when I threw *myself* onto the chopping block. Better to focus on my dominant aspiration. The thing is, all I'd ever really wanted was to be happy. And despite my occasional forays into insanity, I knew I was already there. Aside from that, there was love, but that now meant Simon, and I couldn't focus on that. So I left reality behind and moved on to dreams. Like Martin Luther King, Jr., I too had a dream. Of course, mine was slightly more self-serving, and had yet to be voiced, although I had been silently trying to psych myself up to do something about it for a few years. And really, now that my heart was on the line, why not just go for it and take the whole beating at once?

So I put on a John Denver album. Corny? Perhaps. But it's what

I was in the mood for and sunshine on my shoulders does make me happy. That's the other reason I've stuck around here as long as I have. And as I tried to make peace with the idea that I would probably never really know what Simon thought while reading the words I'd strung together for him, I began to go through all my essays. I wondered what people would make of these stories of mine. I wondered what *my mother* would make of them. But thinking about that would only increase the fear factor, and I already felt like I was hanging off a cliff.

And as I sat there reading about all these seemingly random events in my life, wondering if I really could be a writer like I'd secretly dreamed of being for sixteen years, I knew three things: I knew that I would not be preparing to throw myself on that chopping block if not for Simon; I knew that I needed to be single as long as I had in order to get to this place; and I knew that if I actually did manage to hatch this egg, Tomas would most certainly try to take credit.

acknowledgments

It is not possible to thank all the people who have touched my life and colored these pages. There are people I'd like to thank whose names I don't even remember, but whose kindness I do. Some of them will be written about in the future, fewer will be mentioned now. It's not about love; it's about space.

He already got a whole essay, but I will thank Simon Mathew here for his saltiness, as well as his order to "borrow a pair of testicles for the day and send those essays out." He inspired and emboldened me.

But while Simon was the main catalyst, there was also my good friend Mike De Luca, who, around that same time, and in a fit of rage, told me that I was a pathetic loser who would never amount to anything. In attempting to get published, I wasn't only hoping to impress Simon; I was also desperate to prove Mike wrong. That said, I love him dearly, he apologized shortly thereafter, I've leaned on him for sixteen long years, God knows that's got to get old, and plus, who cares? I'm an *author* now.

Next up, I'd like to thank everyone I've written about here. They are people who have meant a great deal to me, many of them still do, and all of them participated in a life so mind-boggling to me that I had to put it on paper in search of hidden meaning.

I'd like to thank Gillian MacKenzie, my agent and friend, for hearing my voice, assuring me of its value, helping transform an unorganized mess into a book proposal, and just generally making something that should have been daunting, joyous instead.

I'd like to thank Julie Doughty, my editor, for making my dream a reality, for pushing me at times and backing off at others, and for being a hell of a lot more pleasant, relaxed, and patient than I was when I worked with writers.

I'd like to thank Danna Hyams, my former roommate and long-time friend, who, for years, allowed me to write all night long on the only computer I had access to—five feet from her bed—and slept right through it.

I'd like to thank Jane Fleming, who probably would have done the same. Luckily for her, we didn't meet until I had my own place and my own computer. Luckily for me, she too understands my obsessive nature and has been known to bust into my apartment, turn off my computer, and force-feed me.

I'd like to thank Dr. James and Mr. Kee for their brains, humanity, humor, and belligerence. It all makes for good theater.

I'd like to thank Rebecca Ascher-Walsh for helping me navigate this whole weird journey, for providing enlightenment along the way, and for never making me feel like the pain in the ass I know I was as I relentlessly engaged her in discussion and debate on every last sentence of every last essay.

I'd like to thank Stephanie Romanov for her encouragement, enthusiasm and endless positive energy, as well as her unique ability to relax me in front of a camera. Without her, there would be no author photo.

I'd like to thank Kristen Detwiler, Lauren Jacobs, Donna Langley, Claire Rudnick-Polstein, Ariane Sims, Stephanie Striegel, Suzanne Warren and Ana Zins—all friends who have been especially supportive in different ways throughout this past year, listed in alphabetical order to keep me out of trouble.

But most of all, I'd like to thank my family—for the good times, the bad times, a lifetime of memories, and a wealth of source material that I haven't even begun to tap. They're infinitely more interesting than the Waltons, and I love 'em.

And because mothers are so often the easiest people to blame and the last to get any credit, it only seems fitting that I should single mine out now. So my final acknowledgment goes to my mother, who has no doubt been the most influential person in my life. In reading these essays she has probably learned more about me than she ever wanted to know, and definitely more than she ever wanted anyone else to know. Still, she loves me. For that I am grateful. I've made it this long without a child, but I would have never made it this far without my mother. I hope I have made her proud.

THE LAST SINGLE WOMAN IN AMERICA

CINDY GUIDRY grew up in New Orleans and now lives in Los Angeles. *The Last Single Woman in America* is her first book.

Praise for *The Last Single Woman in America*

"A great read . . . quirkily funny essays on the pleasures and perils of looking for love." —*People*

"A sassy set of essays . . .[by] a woman who has found contentment, despite howlingly disastrous relationships." —*USA Today*

"Guidry's funny, fast-talking recollections of her adventures in LA's single scene could well become *Californication* for girls." —*New York Daily News*

"This new essay collection is a hoot, touching on romantic failures, sustaining friendships, the love and the comedy that invariably accompany life." —*The New Orleans Times-Picayune*

"A view of a life in transition. Guidry is forty, single, and has just lost her job. . . . Her ups and downs could be real downers if it weren't for her eccentric friends, sense of adventure, and rowdy sense of humor." —*Body & Soul*, editor's pick

"Wickedly funny. Continuously rib-tickling except for the moments it reminded me that I'm ashamed to be a man." —Paul Dinello, writer and costar of *Strangers with Candy*

"For those who shun self-help books, *The Last Single Woman in America* is sheer poetry. Cindy Guidry speaks to the hidden cynic in all with her unconventional manner." —*Lush Magazine*

"A modern-day Dorothy Parker . . . wickedly observant and outrageously funny." —Ben Sherwood, author of *The Death and Life of Charlie St. Cloud* and *The Man Who Ate the 747*

"Acerbic, witty, and thought provoking." —*Pasadena Star News*

"Guidry has a sharp eye for comic detail. . . . Her observations about sex, gender relations, and the world today are pointed, [and] she handles her characters with gentleness. A fresh and funny first book." —*Library Journal*